HOMEROOM SECURITY

SCHOOL OF EDUCATION
CURRICULUM LABORATORY
UM-DEARBORN

Homeroom Security

SCHOOL DISCIPLINE
IN AN AGE OF FEAR

Aaron Kupchik

NEW YORK UNIVERSITY PRESS   New York and London

NEW YORK UNIVERSITY PRESS
New York and London

www.nyupress.org

© 2010 by New York University
First published in paperback in 2012.

Library of Congress Cataloging-in-Publication Data
Kupchik, Aaron.
Homeroom security : school discipline in an age of fear / Aaron Kupchik.
p. cm.
Includes bibliographical references and index.
ISBN-13: 978–0–8147–4820–6 (cl : alk. paper)
ISBN-13: 978–0–8147–4821–3 (pb : alk. paper)
1. School discipline. 2. Classroom management.
3. Schools—Safety measures. I. Title.
LB3012.K87   2010
371.5—dc22   2009053728

New York University Press books are printed on acid-free paper,
and their binding materials are chosen for strength and durability.
We strive to use environmentally responsible suppliers and materials
to the greatest extent possible in publishing our books.

Manufactured in the United States of America

10 9 8 7 6 5 4 3 2 1

To my brother, Phil,
who could use something dedicated to him,
and to my daughters, Sarah and Alexis,
who will one day be high school students.

CONTENTS

I shudder when I think back to my experiences in high school. Like many other adolescents, I was awkward and insecure, trying to fit in while figuring out who I was and what kind of adult I wanted to be. Even though I grew up in a middle-class suburban community and was sheltered from serious life problems like poverty and violence, I remember feeling overwhelmed by the emotional trauma of being a teenager.

Yet as overwhelmed as I felt then, I imagine that I would feel even more stress if attending the same public high school today, since schools in the United States have changed so dramatically since then. It's not that schools are more violent today than when I graduated high school (in 1990), because they aren't; but the ways that schools treat students has changed. Today's public schools are rife with strict rules and punishment, including zero-tolerance policies, random searches by drug-sniffing dogs, high suspension rates, surveillance cameras, and the presence of police officers. I didn't get into trouble while in high school, so even with today's discipline regime in place I probably wouldn't have been suspended or arrested. But had I passed by an armed officer every day, been subjected to searches by a team of dogs, or walked underneath the constant gaze of security cameras, my awkwardness and discomfort within my own skin would probably have been even greater.

Perhaps this is the wrong way to look at it, though. Maybe public high school students today see things differently, so that police, cameras, dogs, and the like don't add to the normal stress of being an adolescent. I remember that when my friends and I would be out together we were somewhat afraid of the police—even though most of us we were A or B students who rarely did anything illegal. If one of us was driving and we saw a police car, the phrase "watch out, a cop" would end all conversation until the driver could change course. If we were in the mall and saw an officer, we would go in a different direction. But perhaps for today's teens it doesn't matter; perhaps they are so used to having police officers nearby that they don't bat an eye when they see an officer in the mall (or in school). A large reason why I have spent the past few years studying school discipline is to better understand what it means to today's high school students to attend schools that have police and surveillance cameras.

I am also interested in the state of our schools as a parent. I have two small children and want to send them to public schools when they're old enough. Currently, my wife and I are in the market to buy a new house, and one piece of information we seek on each house is the school district for which it's zoned. I began making a spreadsheet for the schools in the areas where we're looking. As I gathered information from the website of each school and school district, I saw that one piece of information some districts give is on suspensions, including the percentage of the student body that gets suspended in any given year. In one district that has three high schools, I saw that one high school suspended 26% of its student body last year, another suspended 40%, and a third suspended 43%. This is in a middle-class suburban area with relatively little crime and violence, and in a district with a good reputation. I find it frightening that suspension rates are this high—to me this suggests that schools are doing something wrong. I can only hope the situation improves before my daughters enter these schools.

Finally, I am also interested in school discipline because it represents an interesting and important academic issue. I am a sociologist who studies juvenile justice—my prior work is focused on punishing children in courts and correctional facilities. But few youth go to court or correctional facilities, whereas the vast majority of American youth go to public schools. Since I'm interested in how our society controls and punishes juveniles, schools seem like the place to be.

These are the reasons why I have studied school discipline: because I'm an academic, a parent, and someone who has still not recovered from his own high school experience. I write this book knowing that although I teach college courses, my experiences teaching college students are far different than what public high school teachers face. Thus, I don't pretend to be an expert on the difficulties of teaching at or running a high school. Yet sometimes an outside perspective can be helpful. My hope is that this book offers such a perspective, and that it contributes to the discussion on school discipline in a way that helps schools out of the problems they now face.

ACKNOWLEDGEMENTS

I received a great deal of help with this book. Most important, I want to thank Nicole L. Bracy and Olivia Salcido for their tremendous assistance. While graduate students at the University of Delaware and Arizona State University, respectively, each spent hundreds of hours collecting data through observations and interviews. Nicole is also a coauthor of chapters 1 and 3, though her insights into how to interpret the data were an important contribution to the entire book. Nicole's and Olivia's judgment and professionalism were amazing, and I am indebted to each of them. A number of other graduate students also contributed to my data collection, data analysis, and writing: Greg Broberg, Megan Denver, Terry Lilley, and Sheruni Ratnabalasuriar.

Several other colleagues and friends helped me develop my thinking about school discipline through conversations and debates, and by reading and commenting on various portions of the draft: Richard Arum, Thomas Catlaw, Jeff Fagan, Aaron Fichtelberg, Ben Fleury-Steiner, LaDawn Haglund, Santhi Leon, Torin Monahan, Michael Mushenow, Yasser Payne, Laura Peck, Caroline Persell, Antonia Randolph, Jonathan Simon, Brad Snyder, and Franklin Zimring. I want to thank Steve Martin for resurrecting what was a project in crisis, and Roberta Gealt for her help with my survey data and analysis. While I was first getting underway with my research, Kerry Clark, Dan Combs, Marcus England, Eugene Garcia, Denise Griffin, and Debi Neat each took time to help direct me. Thanks, as well, to Ilene Kalish, Aiden Amos, Despina Papazoglou Gimbel, Nicholas Taylor, and others at NYU Press for lending their expertise to this book—but in a gentle way, of course.

I have presented pieces of this book at various times over the past few years, but two stand out as particularly helpful in shaping my work. One was in my own department, where my colleagues in the University of Delaware's Department of Sociology and Criminal Justice offered excellent advice for my manuscript; the other was at the Ohio State University's Criminal Justice Research Center, where Ruth Peterson, Laurie Krivo, and their colleagues offered very helpful feedback.

The National Science Foundation supported the research on which this book is based (grant SES-550208). All errors, opinions, findings, conclusions, and recommendations are mine alone and do not necessarily reflect the views of the National Science Foundation. I also received research support from Arizona State University's School of Justice Studies while beginning my work, and then from the University of Delaware as I continued it. I especially want to thank Ronet Bachman and Marie Provine for access to this material support, as well as for their advice and encouragement.

Throughout the course of my research I was hosted by school districts, school administrators, teachers, security staff, police officers, and other school employees at four schools, as well as by students and their parents. To these people who trusted me and took the time to educate me, I sincerely thank you. I wish I could thank you by name, but my promise of anonymity prevents me from doing so. I truly hope you feel that my interpretations of what I observed are fair, and also that my work might even be helpful. I also want to express my admiration for how well most of you do at such very difficult jobs. The school employees I interacted with are generous, thoughtful, and kind to students, almost without exception. Though many of our current school discipline policies may be counterproductive, they are enforced by good people who sincerely try to do right by the children in their charge.

Finally, I want to thank my wife, Elena. I am very fortunate to have such a loving and supporting partner, and one who doesn't seem to mind hearing me talk incessantly about the same subject for years on end.

The schools ain't what they used to be and never was.

—Will Rogers

INTRODUCTION

Too Much Discipline

A six-year-old Latino boy, Albert, was led into the court-room by a bailiff.[1] Albert was very quiet, timidly answering the judge's questions in a soft voice as he stood before the judge along with his mother and aunt. Albert attended first grade at a local school, and had been arrested for threatening a teacher: his teacher refused to give him his "treats," so Albert said he would bring "a gun and a bomb" to school. This prompted the school to call the police and have him arrested. With no argument from the prosecutor, the case was dismissed by the judge, who then complained about how he had been receiving "a Niagara of cases like this due to zero-tolerance policies," which he called "counterproductive."[2]

I wrote this field note about Albert while doing research for a previous book about prosecuting youth in juvenile and criminal courts; his case led me to be curious about school discipline and security. Of course, any child who threatens violence, especially life-threatening violence on such a large scale, should be reprimanded and taught that such threats are inappropriate. The school should also talk to the child's parents, both to let them know about the problem and to determine whether the child has access to weapons. But it seems unlikely that any child of that age could understand the full implications of such a threat. The judge, prosecutor, and defense attorney in this case agreed, as indicated by the fact that they quickly and readily agreed to dismiss the case, and also by the fact that they criticized the school for calling the police to arrest Albert.

Another way to look at this case is to say "better safe than sorry," and to argue that any threat of such large-scale violence should lead to an arrest because there is always some chance that he could follow through with it.

But this position assumes that there are no costs to the school's actions—that there is no harm in responding aggressively, only in not responding aggressively enough—which is dangerously naive. Even though the case was dismissed, one has to wonder how this experience will affect Albert as he matures. He certainly appeared scared. Will he be intimidated by and shy away from teachers, school administrators, or police? Teachers at Albert's school undoubtedly discussed the incident, and it is possible that they might have feared Albert after his arrest and treated him differently—as troublesome and potentially violent—throughout the rest of his academic career. And how might his fellow classmates treat him—with fear and awe or as someone to steer clear of? Each of these possibilities could substantially shape his future life by reducing his attachment to school and increasing the likelihood that he becomes delinquent in the future.[3] One might also wonder how Albert's mother and aunt, who came to court with him, were influenced by the incident, and whether they became more cynical about the police and the school. Moreover, Albert's arrest commanded time and resources from the school, the police, and the courts, each of which is already overburdened, especially in impoverished urban areas like the one where Albert lives.

Considering the potentially harmful consequences of certain reactions to students' misbehavior, it is clear that the full effects of events like this need to be brought to light. That is the aim of this book: to think critically about the full effects of contemporary school discipline.[4]

Most schools across the United States now respond more aggressively to misbehavior than in years past. Zero-tolerance policies, which require punishments for any violation of a certain rule regardless of the severity of that violation, are an important element of the new world of school discipline. For example, Albert may have attended school in a district that has a zero-tolerance rule for threats of violence, meaning that any threat of violence must be reported to the police as a criminal offense. In this scenario, the district probably had in mind older students who have a higher potential for real violence, but no matter, the zero-tolerance rule requires school administrators to follow the rule with a "one size fits all" approach that does not allow them to distinguish between different degrees of seriousness or between juveniles of different ages.

U.S. schools have indeed drawn up more zero-tolerance rules recently, but they have also done much more.[5] Schools now commonly use surveillance cameras, security guards, and police officers. Usually, the security guards work for the school and are unarmed; but schools across the country have also welcomed armed and uniformed police officers, who are stationed on the premises full-time. These officers, often called school resource officers (SROs), are hired by, trained by, and supervised by the police department, not the schools. Schools also commonly use drug-sniffing police dogs to search students or their possessions. Some schools have even taken to strip-searching students.[6] Together these practices constitute a discipline regime that is the new homeroom security.

I examine these trends in detail in the chapters that follow. Though I will discuss a more nuanced understanding for why schools have ratcheted up their security and punishment practices, on the surface at least it is a response to crime and violence in schools. Citizens, and especially parents, are reasonably disturbed and frightened by school crime. These fears rise tremendously when we see an incident as shocking and disturbing as the 1999 killings at Columbine High School, where two students killed twelve people and themselves and injured many others in a rampage that has come to symbolize the worst-case scenario of school violence. Overall our society views youth as innocent and vulnerable, and so it offends our sensibilities to think that they are exposed to violence when in school, especially such a murderous rampage. We also want our schools to provide our children with a quality education, and this requires safety—students who fear for their safety will be absent from school more often, and when they do attend, they will be less able to concentrate on their academic work. For parents, it is anxiety-producing just to send our children to school, where we cannot watch over them and protect them—if we believe that our children are in danger at these schools, our anxiety grows exponentially.

These fears and insecurities are powerful motivators. In response to these fears, many pro-security advocates argue that we need to hire more police to work in schools and purchase more security technology, such as surveillance cameras, since these strategies will help reduce crime and violence in school. Some critics of these strategies point out that fears of school violence do not reflect reality, since schools are among the safest place for children to be; that overreactions to a perceived crisis have resulted in policies that are counterproductive; and that costly, time-consuming delinquency-prevention measures would be better directed toward after-school or community programs.[7]

But the pro-security response to these criticisms is very convincing, since it stokes our fear that vulnerable children will be hurt. Arguments against more security measures often rely on social science research, which is no match in the public arena for the argument that even a single school homicide necessitates enhanced school security measures.

Part of the problem is that most Americans are so wedded to a particular solution to the problem of school crime, despite a lack of evidence that the solution works. Strategies such as police in schools, security cameras, and zero-tolerance measures resonate with widely shared ideas about crime prevention: that more police and punishments will keep us (and our children) safe.[8] Discussions about these strategies usually ignore the fact that they may lead students to perceive school discipline procedures as unfair, even though the existing research tells us that one of the best ways to reduce school crime is to enhance students' perceptions that rules and punishments are just.[9] Moreover, these strategies have been implemented across the United States without any critical discussion or sound evaluation of their effectiveness.

Such a discussion and debate is sorely needed. As I illustrate in the following chapters, schools have so thoroughly embraced new punishment strategies that school punishment is now an organizing principle (though not the only one) on which schools' and school employees' actions are based. School punishment and security goals guide how teachers and administrators interact with students, and they often consider these goals before making decisions about issues such as curricular and extracurricular activities; school events and after-school events; locker assignments, classroom assignments, and even homework assignments.

Problems with Punishment

I argue that schools must watch over students and punish misbehaviors, but our current strategies for doing so are excessive and counterproductive. These strategies are one-dimensional, relying almost entirely on punishment and surveillance, despite evidence that such an approach is problematic and less effective than alternative responses.

My argument stems from research conducted in four high schools located in two states, one mid-Atlantic state and one southwestern state. I studied two high schools in each state: one attended primarily by middle-class white students and one attended primarily by lower-income racial and ethnic minorities. Over the course of two years, my research assistants and I observed classroom activity, hallway interactions, and disciplinary meetings between students and school staff; we interviewed over one hundred people, including students, parents, teachers, security staff, police, and administrators; and we distributed surveys to all juniors at each school. Based on analyses of these data in addition to others' observations of contemporary trends, I present five reasons why the current punishment and security practices in these high schools are counterproductive.

1. Schools Are Overreacting

The current discipline regime is in disproportionate response to the actual threats youth face. Certainly, the high school experience includes bullying, harassment, theft, assault, and other forms of victimization for too many youth, since *any* school violence is too much school violence. Thus, it is reasonable to institute strong security and punishment policies to prevent and respond to crime and misbehavior in school. But in a nation enduring an economic crisis, where the federal government has recently cut taxes at the same time that states have complained about a lack of federal funding for education, where local education funding is often in jeopardy, and where spending on welfare and other social services has decreased, we have limited resources dedicated to addressing the many problems facing American youth.[10] Given these limitations, it makes sense to work efficiently by focusing our efforts where they are most needed and on strategies with evidence of success. Since most juvenile crime occurs away from school, it makes little sense to cut after-school programs that have been repeatedly shown to reduce delinquency, or to add to the number of police officers in schools, a practice that has shown little evidence of success.[11] And yet this is precisely what many communities in the United States have done.

Moreover, the disproportionate fear of violence in schools has created additional challenges. Though serious violence in schools is rare, minor student misbehavior, such as disruption of class or cutting class, is extremely common. The problem is that schools have enacted policies with violence prevention in mind, but these policies are applied mainly to misbehaviors that are only against school rules (not illegal). The result is overkill and a set of practices that ignores real problems in an attempt to punish rather than correct misbehavior.

2. Real Student Problems Are Often Ignored

Schools are so focused on rules that their enforcement and the punishment of rule breakers are ends unto themselves, with little or no attention paid to why students misbehave in the first place. Schools define appropriate responses to student misbehavior so narrowly that teachers, disciplinarians, and administrators tend to pursue only a single goal: following the school's code of conduct and prescribing the appropriate punishment. It is rare to see teachers and school staff engage with students and discuss the causes of students' misbehavior or effective strategies for avoiding future problems.[12]

This does not at all mean that consistent or even strict punishment is bad—in fact, these are necessary for maintaining order. But they are insufficient when presented alone. To be more effective these punishments should be coupled with efforts to address the reasons why students misbehave. For example, I repeatedly heard teachers explain that many students misbehave in class because they do not understand the course material; misbehaving distracts attention away from these students' academic failures, brings them positive peer attention, and absolves them of the need to participate in class. Yet many of these same teachers remove misbehaving students from class without any effort to address the students' academic issues.[13] This ignores the underlying issue and ensures that the students fall farther behind by missing additional class time. Certainly it makes sense to remove such a student so that the teacher can work more effectively with the rest of the class, but it also makes sense to schedule a tutoring session with the student, thereby limiting the likelihood of further misbehavior.

3. Students Are Being Taught the Wrong Lesson

The current school discipline regime discourages students from thinking critically about power relations and governance. They learn in school that their voice does not matter—that they are powerless to change their school environment or even to contest how they are treated when suspected of violating a school rule. Of course, this has always been an element of schooling, since students and teachers/administrators are far from equals within the school power structure.[14] But with a growing regimen of school rules and increasingly severe punishments, the stakes are higher than ever before, making this lesson ever more poignant. To the extent that we learn about our roles as future citizens while in school, this lesson encourages passivity and the uncritical acceptance of authority, which bode poorly for future levels of democratic participation in society.

Additionally, the rules and procedures used in school socialize students to tolerate and even expect similar practices outside school. If increasing numbers of students attend schools with police officers, surveillance cameras, and random searches by drug-sniffing dogs, these and other similar security practices will seem normal to them. This is important with regard to broader social control practices and debates about the balance between liberties and securities. For example, a citizen may or may not support the U.S. government's ability to listen to citizens' phone conversations without warrants, depending on his or her level of trust in the government, fear of terrorism, and concern for civil liberties. Regardless of which side of this debate prevails, simply having debates like this is healthy for a democracy because it allows room for the expression of diverse views. But as a result of socializing high school students to accept invasive security practices in the name of school crime prevention, debates like this one, or about future social control issues, are likely to either disappear or shift toward greater acceptance of surveillance.

4. Student Misbehavior Is Likely to Get Worse with These Policies

Ironically, school punishment practices have the potential to increase rather than decrease student misbehavior. One of the most consistent and important findings of social science research on why students follow school rules (as well as why people obey laws, generally) is that they believe these rules/laws are fair, well-communicated, evenly applied, and result in fair outcomes.[15] The legitimacy of rules depends to a large extent on their perceived fairness, and this in turn shapes people's willingness to obey the rules. By enacting overly harsh punishments, failing to listen to students when they get in trouble, denying them a voice in shaping school rules or in how they are treated in school, and inconsistently enforcing rules, schools damage the perceived legitimacy of school rules and punishments, thereby making misbehavior more likely. Though my research is not able to address the long-term implications of this and whether school crime increases as a result, a healthy body of prior research leads us to expect that it will.

5. At-Risk Students Are at Greater Risk

Increasing levels of surveillance and punishment in schools means that students who were already at risk for a variety of problems—including suspension, expulsion, arrest, school failure, and dropping out—are now at an even greater risk of experiencing these problems. An extensive body of prior research convincingly demonstrates that school punishments are not evenly distributed throughout student bodies. Rather, low-income students and youth of color are more likely than middle-income and white youth to be punished in school.[16] Rather than trying to address the reasons why they are most likely to be punished or trying to help these students succeed in school, our current practices seek to exclude them from school. This only enhances their problems and limits their ability to compete academically and professionally.

Even if one defends this disproportionate punishment by claiming that these students are punished more than others because they misbehave more, rather than because they are unfairly targeted (though most existing research does suggest unfair targeting), this practice is still a problem.[17] This logic absolves public schools from their duty to teach children proper modes of behavior, a duty American public schools have always assumed, and its adherents pretend that schools are responsible only for teaching academics, since behavior problems are often handled by removal from school.[18] Additionally, by seeking to exclude from the school (through suspension, expulsion, and the like) those at risk of behavioral failure, this strategy runs contrary to other educational reforms. Consider, for example, the No Child Left Behind Act.[19] The first issue this legislation addresses (Title I) is "Improving the Academic Achievement of the Disadvantaged." Rhetoric surrounding the act also has focused on how to improve underperforming schools, which tend to be clustered in poor communities and inner cities.[20] Thus, though many disagree with its methods, the primary thrust of this major educational reform is to improve education for the disadvantaged, or for those most at risk of academic failure. In a rejection of this logic, our recent school punishment reforms seek to absolve schools of the duty of correcting the behavior of students most at risk of violating school rules, and to suspend, expel, and arrest these students instead.

How Did We Get Here?

In short, I argue that much of the new homeroom security is a response to fear and general insecurities rather than careful, evidence-based deliberation. Though it is compelling to argue that contemporary school punishment and security is a response to Columbine and other school shootings, such an explanation oversimplifies a complex trend that began long before Columbine. As the legal scholar Jonathan Simon argues in *Governing Through Crime*, the fear of crime has dominated American governance in recent decades, to the point where policy-makers have mobilized fear of victimization in order to pass laws related to a wide variety of social issues, including education.[21] As a result, school discipline policies are overly simplistic reactions to fears that appease demands for harsh accountability. Though they may be well-intentioned, these policies often are not based on evidence of what actually works to help the problems schools and students face.

Of course once policies are written, there is a great deal of flexibility in how individual teachers, school security personnel, and school administrators put them into practice. The problems that I list above come about not because people intend to do harm, but because of good intentions gone awry. Almost without exception, the individuals I met in the course of my research are dedicated people who care about the welfare of the children in their schools. Given the relatively low pay and the stringent demands of being a public high school teacher, it is hard to imagine anyone working there unless he or she has (or had, earlier in his/her career) a strong desire to help youth.

How, then, do good people execute policies in such a way that produces these problems? Part of the answer is, again, fear. School staff may be afraid of school crime and feel a need to respond harshly; they may fear liability for not enforcing punitive school rules fully; or they may respond to stereotypes by either fearing African American or Latino/a youth who dress in ways perceived as threatening (e.g., do-rags or baggy pants), or perceive these youth as being more confrontational and less respectful.[22] Another part of the answer is that school staff have insufficient time and resources to do their jobs properly, and are forced to take shortcuts, such as removing a student from class rather than taking the time to talk to him or her about why his/her behavior is inappropriate. These kinds of regrettable school discipline moments are similar to regrettable parenting moments; a parent who punishes a child or forbids the child to do something and when asked why, responds only by saying "because I said so," is similar to the administrator who suspends a misbehaving student without explaining the reason for the rule or why the punishment is necessary. Both individuals may be acting out of frustration, and both responses are understandable reactions to annoyance or impatience with a misbehaving child.

School staff tend to develop shared perceptions of the problem of student misbehavior and how they should best respond to it. Unfortunately, these perceptions often are shaped by fear and the frustration of insufficient time and resources, and as a result, responses to misbehavior can cause more problems than they fix. Yet this does not mean that school discipline efforts are entirely counterproductive. For example, if it is true that police in schools are able to reduce students' fears or effectively mentor students, or that zero-tolerance policies are able to limit unfair uses of discretion in handing out punishments, then these practices can help. But as I argue throughout this book, we need to consider these benefits alongside the harms they also cause, rather than uncritically accepting contemporary methods. When we do so, we see that for many of our current practices, the negatives outweigh the positives.

Organization of the Book

Chapter 1 discusses the changes in school discipline that have taken place recently, as well as competing explanations for these trends, focusing on recorded levels of school crime across the United States, public fear of school crime, and perceptions of general failures in public education. Given that fears of crime have risen and punitive policies have grown without corresponding increases in actual crime, the most satisfying explanations for the new school discipline regime focus on postmodern insecurities and anxieties over crime, poverty, and school failure. The chapter presents prior evidence on the effects of this new discipline regime, such as evidence that racial and ethnic minorities and low-income students are more likely than white students to be punished in schools, and reviews school crime prevention efforts that appear to be effective based on existing evidence. Finally, as a way of understanding the significance of contemporary school discipline, I discuss sociological and philosophical work on the functions of mass education, including the work of John Dewey, Emile Durkheim, and Michel Foucault. This body of work clarifies the ways that schools socialize students to learn their roles in society and raises questions about what life lessons students might take away from contemporary school discipline and security.

In chapter 2 I move from the general to the specific by focusing on the results of my empirical research, where I begin by describing the four high schools, in two states, that I studied. The chapter discusses the communities in which these schools are located, the student demographics, school characteristics, and the policies and practices each school has implemented to detect and punish misbehaving students.

Chapter 3 considers the effects of a particularly important (and symbolically powerful) school security initiative: full-time police officers in public schools. The chapter discusses how these officers interact with students and what effects their presence has on schools. Though they bravely attempt to counsel and mentor students, often police have neither the skills nor resources to do so effectively. Their presence escalates disciplinary situations, both by introducing a law-and-order mentality to the school and by facilitating the arrest of students whose crimes may otherwise have been considered too minor to warrant calling the police (e.g., involvement in a fistfight). Yet despite these real problems, their presence helps in some ways; though they seem unable to prevent most misbehavior, they do ease fears and insecurities of almost all stakeholders, including students, teachers, parents, and administrators. This benefit needs to be considered along with the drawbacks in an informed, critical discussion about whether our schools should have full-time police officers on campus.

I continue in chapter 4 by sketching out one of the important lessons about contemporary school discipline: that the current emphasis on rules and punishments eclipses other school goals, often including even pedagogical goals. Rules are enforced for their own sake, with no corresponding attempt to solve underlying problems, teach students why the rules are in place, or resolve conflicts. Though zero-tolerance policies legitimize this climate, they do not cause it, since there is evidence of this problem occurring prior to their implementation. Similarly, the problem is not caused by the presence of police officers, though their presence does exacerbate it by introducing a stern law enforcement perspective that takes priority over a treatment- or resolution-oriented one.

Many scholars who look carefully at education argue that schools reproduce existing social inequalities. In chapter 5 I argue that this is true, in part, but somewhat of an oversimplification with regard to school punishment. That is, race/ethnicity, class, and gender shape school punishment, but not in some of the ways that one might expect. Rather, some of the punitive practices that were historically used only in mostly low-income or minority schools are now used in middle-class white schools as well, even if they are used in different ways and have different consequences. When comparing experiences of individual students, however, we see that biases about racial/ethnic minorities, poor students, and female students substantially shape school discipline within schools. As a result, the contemporary discipline regime further marginalizes students who enter school already facing social and academic disadvantages.

In the concluding chapter, I offer suggestions for school punishment and security that would be more effective at preventing school crime and misbehavior. Such strategies would be strict, but more fair and consistent; they would not include zero-tolerance policies; they would include more rewards for good behavior; they would involve counseling, treatment of students' underlying problems, and conflict resolution; and they would involve students as partners rather than objects of punishment. I also address the issue of police in schools, and suggest that on balance, they would best be restricted only to schools with demonstrated crime problems. There are ways that we can better protect children in schools from harm, and one important mission of this book is to discuss these methods.

1

A NEW REGIME

with Nicole L. Bracy

The following appeared in a recent op-ed piece published in the *Boston Globe*:

A 13-year-old girl was handcuffed and arrested at Brocton [Massachusetts] High School last June for wearing a T-shirt. The T-shirt, which she was asked by school officials to remove, bore the image of her ex-boyfriend, 14-year-old Marvin Constant, who had recently been killed in a Boston area shooting. The girl refused to remove the memorial shirt and was arrested for "causing a disturbance."

In Texas, 14-year-old high school freshman, Shaquanda Cotton, was sentenced to seven years in prison. Her crime was pushing a hall monitor out of the way when she was stopped from entering a school building. The official charge was "assault on a public servant."

While extreme, these cases are not unusual. In Massachusetts and across the country, an increasing number of incidents that traditionally have been handled in schools by trips to the principal's office are being dealt with by law enforcement officials and judges in the juvenile justice system. Countless school children, particularly children of color in poverty-stricken zip codes, are being pushed out of schools and into juvenile correctional facilities for minor misconduct.[1]

This is the new homeroom security. Public schools today look very different than those of just a generation ago; they have undergone a host of changes over the past fifteen years as concerns about security and safety have permeated American consciousness. These changes have been twofold: first, schools have ratcheted up their punishment policies, clarifying what are and are not acceptable behaviors and enforcing these rules with tougher penalties for students who violate them; and second, schools have introduced security forces (such as security guards and law enforcement officers) and surveillance technologies (such as metal detectors and security cameras) to deter students from misbehavior and catch those who do misbehave. In the effort to protect our youth, schools have borrowed a variety of policies and practices from the criminal justice system.[2]

Zero-tolerance policies, which require schools to suspend or expel any student caught violating a rule, are a significant part of this new regime. Such policies are controversial because they establish categories of offenses that are met with set punishments and often don't allow for extenuating circumstances or exceptions. A student who forgot that he left a pocket knife in his backpack after a weekend camping may be given the same punishment as a student who brings a gun to school. Zero-tolerance policies are important because they can lead to serious consequences for student misbehavior, but also because of their symbolic value; as the name implies, a zero-tolerance policy communicates that "tolerance," once a value we wanted to teach our children, is now out of the question when it comes to certain categories of misbehaviors or crimes.

Another way that schools have demonstrated their commitment to safety is by making law enforcement officers part of their school staffs. Currently, the most common type of law enforcement officer found in schools is the school resource officer (SRO), a sworn, armed, uniformed police officer placed in a public school. Although law enforcement is the primary responsibility of SROs, their role is not entirely law enforcement–related. The National Sheriffs' Association describes the responsibilities of an SRO as including "law enforcement, problem solving, teaching, counseling, and crisis management."[3] It is common for such officers to counsel students, organize extracurricular activities for them, and teach law-related courses.

Many public schools have installed security cameras throughout the interiors and exteriors of school buildings. According to the National Center for Education Statistics, during the 2005–2006 school year nearly 70% of public high schools used security cameras to monitor the school. By comparison, just six years earlier (the 1999–2000 school year) only 26% of public high schools had security cameras.[4]

It is also increasingly common for schools to use drug-sniffing dogs around campus; 41% of middle schools and 61% of high schools used drug-sniffing dogs at least once over the 2005–2006 school year. Other security measures that exist on school campuses, but are somewhat less common, include metal detectors and bans on student backpacks. Approximately 5% of all schools and 11% of public high schools in 2005–2006 report using metal detectors to randomly check students for weapons as they enter the school building in the morning, and 6% of schools either required that all student backpacks be transparent (clear plastic) or prohibited students from bringing backpacks to school at all.[5]

Not surprisingly, considering these new security measures, the numbers of students being suspended and expelled from public schools have increased dramatically. In a 2001 report from the Justice Policy Institute, the authors find that school suspensions and expulsions nearly doubled from 1974 to 1998 while rates of student victimization remained stable, leading them to conclude that suspensions and expulsions are not the result of increasingly high levels of victimization at school.[6] The additional suspensions are largely a response to non-violent misbehavior, not serious incidents such as violence, as schools have become tougher on less serious offenses than in years past.[7]

Despite common rhetoric about the growing dangers inside schools, school crime has been declining over the past two decades.[8] In 1992, the rate of crime against students (both violent and non-violent combined) at school was 144 incidents per 1,000 students. By 2005, the rate had dropped to 57 per 1,000 students.[9] In fact, schools are among the safest places for youth to be; students are much more likely to be affected by violent crime outside of school than inside.[10] In 1996, the Centers for Disease Control reported that there was less than a one in a million chance that a student would be killed or commit suicide in or around school.[11] By 1999 this rate had decreased to one in 2 million, and by 2006 the chances of a student dying at school by suicide or homicide was one in 3.2 million.[12] Not only is crime in schools down, but students also report feeling safer in schools today than they did a decade ago. The percentage of students between the ages of twelve and eighteen who report being afraid of getting attacked or harmed at school declined from 12% in 1995 to 6% in 2005.[13]

It might be tempting to assume that the decreases in school violence are due to the changes in school discipline, but the existing evidence suggests that this assumption is false. Several researchers have investigated the types of strategies that best prevent crime and violence in schools. Though these researchers have used a variety of different methodologies for studying this question and conducted their studies in different locations, their results converge on a set of conclusions about what schools can do to reduce rates of student misbehavior; criminologist Denise C. Gottfredson offers a comprehensive review of this research in her book *Schools and Delinquency*, from which I borrow in the following paragraphs. One of the most consistent findings is that schools must impose firm, clear, and consistent rules. Students must be punished for misbehaving, the punishment must be sufficiently firm that students understand their rule violations are serious, and everyone must know what kind of punishment to expect when they break school rules. This means that the rules and punishments must be effectively communicated to students and school staff, and that the punishments for breaking the rules must be consistently applied.[14]

A second consistent theme in this research is that schools can reduce student misbehavior by creating an inclusive, democratic, or positive psychosocial climate for students.[15] Schools with the following characteristics are shown to have lower rates of student misbehavior than other schools:

- Students perceive that they have the ability to shape school policies;[16]
- Students perceive the rules to be fair and clear;[17]
- Schools reward students' positive behavior, not just punish them for misbehavior;[18]
- Schools enhance students' behavioral problem-solving skills (modeled after approaches to problem-solving policing);[19]
- Schools are communally organized, whereby there is a system of shared values and a pattern of caring relationships among students and staff.[20]

A number of studies conclude that when schools are able to create a climate that rewards positive behaviors, allows students a voice in their treatment and in school governance, maintains a sense of fairness among students, and treats students with respect and care, student misbehavior is reduced. As Gottfredson states: "Delinquent youth cultures flourish in schools that do not or cannot establish and maintain a 'communal' social organization. Communal schools are characterized by a system of shared values among members of the organization, particularly relating to the purposes of the institution, expectations for learning and behavior, and expectations for student achievement; meaningful social interactions among school members; and a distinctive pattern of social relations embodying an 'ethos of caring' and involving collegial relations among adults in the institution."[21]

The research consistently shows that firm and consistent rules are important but insufficient. Schools also need to pay attention to how they enforce rules and how adults and children interact within the schools. By creating a climate in which students learn positive behaviors and problem-solving skills, in which they have meaningful interactions with adults, and in which they feel fairly treated, schools can reduce student misbehaviors.

These research findings follow directly from one of today's most popular and influential criminological theories: control theory. Though the roots of this theory extend back to Thomas Hobbes and the enlightenment era, its modern version is usually attributed to the criminologist Travis Hirschi's social bond theory. Hirschi noted that if youths are bonded to social institutions like schools—if they internalize the norms of the schools, feel they have something to lose if they violate the school's rules, and use their time constructively in school activities—then they are less likely to break school rules or criminal laws.[22] When schools build a positive, communal school climate, they improve students' bonds to the schools and thus reduce misbehavior.

This research result is also consistent with a separate body of work on procedural justice that shows that if citizens are treated fairly when confronted with an authority, they are more likely to perceive the authority to be legitimate and, subsequently, to abide by rules. For example, people have greater confidence in the police and courts when they believe these officials act fairly, and as a result they are more likely to perceive laws as legitimate and abide by them. The theory has been repeatedly tested and validated, often in the context of police-citizen interactions; the research consistently finds that citizens' views of justice are shaped at least as much by how they are treated (e.g., whether an officer treats them respectfully and listens to them) as by whether they are arrested.[23]

The extension of the theory to schools is clear. If schools treat students respectfully and fairly, students are more likely to perceive the school's authority as legitimate and to follow school rules. As Gottfredson states, "By modeling appropriate behavior and establishing a fair and just discipline system, school staff enhances student beliefs in the validity of rules and laws."[24]

Unfortunately, the reality of school discipline often directly contradicts this understanding.[25] Schools often enforce discipline in ways that fail to respect students, that erode a communal climate, that increase students' powerlessness and alienation, and that are likely to undermine students' perceptions of legitimate school authority. This explains why prior studies suggest that tougher rules, more suspensions, and increased security have little or no effect on student misbehavior. In fact, several studies now show not only that zero-tolerance policies don't work, but that they can actually make things worse, as students may rebel against punitive disciplinary policies that they perceive to be unfair.[26] Rigid school disciplinary policies can alienate students by creating an adversarial relationship between students and adults who work in schools, making students feel uncomfortable going to teachers/staff when they have a problem.[27] Moreover, some students may face real psychological harm if subjected to intrusive security and discipline measures like strip searches or corporal punishment.[28]

Contemporary school discipline may also be ineffective because often it is unfair. Several existing studies very clearly, consistently, and convincingly illustrate how strict discipline policies disproportionately affect students of color and poor students.[29] One early and well-cited study finds that black students are twice as likely to be suspended as white students and, independent of race, being poor also increases a student's probability of being suspended.[30] Other research concludes that black students' disproportionate likelihood of receiving school punishment is influenced by the fact that they receive lower grades, are perceived as less well-behaved, and have been disproportionately sanctioned at school in the past.[31] Evidence also suggests that students of color are more likely to be referred for discipline because teachers and other school staff perceive their behavior to be more threatening, disrespectful, and inappropriate compared to the behavior of white students.[32] As educational researcher Russell Skiba and colleagues state, "In the absence of a plausible alternative hypothesis, it becomes likely that highly consistent statistical discrepancies in school punishment for black and white students indicate a systematic and prevalent bias in the practice of school discipline."[33]

In addition to being ineffective (and possibly counterproductive) at deterring misbehavior and being inequitably applied, the new regime of school punishments may harm students' academic chances as well. Students who are suspended or expelled are more likely to drop out of school altogether, thereby reducing their opportunities for employment and other successes later in life.[34]

Critics of these modern school policies also cite increasingly obvious parallels between schools and the criminal justice system, and the increasing likelihood that youth punished for school misbehavior are sent to the juvenile or criminal justice system. By relying on police officers, ramping up punishments for misbehavior, and subjecting students to invasive surveillance (such as cameras, metal detectors, searches by drug-sniffing dogs, and the like), schools have created what some call a "school-to-prison pipeline."[35] Student behaviors that once were dealt with by teachers, administrators, and counselors—such as minor fights between students, disruptive classroom behavior, or truancy—are now outsourced to be dealt with by criminal justice agencies.[36] What's more, the risks of criminal justice involvement are not equally distributed, as students of color are most likely to be arrested as a result of a school-based incident and funneled into the criminal justice system.[37] In light of these consequences, organizations like the American Bar Association, the American Civil Liberties Union, the American Psychological Association, and the National Council on Crime and Delinquency have publicly denounced the use of zero-tolerance policies in schools.

Critics of the new regime of school punishment and security also claim that many of these practices erode students' rights. In 1969, the Supreme Court in *Tinker v. Des Moines* ruled that a Des Moines school's policy prohibiting students from wearing black armbands in protest of the Vietnam War was unconstitutional, as it violated students' First Amendment rights.[38] The Court famously pointed out in their decision that students "do not shed their constitutional rights . . . at the schoolhouse gate." Yet it is unclear whether or how the new school–criminal justice system partnerships and enhanced school penalties for misbehavior affect students' constitutional rights. This is especially true with regard to police in schools, since schools and police are traditionally held to different legal standards when it comes to questioning students about a crime or searching students and their property. Historically, schools have been granted greater leeway than police to search and question students, since they act in loco parentis and therefore are presumed to have students' best interests at heart.[39] Schools can search students under the lesser "reasonable suspicion" standard and can question students about a crime with few restrictions. Police officers, on the other hand, are held to much higher standards of proof—they typically need "probable cause" that a crime has been committed before they can search a citizen, and are required to Mirandize a suspect (in custody) before questioning him or her about a crime. Now that schools and police work together on a daily basis, it is unclear under what circumstances law enforcement standards apply and in what circumstances school standards apply. As a result, students' rights may be in jeopardy if schools and police partner in ways that place more emphasis on their own goals of safety and order than they do on the legal protections intended for youth in schools.

The preservation of students' due process rights is also a concern with regard to the growing use of punishments that exclude students from class. In *Goss v. Lopez* (in 1975), the Supreme Court recognized education as a property right protected by the Fourteenth Amendment when it ruled that the due process rights of nine students were violated when they were suspended from school without a hearing.[40] Just like suspected criminals, students have the right to be notified of the charges against them and have an opportunity to tell their side of the story before being suspended or expelled from school. The suspension and expulsion of millions of students in American public schools each year raises questions about whether these students have received adequate due process. Some schools may find the due process requirements, such as giving students a hearing before they are suspended, to be too cumbersome or time-consuming, and students and parents may not be sufficiently versed in the law to demand it.

Recently the Supreme Court has also taken issue with how schools conduct searches of students. In *Safford Unified School District #1 v. Redding*, the Court considered the case of a thirteen-year-old middle school student who was subjected to a strip search. After another student reported that Redding gave her prescription-strength ibuprofen, school officials searched Redding's possessions and pockets. Finding nothing, she was then asked to remove her clothes, and to "pull her bra out and to the side and shake it, and to pull out the elastic on her underpants, thus exposing her breasts and pelvic area to some degree."[41] No pills were found. The Court ruled the search unconstitutional; writing for the majority, Justice Souter stated that "the intrusiveness of the strip search here cannot be seen as justifiably related to the circumstances."[42] The fact that five Justices joined Souter in his judgment, including conservatives Roberts, Scalia, and Alito, suggests some consensus that (in this case at least) schools' efforts at rule enforcement can go too far.[43]

Of course, given the popularity of contemporary school discipline and security policies, it is obvious that there are many proponents and defenders of these policies as well. While zero-tolerance policies receive a significant amount of criticism from researchers, they tend to be favored by the people who are involved with students on a daily basis: teachers and administrators. A 2004 study of 725 U.S. middle and high school teachers found that 93% of teachers supported the imposition of zero-tolerance policies.[44] Supporters of zero-tolerance policies point to the potential deterrent effect these policies may have; knowing punishment is imminent, students may be more likely to think twice before breaking a rule. Contrary to criticisms that they are often unfairly applied, proponents argue that zero-tolerance policies are one of the fairest ways to mete out punishments, since all offenders are treated equally under these "one size fits all" rules.[45]

Those who support the introduction of police into schools argue that having a police officer on the premises increases the likelihood that misbehaving students will be apprehended, and therefore deters students (and outsiders) from committing crimes at school.[46] In light of highly publicized incidents of school violence like the 1999 shootings at Columbine High School, police presence on school campuses may help to assuage some of the fears of parents, school staff, and students who are increasingly concerned about school safety.[47] Further, having a police officer on campus also benefits school administrators by providing an immediate responder when crimes do occur on campus, eliminating the need for schools to call 911 and wait for a patrol officer to respond.

From the perspective of law enforcement agencies, having police in schools can promote the legal socialization of youth by giving students the opportunity to have positive interactions with police officers, which could lead to improved relations between youth and the police.[48] Moreover, through the course of working in schools and getting to know students, police may be able to use information they learn from students to help solve crimes at school and in the community. These goals are consistent with the community policing model on which SRO programs are built, though it is not entirely clear whether these goals are realized and whether they translate into actual benefits to students (versus being beneficial only to police departments).[49] Studies that examine students' perceptions of their SROs, for example, conclude that students do not regard their school's police officer as a typical officer and that SROs have no impact on students' overall perceptions of the police.[50]

Though it is true that contemporary school security and punishment can have some of these positive effects, I find that these positives are largely outweighed by their negative consequences. To better serve students and to have more orderly and fair schools, we ought to be able to consider both positive and negative aspects of school discipline, and to have a dialogue that balances fear and assumptions with evidence.

Explaining the Rise of School Punishment and Security

The recent buildup of school punishment and security mirrors changes seen throughout Western society, as the United States and other nations have made formal social control a central feature of the social landscape. In *The Culture of Control*, sociologist David Garland illustrates how the distinctive social organization of the past few decades (e.g., changes in employment patterns, residential patterns, inequality, and crime rates) and the rise of socially conservative politics have shaped contemporary crime control. One very visible result is that the United States now incarcerates over two million people, though modern crime control works in many other ways as well. For example, Garland states: "The most significant development in the crime control field is not the transformation of criminal justice institutions but rather the development, alongside these institutions, of a quite different way of regulating crime and criminals. Alongside policing and penality there has grown up a third 'governmental' sector—the new apparatus of prevention and security. . . . This small but expanding sector is made up of crime prevention organizations, public-private partnerships, community policing arrangements, and multi-agency working practices that link together the different authorities whose activities bear upon the problems of crime and security."[51] Schools are now a part of this "governmental" sector.

Legal scholar Jonathan Simon's book *Governing Through Crime* continues in this vein by illustrating how crime control has become central to policymaking. Simon argues that crime control has become a paradigm through which policy-makers govern a variety of different policy areas. Since being confronted with the crisis of the weakening New Deal political order (due to social changes of the 1960s and 1970s), politicians have been forced to find a new discourse for their agendas. They turned to the issue of crime and victimization, finding that by capitalizing on the public's fears and insecurities they could mobilize support for their policy initiatives. Indeed, one chapter of *Governing Through Crime* is dedicated solely to the changes in school discipline and how they are a part of this larger trend. He argues that policymakers have approached concerns and anxiety over schools by focusing first and foremost on crime and violence.

To understand the recent shifts in school punishment and security, we need to take an even broader view. School discipline and security are but one branch of a larger assault on public education that stems from a lack of confidence in the schools. Just as Simon argues that governing through crime is shaped by insecurities due to the breakdown of the New Deal style of governance, so must we look at school security measures as a response to broad insecurities.

This is easy to do. Since its inception, U.S. public education has been at the center of many of the nation's most significant social crises. Public schools first spread throughout the United States as a response to the perceived crisis of immigrants flooding the country in the late nineteenth century.[52] Schools were pioneered as a way to "Americanize" the lower-class and immigrant youth, who many social reformers believed were degrading the country's moral fabric; schools taught these youth middle-class norms, kept them off the streets, and fostered in them an American identity. As noted by education scholar James G. Cibulka: "The social foundations of education Progressivism have been critiqued as partisan. . . . The social roots of this reform movement were White, Protestant, and middle class. It was rooted in small-town America and sought to reclaim civic virtue amid the tumultuous changes of an industrializing, urbanizing America."[53] A clear illustration of this is the Pledge of Allegiance—a promise to be a flag-respecting American, without any reference to academic learning—that students across the United States still recite daily.

Public schools especially came into the political spotlight at the beginning of the civil rights era, with the Supreme Court's *Brown v. Board of Education* decision. Though schools may not have actually desegregated in 1954, this landmark decision thrust public schools directly into the heated national debate about race and racial segregation. That this decision is one of the best-known moments of the civil rights movement suggests that schools are a primary location where social conflicts are played out.

We also see this with the perceived crisis of communism early in the cold war. In 1957, the Soviet Union launched the first artificial satellite, *Sputnik*, into orbit, igniting a wave of concerns that the United States was falling behind the Soviet Union technologically. One primary response was to blame public schools for failing to maintain American superiority in the natural sciences and math. This concern spurred passage of the National Defense Education Act, which allotted nine hundred million dollars in federal funds toward math, science, and foreign language instruction in schools and colleges.[54] Indicating its perceived value, public education was viewed as central to national defense during a time of concern about the spread of communism and the threat of nuclear war.[55]

The perceived crisis of the past fifteen years, during which we have seen a massive buildup of school discipline, may not be a response to a single event or a single issue, but public schools have nevertheless become a stage for the airing of public anxieties and conflicts, including racial conflicts, fear of crime, and concern over growing needs of youth. The first of these, racial conflict, was abundantly clear in the aftermath of *Brown v. Board of Education.* The resulting violence and need for National Guard troops to escort black students into an Arkansas school in 1957 to protect them from violence at the hands of segregationists say a great deal about the intensity of the desegregation battles fought in schools and the public fear that underlies resentment toward desegregation.

But this fear is not limited to such dramatic events of an earlier era. Recent data show that as greater numbers of racial/ethnic minority students enter public schools, many white students flee public schools for private schools. For example, in 1968, white students represented 37% of the Chicago Public Schools' student body, and 35% in St. Louis; by 2000, they were less than 10% and 17% respectively.[56] In New York City—the nation's largest school district, with over one million students—14% of public school students are white, despite the fact that 37% of the city's under-eighteen population is classified as white.[57] As the author Jonathan Kozol powerfully argues, contemporary schooling is scarred by battles over race, as advantaged districts with mostly white students struggle to protect their financial advantages and prevent intrusion by minority students. He writes: "When Asbury Park [New Jersey]—predominantly non-white—asked to rent facilities in a white district, the white district was willing to take only 'a small number of students' and insisted that they 'be kept separate.' Similarly, the schools of Irvington, where 92 percent of children are non-white, tried to rent rooms for their children in three suburbs, all of which were white, when building shortages left children without schools. 'The schools sought by Irvington were vacant' the court notes. 'The districts simply did not want [the] children.'"[58]

The second of these issues, fear of crime, is highlighted by prior scholars such as Simon as well as by legal scholars William Lyons and Julie Drew in their book *Punishing Schools*.[59] The most visible focal point for this fear is Columbine, since the 1999 tragedy represents every parent's and educator's nightmare scenario. Yet fear of crime is much broader than this, and is also represented in more subtle ways, such as through concerns about immorality among today's youth. Concerns about the immorality of what today's youth wear (particularly skimpy clothing for girls), music with violent or sexual lyrics, and a seductive style of dancing mirror the concerns voiced a generation or two ago about fashion items such as miniskirts and tank tops, not to mention the outrage over the immoral music and dance moves of artists like Elvis Presley in the 1950s. As the sociologist Karen Sternheimer argues in *Kids These Days*, each generation of youth receives a similar morality-based criticism, as each generation of adults believes that the current youth are depraved. She describes how general insecurities are expressed through fear for and of youth, and how targeting youth as a problem population works "to absolve adults of responsibility for creating the often dangerous and difficult conditions many young people must endure."[60] In truth, though, youth tend to change much less, generation to generation, than most people assume. A recent survey in Arizona, for example, finds that current teenagers use fewer drugs, have less sex, and drink less alcohol than did teenagers a generation ago.[61] Assumptions of a generational decline in morality contribute to the perception that today's youth are out of control and threatening, adding to public anxieties over youth and public schools.

The third anxiety has to do with changes in family dynamics, social structure, and the welfare state that have led to growing needs among youth. Many disadvantaged youth come to school hungry or improperly clothed, forcing schools to either feed and clothe them or respond to their resulting behaviors (it is hard to concentrate in class if you are hungry).[62] Though it is unclear how much this represents a difference from before, several changes over the past thirty years suggest that the problem has in fact grown, especially in impoverished urban areas: the elimination of industrial labor jobs, a growing gap between rich and poor, reductions in public benefits, and a decline in standard of living for the poor.[63] Yet the overall problem is not restricted to disadvantaged youth. With the growth in both the number of mothers in the workforce and the average workweek for parents, many youth have less parental supervision than typical for prior generations. As a result of these trends schools are under pressure to do more than simply educate students: they are expected to provide social services for youth, supervise them, and parent them as well.

It would be myopic to assume that these pressures are new, since the initial vision for schools was to "Americanize" immigrant and lower-class youth; this vision very clearly involves schools intervening in students' lives well beyond academics. Rather, changes in postwar American society, such as the growth of working parents and single-parent families, have altered how schools inter-act with students in ways that potentially add to their burden, or at least cause school officials and the public to perceive the school's burden as hav-ing grown. This perception was voiced to me several times throughout my research, as school officials feel pressure to do much more with youth than they are capable of doing. Consider as an example the following statement by a teacher, who discussed student behavioral problems as a consequence of immature parents (who became parents while teenagers):

[Students] need discipline and structure. They cannot be allowed to just say what they wanna say, when they wanna say it, how they wanna say it. [That] can't happen—it can't happen, and it is happening everywhere. I mean, you've heard it. You know, I walk down the hall and two kids are arguing and the *f* word comes out every other word. I don't know if they realize that doesn't happen in the real world. I mean, [if] you [say that] in the middle of the mall, [then] security's gonna escort you out of the mall. . . . I mean, I know why it's happening, I just don't know how to stop [it], you can't stop it. I mean you have a fifteen-year-old kid, and we discussed this the other day. It was so funny, I had ten girls in this class, in the back of the computer lab, one of them said, "My mom just turned thirty-two." The other girls were talking, the oldest mother of those ten children [gave birth when she] was seventeen. So these kids are having kids, but they've never passed the maturity, you know at age fifteen you're still very immature, and you're in school. Then you leave school because you're having a baby and don't come back, you've missed the maturity process, so these kids are being raised by women who've never been allowed to mature because they've left the process. So we're not gonna win this game. (I)[64]

These far-reaching public anxieties each find expression in concern over who attends public schools and what the schools do. One of the principals I interviewed helped explain this; when addressing why parents often become angry at school administrators, he stated:

You have to understand something: the local school is the closest thing to government that a person can actually get their hands on. So when they're mad about government, whether it be at the federal level, the taxes they gotta pay, the decisions that are made . . . the local school is the closest thing they can actually get their hands on when they're mad and angry about how their life is being determined. (I)

Concerns about social changes as diverse as crime rates, employment patterns, youthful immorality, desegregation, and poverty all lead to criticism and discontent over what schools do.

Unsurprisingly, confidence in public education (by some measures) is low. In a June 2008 nationwide Gallup poll, only 33% of respondents reported that they have "a great deal" or "quite a lot" of confidence in public schools.[65] In 1973 (the first year with data available) 58% of adults answered similarly to the same question.[66] Journalist Peter Schrag describes this lack of confidence in American public schools by referencing the list of demands Americans have placed on their schools since 1951:

Win the Cold War; beat the Germans and the Japanese in the battle for economic supremacy; outduel the Chinese and Indians in the training of scientists and engineers; Americanize millions of children not just from Southern and Eastern Europe . . . but from a hundred Third World cultures . . . ; make every child "proficient" in English and math; educate the blind, the mentally handicapped, and the emotionally disturbed to the same levels as all others; teach the evils of alcohol, tobacco, marijuana, cocaine, heroin, and premarital sex; prepare all for college; teach immigrants in their native languages; teach driver's ed; feed lunch to poor children; entertain the community with Friday-night football and midwinter basketball; sponsor dances and fairs for the kids; and serve as the prime (and often the only) social-welfare agency for both children and parents. . . . Given the mandates, is it any wonder that so many Americans think the schools are lousy?[67]

Perhaps the most significant symbol of the lack of confidence in education in recent years is the No Child Left Behind Act (hereafter NCLB) of 2001.[68] NCLB mandates accountability through high-stakes standardized tests for an educational system perceived to fail at both reaching sufficient performance standards and ensuring equity across schools. The stakes are high because schools that fail to meet designated passing rates or adequate yearly progress are punished financially and possibly forced to restructure or close.[69]

Though NCLB is based on a worthy goal—improving educational outcomes through testing, assessment, and accountability—its critics have been fierce. In addition to claims that it is an unfunded mandate and that schools are unfairly judged through NCLB, many complain that it changes school curricula in a way that forces schools to "teach to the test."[70] This means that schools narrow their curricula to focus only on subjects included on the standardized tests, and that rote instruction replaces training in critical-thinking skills. Since schools are punished if they fail to meet their standardized test marks, these are rational responses to the incentives they are given. Yet one must wonder about the harm of changing teaching styles and narrowing the curricula in these ways.

In addition to changing how schools teach and what courses are offered, NCLB rewards schools for altering their student bodies. Schools who can restrict their student bodies to the best test takers will improve their scores and be financially rewarded (or at least escape punishment). It would be unconstitutional to do this wholesale, since public schools cannot decide which students are the worst test takers and simply expel them. Yet prior research does suggest that the pressure put on schools by NCLB does encourage them to "push out" a number of poor-performing students; given the established correlations between poor academic performance and behavioral misconduct, this can mean that NCLB encourages schools to remove misbehaving students.[71]

Thus, the political pressure of NCLB, the social anxieties that surround school, the lack of confidence in public educational systems, and the fear of crime are all intertwined. Collectively, these issues lead to great insecurity about and within public schools, a condition that gives rise to "governing through crime." As Simon states: "At its core, the implicit fallacy dominating many school policy debates today consists of a gross conflation of virtually all the vulnerabilities of children and youth into variations on the theme of crime. This may work to raise the salience of education on the public agenda, but at the cost to students of an education embedded with themes of 'accountability,' 'zero tolerance,' and 'norm shaping.'"[72] To understand punishment and security in contemporary public high schools, one must realize that schools face this assortment of problems as school staff struggle to cope with rising expectations, anxieties, and pressures.

Simon's work also helps us understand why school punishment and security have become dominant expressions of these widely varying insecurities. He discusses a national governors' conference convened in 1990 by president George H. W. Bush outlining six goals of public education to be achieved by the year 2000. These six goals speak to the need to raise graduation rates, for higher preparedness among children entering school, to raise science and math achievement rates, and other sound pedagogical goals; only the sixth goal relates to school security by stating, "Every school in America will be free of drugs and violence and will offer a disciplined environment conducive to learning."[73] Simon argues that this one goal became central to the modern reshaping of schools because it evokes fears of largely poor and minority school populations in crime-ridden neighborhoods; it links drugs and violence, which makes the problem relevant to all segments of the population; and it links these problems to school achievement, thus presenting discipline and security as avenues for raising academic standards.

It is important to note that this explanation for the growing prominence of school discipline and security relies on changes that began decades ago and have accelerated since 1990. This shift is the product of many subtle changes in social relations, social structure, and cultural dynamics, as described by both Garland and Simon—not the simple consequence of tragedies such as the incident at Columbine High School in 1999. Columbine High certainly caught the public's attention: it was prominently covered by the national news media, it involved extreme violence, it happened in a middle-class white community (thus defying the expectation of school violence occurring only in poor urban areas), and it exposed the security vulnerabilities of high schools. It was a horrible tragedy and it was very frightening. Yet it would be a mistake to think that police officers in schools, zero-tolerance policies, rising suspension rates, and other punishment and security initiatives are the result only of this one incident. Though Columbine might have accelerated these forces and made school discipline and security even more central than before, especially as a story for the media, the trends were already in progress.[74] To realize this, one need only see the surveillance camera footage of the Columbine High shooting, showing armed school guards searching for the attackers during the incident. The point is that both the security cameras and the armed guards were already there (and failed to prevent the massacre from happening).

Zero-tolerance policies began to emerge in the 1980s—long before Columbine—and then became common after Congress passed the 1994 Safe Schools Act, which required public schools to expel for at least one year any student bringing a weapon to school, or else lose their federal funding.[75] As one would expect, schools across the country rapidly got on board; by 1997, over 90% of public schools had zero-tolerance policies for firearms and weapons.[76] Since then, however, many schools have voluntarily expanded zero-tolerance policies to include non-violent and non-criminal behaviors such as excessive absences, persistent defiance of authority, and defacement of school property.[77]

The first SRO program also began long ago, in the 1950s, though full-time police presence in schools across the country was still quite rare until a series of federal funding and legislative initiatives in the 1990s.[78] The Safe Schools Act of 1994 spurred the growth of this program by dedicating money to public schools that develop violence-prevention programs, which create partnerships with community agencies, including law enforcement. Additionally, a 1998 amendment to the 1968 Omnibus Crime Control and Safe Street Act encouraged school-police partnerships through the SRO model.[79] Thus, legislation that predates Columbine led to growth in the numbers of police in schools, and by 1999 54% of public school students between the ages of twelve and eighteen reported having a daily police or security presence. This trend accelerated after Columbine, thanks to additional federal funding; by 2005, 68% of students reported an officer or security guard in their school.[80] But clearly these trends were well underway prior to Columbine.

Understanding the Significance of the New Discipline Regime

There has been a great deal of academic writing on schools by scholars in several fields—sociology, philosophy, history, education, and political science—that illustrates the importance of schools in shaping the future lives of youth and in helping determine what our society looks like. This work clearly demonstrates how changes in school discipline are important not only for whether and how they prevent crime and punish students caught misbehaving (though these topics are extremely important), but also because they might reshape the school environment in ways that have far-reaching effects. Because the school environment has the potential to affect our national economy, political participation, and social inequality, it is an important issue for everyone, not just students or parents of students who are punished in school.

Schools do much more than teach academics. They also teach children how to think, how to act, and how to get along in the world. As sociologist Emile Durkheim stated, "The school has, above all, the function of linking the child to this society."[81] His statement was part of a series of lectures at the Sorbonne in 1902–1903 that were then printed as the book, *Moral Education*. In these lectures Durkheim discusses how schools are vitally important for the continuing health of society. Through the exercise of their authority schools teach morality, which, Durkheim argued, can only exist in relation to the social unit, since morality requires acting on behalf of others. Schools thus provide the foundation for an ordered society. When one considers Durkheim's larger body of work, the importance he places on school seems even more impressive. Durkheim argued that society is more than the sum of its parts—that there is an inescapable "conscience collective" that binds us together, allows for orderly interactions, and gives meaning to social life. The fact that Durkheim saw the school as the mechanism through which the conscience collective is developed illustrates the importance he placed on the institution.

Durkheim was certainly not alone in recognizing how modern society requires mass education. The philosopher John Dewey, for example, is well-known for his work on public education as a foundation of democratic society.[82] Because the school teaches free exchange and communication of experience, it equips citizens with the skills necessary to maintain democratic government. While in school students learn how to think critically, how to communicate their ideas, and how to solve problems; democratic society requires citizens to have these skills so that the public can participate in the government process by expressing their needs, being able to critically evaluate governmental policies, and recognizing progress. Thus, the school prepares us for life in society, particularly a democratic one in which citizens participate in government.

Historians of education have noted that preparing young people for future social life has been a primary goal of public schools since the spread of compulsory education in the nineteenth century. In *The One Best System*, historian David Tyack details the transformation from village school systems of the early nineteenth century to corporate-bureaucratic school systems run by educational experts. He describes how the changing organization of schools paralleled changing social and economic conditions in the United States. As society moved further into an industrial age, schools followed suit by adopting a bureaucratic organizing principle, with standardized curricula and increased supervision/direction from school administrators. Business leaders often led and funded school reforms during this era, and the resulting model of education taught youth the logics of an urban-industrial society. Schools demanded habits such as punctuality, silence, and precision, since these behaviors would be demanded of students in their future roles as factory workers. The phrase "toe the line" comes from this type of physical discipline in schools that prepared students for the demands of assembly-line physical labor: students in some schools were required to stand rigidly with their toes precisely on a line drawn on the floor while reciting lessons.

Though schools socialize youth into society by instilling in them valued skills and behaviors, this process happens very differently for different youth. Critical analyses of education suggest that one's social position determines the types of lessons received in school. Since schools grease the wheels of industry, they must prepare students differently depending on their eventual roles within the mode of production. This perspective has been discussed in many texts, perhaps the most famous of which is *Schooling in Capitalist America* by economists Samuel Bowles and Herbert Gintis.[83] Bowles and Gintis argue that because the relationships of authority between school administrators and teachers and between teachers and students mirror the relationships of an occupational division of labor, schools socialize students into the relations of dominance and subordination demanded within an industrial economy.

Schools train people to be laborers, and they reinforce the social inequalities along lines of race, ethnicity, social class, and sex that exist in the labor force. Moreover, they replicate inequalities and fulfill economic demands while appeasing the working class—since their children receive a free education that, in theory, allows anyone to rise in social status—thus reducing the likelihood of workers rising up against their employers.[84]

Sociologists Pierre Bourdieu and Jean-Claude Passeron add to this perspective by elaborating a theory of social reproduction that explains how schools reproduce existing social inequalities through an unequal distribution of cultural capital.[85] Here cultural capital refers to the skills, behaviors, and preferences that have economic and social value, and that come about through social inequality.[86] This social value placed on preferences or behaviors is arbitrarily established but enforced through a structural hierarchy. For example, there is nothing inherently better about ballet than hip-hop dancing, though the dance that tends to be preferred by dominant groups (ballet) bears greater social status than the dance preferred by subordinate groups (hip-hop). Schools make this system seem legitimate by emphasizing the value of the dominant groups' interests and behaviors. In other words, schools teach students that some skills and behaviors are superior to others, and the students who best master these behaviors are rewarded by the school; yet the students who best master these behaviors are also the ones in whom they were already deeply ingrained, due to their position within the social power structure. Because the school appears to be a meritocracy, this unequal treatment appears to be fair, as if the objectively most talented students naturally come out on top. Really, Bourdieu and Passeron argue, the process simply mimics and reproduces existing social inequalities, thereby making these inequalities appear to be the legitimate and fair result of a meritocratic school system.

This problem of schools reinforcing social inequality is made even worse by the fact that it works in such subtle, usually hidden ways. Educational inequities seem normal and acceptable because they mirror the outside world. As education scholar Michael Apple states, "The problem is hegemonic—we're blind to it because it is understood as natural."[87] Expectations and standards are communicated very subtly in undetected ways, such as in linguistic codes. For example, James Paul Gee shows how all language has a social context, and how the language we use contains symbols that indicate our membership in various social groups. By privileging only a single mode of discourse, schools maintain the social power of groups who have already mastered this discourse: "All texts—spoken or written—construct a favored position from which they are to be received. . . . In this sense, all texts . . . are also about solidarity; that is, the construction of the 'right' sorts of listeners and readers, ones sufficiently like the social identity the speaker or writer has adopted for the construction of that particular text."[88] Because schools teach norms and expectations in such subtle ways, scholars refer to this as the "hidden curriculum."[89]

Several excellent studies have illustrated how this unequal socialization process works in practice to perpetuate existing social inequalities. One of the best known is sociologist Paul Willis's *Learning to Labor*.[90] By studying a group of working-class English boys, whom he calls the "lads," Willis advances our understanding of how working-class youth are socialized into working-class futures, while middle-class youth are socialized into middle-class futures. The lads perceive the school as hostile to them, and they (astutely) see the small likelihood that academic success will lead to promising careers for them. As a result, they reject the school's middle-class behavioral expectations and academics, opposing the school's authority as a way to assert their independence. In other words, the school rewards only white-collar norms of academic study and acceptance of authority, not the behaviors the lads see at home and in their community: manual labor, practical ability rather than theoretical knowledge, and an oppositional culture. In response to the school's disapproval, the lads reject the school's goals and its authority, instead pursuing working-class jobs. Thus, the lads participate in this social stratification process by rejecting the structural and cultural norms that they perceive to be hostile to them.

More recent studies also illustrate how the norms that are rewarded and taught by the school reproduce existing social inequalities, and how these inequalities exist along race/ethnicity and gender lines in addition to those of social class. In a recent ethnography of racial/ethnic minority students in public schools, sociologist Prudence Carter demonstrates how minority students often find a cultural conflict at school. Cultural issues such as standards of dress, language, and musical taste among students of color often meet disapproval in the school, despite the fact that they have nothing to do with academic learning. This forces students to choose between their cultural norms and the norms rewarded in the school. Though some students are able to successfully navigate back and forth between these two codes—Carter calls them "cultural straddlers"—others feel marginalized and may either retreat from school involvement or defy the school's authority.[91]

This body of theory and research makes a very powerful argument about how schools are tied to broader society. On the one hand, schools are shaped by social influences, since the norms that define schools' behavioral expectations, instructional content, and pedagogic approach are based on those of powerful groups in society. These norms are not shared by all members of society, thus the school privileges some groups over others in a way that mirrors broader social inequalities. On the other hand, schools themselves exert an influence on broader society by applying this unequal treatment to youth. This process rewards the students who conform to these norms and punishes those who don't, all while making this reward and punishment system appear to be the result only of hard work and natural ability. This acts as training for students, as they are socialized into future roles and expectations for their adult lives. Some learn how to display the behaviors that garner approval of authorities, while others learn that their behaviors or preferences are looked down on by authorities.

With this brief summary of how schools mirror and reproduce social inequality in mind, it becomes clear how school punishment and security have much broader effects than crime control alone. The way that schools police and punish youth borrows from and reproduces broader social relations, much like prior scholars discuss related to the school's pedagogy. The presence of police and technological surveillance mirror what is currently going on outside schools, particularly mass incarceration and post-industrialization.[92] Youth today enter a society in which there are over two million Americans behind bars, and where traditional industry and labor have been replaced with a logic of global capital that prioritizes new practices, including labor outsourcing, just-in-time production, decentralization, computerized automation, and temporary employment. Today's workers have greater flexibility than workers of generations ago (e.g., telecommuting, electronic rather than personal oversight, etc.), but in ways that contribute to their financial risk, responsibility, and employment instability. These trends are reflected in contemporary school security, particularly through the introduction of police and technological surveillance. These security practices enhance the link between school and the criminal justice system, introduce students to the risk of incarceration through greater frequency of police involvement in their lives, and lead to greater control over youths' actions through electronic monitoring.[93]

Not only do school security practices borrow from trends in labor markets and punishment, but they also socialize students into this new regime, so that students no longer think twice about having police in schools or being filmed by surveillance cameras. This means that when they leave school, students are less likely than members of previous generations to be alarmed at frequent police presence in their neighborhoods or surveillance in the workplace. By teaching students what to expect and how to respond to these social control mechanisms (e.g., learning to take drug tests without complaint), schools socialize youth into future adult roles and responsibilities. This mirrors precisely what scholars such as David Tyack and Paul Willis discussed about schools preparing youth for industrial labor, only the content of the learning has changed with the times.

In an essay about how the prison and the ghetto have come to resemble each other and to work together in the marginalization of African American communities, sociologist Loïc Wacquant discusses how urban schools socialize lower-income and minority youth into the carceral state:

> Public schools in the hyperghetto have similarly deteriorated to the point where they operate in the manner of *institutions of confinement* whose primary mission is not to educate but to ensure "custody and control." . . . Indeed, it appears that the main purpose of these school [*sic*] is simply to "neutralize" youth considered unworthy and unruly by holding them under lock and key for the day so that, at minimum, they do not engage in street crime. . . . The carceral atmosphere of schools and the constant presence of armed guards in uniform in the lobbies, corridors, cafeteria, and playground of their establishment habituates the children of the hyperghetto to the demeanor, tactics, and interactive style of the correctional officers many of them are bound to encounter shortly after their school days are over.[94]

Wacquant describes the prison as the mechanism for maintaining the social and economic marginalization of African Americans, and how this is now made possible because of the integration of the ghetto and the prison. He describes how ghetto schools have incorporated physical properties of prisons (e.g., locked doors, metal detectors, barbed wire), technologies such as cameras, and security forces, making them function much like prisons. In doing so, they prepare lower-income minority youth who live in the ghetto for the likelihood that they will be involved with the criminal justice system.

As Wacquant's argument clearly shows, we need to consider how this socialization process differs for different students. We would expect minority students and lower-income students to receive close scrutiny, to be punished quickly and severely, and to be disciplined in ways that lead them to expect stern authority governing their lives. In contrast, we would expect white students and middle-income students to be given more leeway in schools, to be given relatively mild punishments for misbehavior, and to interact with school security in ways that teach them how to manage risk and receive protection from external threats. In this way, schools would prepare the former group of students to live under close watch by the state, enduring bleak economic futures, frequent police surveillance, and harsh punishments for misbehaviors; the latter would be taught skills that empower them to avoid, manage, and control such risks, or to use these elements of control to their social, professional, and economic advantage.[95]

This holds true when we look at the individual level. That is, minorities and lower-income students are indeed more likely than others to be punished in school, even when they commit similar infractions. But Wacquant's argument suggests that this is an issue for entire schools, not just individuals, since whole communities are being marginalized and socialized into the carceral regime. Though schools can and do respond in different ways to different students within the same schools, we also need to think about how entire schools set and enforce security and discipline policies, and how these schools vary from other schools in different communities.

Very few studies have done this, and those that have find that schools with mostly middle-class white students enforce discipline very differently than those with mostly lower-income minority students. Legal scholars William Lyons and Julie Drew, for example, compare two schools: "Suburban High School," with mostly middle-class white students, and "Urban High School," with mostly lower-income minority youth.[96] They argue that discipline varies across these two schools because of how each school community thinks of conflict within their walls. At Suburban High, conflict is considered to be minor, usually revolving around students' romantic problems, because the similarity of students (and absence of minority or poor students) causes them and school staff to perceive everyone there as having common values. This creates a collective sense of security. In contrast, at Urban High students and staff express more fear and perceive more conflict, which makes punishment situations more tense and conflict-driven. Their analyses go on to suggest less of a disparity than one might assume, since the main themes that they express in their book—that a zero-tolerance disciplinary climate erodes democratic dialogue, fails to solve students' problems, and reproduces existing social inequalities—are found in both schools.

In sum, when we think about how this prior research relates to school discipline, there is reason for concern. The potential impact of school punishment and security is particularly important in shaping how young adults interact with authority figures, including employers and the state, and contemporary school discipline has the potential to teach dangerous lessons. One such lesson is to accept existing power relations uncritically, without challenging authority. Students may become young adults who think nothing of electronic surveillance, drug tests, and other controlling measures that they became accustomed to in school and that they may find in the workplace. Coming of age in an environment where having "zero tolerance" is proudly trumpeted, where complicated behaviors and problems are assessed through rigid, one-size-fits-all rules, and where consequences for relatively minor misbehavior can be severe (suspension, expulsion, arrest), surely has an effect on how one understands authority. Contemporary schools require that students both relinquish power to challenge authority and internalize the harsh consequences of violating school rules.[97]

Michel Foucault described this mode of discipline, most famously in *Discipline and Punish*.[98] Foucault traces the historical shift in responding to criminal offenders from the gallows to the prison—from a model of physical punishment to the emergence of the prison as a response to crime. For Foucault, a history of the prison provides a window for discussing power and discipline in modern society, since the prison is the most evident display of these forces.[99] His vision of discipline is one that reaches the "souls" of individuals in addition to their bodies. Those who wield power seek to alter deviants' souls by normalizing or correcting them, which is done by having subjects internalize discipline, thereby becoming docile and obedient to authority. In order to do this, authorities collect information about their subjects, which is then used to highlight deviance, punish the offender, and correct the offender by bringing about the desired behavior. Constant surveillance allows authorities to have thorough knowledge about their subjects and to supervise their actions.

Foucault discusses the school as part of this discipline process. Though the prison may be the epitome of modern discipline, the school also contributes to it, as do other institutions such as the family, work, and health care institutions. In various ways, each institution supervises, trains, and disciplines in a way that seeks to correct one's soul—to have subjects internalize authority in such a way that they routinely obey it.[100] The buildup of surveillance, rigid security, and harsh punishments in public high schools threatens to strengthen this discipline process and create docile workers who leave school uncritical of the power exerted over them by authorities.

These power relations are neither new nor unique to contemporary schools. Foucault considers discipline of the soul to be a necessity for the development of modern democratic society, since the freedoms allowed in a democratic society would not be possible without the order produced by discipline. But it is important to realize that something has changed in public schools across the United States over the past two decades, and these changes accelerate the power dynamics Foucault describes. Practices such as surveillance cameras, drug-sniffing dogs, and police presence in schools are clear embodiments of the tools Foucault described as necessary for achieving discipline. Because of enormous increases in the use of these tools, we risk changes in the labor market that give even greater power to employers at the expense of employees, since young adults may be raised to internalize discipline and expect strict accountability more so than before. When one considers other recent trends in the U.S. labor market, such as the decline in the influence of labor unions as well as the outsourcing of jobs overseas, the potential for greater internalization of authority among young workers is disconcerting.

One can also imagine how school discipline and security may be reshaping other features of social life, such as civic participation. If it is the case that students are socialized into powerlessness, whereby they learn that they are impotent to do anything but follow authority, then this could have a marked impact on citizens' participation in government, including declines in voting rates, political protest, and participation in local government (town assemblies, school committees, PTAs, etc.). In *Why We Vote*, political scientist David E. Campbell considers how school shapes one of these behaviors: voting.[101] His analyses suggest that students who attend schools with more inclusive, civic climates are more likely to vote than others over the course of their lives (though the effect does not appear immediately). Schools that do a better job of empowering students to appreciate their role as citizens of a school also do a better job of empowering them to appreciate their role as citizens of a nation. Thus, one should be concerned about the potential for schools to be run in an authoritarian way rather than a democratic way, since this could alienate students in a way that teaches them to be passive citizens and makes them less likely to participate in civic life. It is entirely possible that by introducing zero-tolerance policies, police, surveillance cameras, and other school punishment and security policies, we are altering our future political landscape by reducing the future participation of today's youth.

One can also imagine changes in civic participation other than voting practices. If school discipline takes on an authoritarian tone, then it is likely to create citizens that do not see themselves as part of a national community in other ways as well. Actions such as living in gated communities and buying SUVs, each of which connote both fear of external threat and the pursuit of individual advantage at the expense of the communal good, might become even more common.[102] In sum, the bond that ties individuals to their communities becomes stronger when youth learn in school how to be active community members; but if schools treat youth as potential criminals rather than worthy citizens, they might be weakening this bond.

Finally, it is also clear that students' involvement with school punishment and security shapes their relation to formal social control outside schools. One way that this might happen is for schools to act as accomplices to the criminal justice system.[103] In this capacity, schools sort and label certain students as criminals, and both institutions work together to marginalize entire communities. Foucault's description of schools as part of a carceral continuum also characterizes schools as working alongside the prison to instill discipline in society.[104] This effect might be a long-lasting one, whereby the lessons students learn in school about the ubiquity and omniscience of authority might shape their adult lives, making them generally more compliant and less likely to challenge social control mechanisms.

What's more, these negative potential consequences are likely to be concentrated among lower-income and minority groups.[105] If poor students and youth of color become less protected in the workplace, less likely to vote, and more compliant to authority, then they would be even less likely than they are now to challenge social hierarchies, thereby causing current social divisions to grow.

Obviously, this discussion focuses only on the negative possibilities: that contemporary school discipline and security have far-reaching negative effects. It is also possible that police, surveillance cameras, zero-tolerance policies, and the like socialize students to be less fearful, better integrated into society, more moral, and better able to successfully navigate their futures because they have properly internalized social rules and norms. This more optimistic conception is consistent with Durkheim's view of the importance of school discipline for teaching morality.[106] Yet Durkheim also emphasized that school discipline must be done in a way that allows students to participate in dispensing justice and is perceived by them to be fair. Unfortunately, this is not what I found in my research. Rather, school rules are enforced in ways that put students at risk of unnecessary punishment, fail to address students' real problems, and exacerbate existing inequalities.

2

PROTECTING OUR CHILDREN

Discipline Practices at School

At Landsdowne Junior High School, the *St. Louis Sun* reports, "there are scores of window frames without glass, like sockets without eyes." Hallways in many schools are dark, with light bulbs missing or burnt out. One walks into a school, a member of the city's board of education notes, "and you can smell the urinals a hundred feet away . . . "

A teacher at an elementary school in East St. Louis has only one full-color workbook for her class. She photocopies workbook pages for her children, but the copies can't be made in color and the lessons call for color recognition by the children.

A history teacher at the Martin Luther King School has 110 students in four classes—but only 26 books. Some of the books are missing the first hundred pages.[1]

This bleak description of schools in East St. Louis, Illinois, a poor area in which most of the residents are African Americans, comes from Jonathan Kozol's book *Savage Inequalities*.[2] In other passages he describes schools in wealthier areas that have all the supplies they need and are in excellent physical condition. Such disparities in schools' physical conditions surely lead to differences in how schools are run. I can only imagine how difficult it must be to convince students in one of these East St. Louis schools of the importance of education, to supervise groups of children in dark hallways, or to ask them to respect one another when they suffer the disrespect of having to attend such decrepit schools. The four schools I studied face different circumstances and challenges that are also important to discuss in order to understand how each polices and punishes students.

Unionville High School

Unionville High School is located in a mid-Atlantic state. When its school district approved my research, I had listed Unionville High and another school as equally appropriate research sites. The district officials specifically requested that of the two, I visit Unionville High. As my research assistant and I entered the school and spent time there, the reason why became apparent: the school has a reputation as being a disorderly, low-performing, and violent place. When I met the administrators who would serve as my contacts for the next several months and answered their questions about why we were at Unionville High, several of them grinned and asked how I had chosen the school as a research site. I told them that it was an appropriate demographic comparison to a school I had already studied in another state, and that the district officials requested Unionville High rather than another school. At this, the school employees usually laughed knowingly, and talked about how Unionville High has a reputation for being violent and disorderly, which is why (they assumed) the district wanted me to study it.

This knowing laugh made me think that only outsiders perceived Unionville as disorderly, and that these insiders knew better. I soon realized that this is untrue. Staff members told stories of weapons being common at school, as well as rampant drug use in bathrooms among students—some stories even described staff members who smoked marijuana with the students in years past. Students echoed this negative assessment, such as the following white female student:

STUDENT: The kids in this school are just awful.

INTERVIEWER: Yeah? Tell me, how are they awful?

STUDENT: They're disgusting, their attitudes and lack of respect. I just, I don't how their parents even raised them like that, they're just rude.

INTERVIEWER: Like what kind of rudeness? Like what kind of, how does that show itself?

STUDENT: Like, let's say if I was in the hallway and a dean came up to me and was like, "Let me see your pass," the student would cuss at them, yell at them, walk away. I was in the hallway with [the Junior ROTC instructor] the other day and these two kids walked up, you know, act-

FIGURE 2.1

Frequency of Suspensions, by Category, at Unionville High

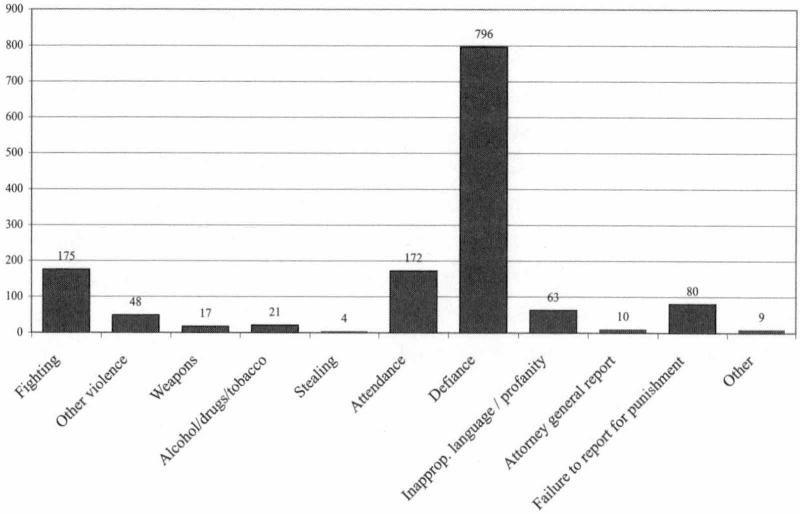

ing all arrogant and stuff, and [the instructor] asked them you know, "Do you have a pass?", like repeatedly, and they just ignored him and kept on walking. That is just the utmost disrespect I've ever seen in this school.

INTERVIEWER: Hmm, so they just don't respect the adults in the school?

STUDENT: No, not at all. (I)

Based on my observations over time, it is understandable why school officials and students talked about the disorder at Unionville High. Though I never observed serious violence, weapons, or drugs firsthand, I did observe a great deal of minor incidents—more than at any of the other three schools. These incidents fall short of actual crime and often short of school rule violations, but they contribute to a chaotic, unruly feeling, such as physical play between students, yelling, profanity, and disobedience to school staff.

The response to disorder at Unionville High is striking, as shown in figure 2.1, which uses data on suspensions for the 2005–2006 school year that were supplied by district officials. This figure is overwhelmed by the enormous number of suspensions for defiance (n = 796), which includes behaviors the school labels "defiance of school authority," "disruption of the educational process," and "inappropriate behavior." With 180 school days in a year, this amounts to more than 4 suspensions per day for this type of minor-level misbehavior. There were also 175 suspensions for fighting, and 172 for attendance violations.

With regard to race/ethnicity and class, school staff talk about Unionville High students in a way that surprised me—they frequently speak about the students as if they are nearly all racial/ethnic minorities and poor. Yet according to the Institute of Education Statistics, the student body is 36% white, 49% black, and 11% Hispanic, and 41% receive free or reduced-price lunches (see table 2.1). Whites are in the minority here, and nearly half the students are classified as poor for the school lunch program, but school officials talk about the student body in terms that made me expect a much lower percentage of white students and higher percentage of poor students. For example, the police officer there once commented on how the school

TABLE 2.1

Comparison of Sampled Schools (2004–2005 School Year)

	Southwestern state schools		Mid-Atlantic state schools	
	Frontera High	Fairway Estates High	Unionville High	Centerville High
Total students	2,227	2,739	1,506	2,067
Student/teacher ratio	16.5	23.1[a]	15.4	18.1
Race/ethnicity (%):				
White	3.5	82.5	36.3	73.5
Hispanic	91.7	11.1	10.9	3
Black	3.1	2.3	48.9	20.8
Asian	0.4	2.4	3.7	2.4
American Indian/Alaskan	1.2	1.7	0.2	0.2
Free or reduced lunch eligible (%)	93.8	18.1	41.2	9.1

Source: Institute of Education Statistics, U.S. Department of Education.

[a] If one calculates the student/teacher ratio using the populations listed on Fairway Estate High's website rather than using the U.S. Department of Education data, the ratio is 18.3, which is consistent with the other three schools.

district "dumps all of the worst kids" at Unionville High, and that the students at Unionville come from the "lowest socioeconomic statuses" in the area. By emphasizing the level of disadvantage among the students at Unionville High, the staff's rhetoric is consistent with how many of them speak about Unionville High generally: as a school in trouble.

Unionville High faces academic challenges as well. During my time there, it was on "academic watch" under the state's accountability/testing system, as it had not met adequate yearly progress goals. The state's 2007 goals for percentages of students who meet or exceed standards in English and math were 68% and 50% respectively; Unionville students failed to meet both of these goals, with 54% meeting or exceeding the English standards and 36% meeting or exceeding the math standards. Additionally, the school's graduation rate is only 72%, below the state goal of 78%.

Another problem facing Unionville High is the physical structure itself. The school consists of a single building, built in 1973, that is surrounded by parking lots, tennis courts, and athletic fields. Inside the building some of the paint is faded and chipped, and the lighting is poor in many places. School staff members pointed out to me where temporary walls were erected to create additional office or class space, since the school was designed for fewer students and staff than it currently houses. In addition to this dismal appearance, I often saw trash in the hallways and occasionally graffiti on walls. Subscribers to the "broken windows" theory of crime—that residents of communities take cues from their environment, such that litter, graffiti, or broken windows in an area make one more likely to commit crime—would argue that the physical environment encourages misbehavior at Unionville High.[3]

The school's architectural layout presents challenges as well. When I first arrived at Unionville and looked at a map of the school, I was confused by the byzantine array of corridors and separate wings. The school has two floors, and each of these floors is divided into two circular sections. Each section has its own cafeteria. There are several stairways in different parts of the school, and multiple paths one could take from one wing to another. More important, with so many turns in the hallways, staff members monitoring the halls find they have very little visibility, since there is always another corner around which a student can hide.

There is also very little oversight of the front entrance. Though there is a desk by the door with a clipboard and sign-in sheet for visitors, there is usually nobody monitoring the entrance. All other doors are kept locked (though students can open them from inside the school).

As one might expect based on student demographics, Unionville High is located in a relatively poor neighborhood. It is in the suburbs, about ten miles from a mid-sized city, but the suburbs are home to a large number of townhouses and trailer parks. The single-family homes near the school are small and stand in stark comparison to the 3,000–4,000 square foot mansions immediately surrounding Centerville High.

But looking at the immediate neighborhood does not fully explain Unionville High, since a large number of its students are bused in from the nearby city. This practice dates back to the 1970s, when the area schools were forced to desegregate. In response, the public high schools in the city eventually closed, and the city's resident children were sent to high schools in three different neighboring districts. Children in some of the poorest neighborhoods of the city were sent to Unionville High's district, which continues today. This is important for understanding dynamics at Unionville High not only because it means that there is a good deal of poverty and a large number of racial/ethnic minorities among the students, but also because it means that many parents—and especially parents of the most disadvantaged students—do not live near the school. This adds to the difficulties parents already face in interacting with school officials or attending school events. It also imposes greater social distance between groups of students, since they live far apart.

Some contend that the inner-city youth who are bused to Unionville High make the school a more disruptive place, as these youth are more likely than others to commit crimes. One white male staff member, for example, told me very confidently that these students are the ones who bring marijuana to school:

You can't buy weed in [the neighboring community]. The weed that's for sale [near the school] they can't afford. You want the cheap weed that these kids are smoking, it's gotta come from [the nearby city]. They don't have cars, luckily we provide transportation [buses]. (I)

The school is located on a busy, four-lane, divided highway. In front of the school on the street there is a street sign that is supposed to say "drug free school zone," except that the word "free" has been crossed out with spray paint. The school sits immediately next to a townhouse complex, and across the highway is a strip mall with a Burger King, grocery store, pharmacy, and other small stores. Thus, there are plenty of entertaining destinations for students who skip class, as long they are willing to cross a busy highway (where there is no crosswalk)—I often noticed students drinking from Burger King cups in school.

The political climate surrounding Unionville High should also be noted. I began the observations during a difficult time for this school district. The superintendent had recently left to take a position in another state, and the new superintendent requested a budget audit, which found that the prior superintendent had disguised questionable financial transactions and a twelve-million-dollar deficit. This weakened public confidence in the district and put it in fiscal constraint at the same time that the housing market was collapsing and the economy was heading into a deep recession. These problems left their toll on Unionville High in the form of insufficient funding for supplies and programs, as well as a lack of job security for school staff. Erosion of staff morale was evident in the spring, when several of the staff with whom I interacted regularly were informed that they would not be rehired for the following year.

Leadership at Unionville has been inconsistent as well. I began research there shortly after a new principal took control of the school, a few months into the 2006–2007 school year. This was the fourth principal in the past four years, leaving a great deal of inconsistency in how the school was run. Some students noted this during interviews, such as the following black female student who complained about the current principal:

I don't really like him. He's not fair at all, every single principal in this school was not fair I think. We had, I was here for four years, four different principals each year and every principal tried to change up the school in a way that was not even important. He changed, we had so much spirit in this school, like artists who had like a [mural] on the wall, or like school spirit, he painted all the stuff white, and we were not supposed to have certain posters on the wall, in the classrooms. It's like, it was hard, like this school was like jail. And like if he'll see you in the hallway, he'll question you. Like, if you go to him with help, he never gets back to you. There's some teachers who don't like to help you at all, so you have no choice to go to him because he is the principal. . . . I don't think any of the principals is fair, but they all left, so it's like you can't count on nobody in Unionville. Unionville is just one big mess. . . . I wish I never even came here. (I)

Discipline Policies and Practices

All these challenges faced by Unionville High—political turmoil, inconsistent leadership, disorder in the hallways, a deteriorating physical structure, parents who live far away, and a relatively disadvantaged student body—are important for understanding how punishment and security work here. They set the stage for a punitive discipline regime that responds to the perceived chaos by trying to provide a regimented order. The situation at Unionville High illustrates clearly how contemporary school discipline is fueled by insecurities surrounding school and a lack of confidence in public education; with all the problems the school faces, one of the few things a principal can do is implement tough policies that promise to "right the ship."

Of course, since school discipline has changed throughout the United States, it is obvious that these particular challenges faced by Unionville High have not created its punitive discipline climate—but these factors have influenced the school's draconian climate, and possibly made it worse. Unionville High relies on exclusion of students far more often than the other three schools I studied—its suspension rate is a staggering ninety-six suspensions per hundred students (including repeat offenders), with 43% of the student body suspended at lest once in 2005–2006 (see figure 2.2). The themes I discuss throughout this book are present in Unionville High and elsewhere, but punishment is given out more often at Unionville than at other schools. Other schools punish students without listening to them, escalate misbehavior problems, and enforce authority without dealing with problems, all of which is qualitatively similar to how this happens at Unionville High—but the other three schools do it less often. In part, this is directly caused by the higher rates of disorder; but it also seems due to a tougher stance on student misbehavior in an attempt to create order out of chaos.[4]

FIGURE 2.2

Suspension Rate (per 100 youth) in Each School (2005–2006)

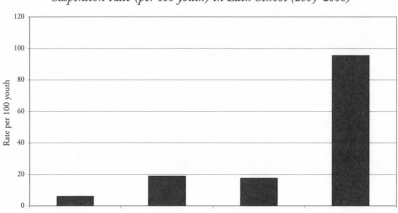

The method of punishing students at Unionville does not vary substantially from the other schools I studied. Like other schools, most of the rule enforcement and punishment is handled by employees who are called "deans of discipline," staff members whose primary responsibilities concern responding to student misbehavior. There are three deans of discipline at Unionville High; each is assigned students based on an alphabetical range, and each has an office where students go if given a "referral" and removed from class.[5] The deans then respond by assigning punishments based on their judgment and the school's code of conduct. They have a great deal of discretion in punishing students—assistant principals are required to sign all suspension forms, but I routinely saw the deans forego this.

When I began observing at Unionville High, one of the deans, an African American woman, also performed other duties: she spent a great deal of time with students entering the school from alternative placements, as well as those facing expulsion. During my stay, another dean, a white male, was hired and she concentrated solely on her other duties. At this point, all three deans were white males, and like at other schools, these men were very involved in athletics. One was a former college football player and is the current defensive coordinator for the varsity football team, and another is the school's athletic director and golf team coach.

The fact that two of the three deans are coaches is important. Disciplinary roles can be "free hires" for administrators, in that they can hire somebody who has skills in another area (e.g., coaching), and give that person duties as a disciplinarian in order to justify a full-time salary. I discussed this with an administrator and former dean of discipline in another school, within the same district as Unionville High, who told me that deans tend to be coaches for two reasons: (1) because coaches often have a disciplinary mindset and thus they seek out the position, and (2) because it allows a full-time position for a coach. In other words, disciplinary roles are not filled by looking for candidates with backgrounds that lend themselves toward effective discipline (e.g., consistency, empathy, listening skills, patience, etc.). Instead the positions tend to be filled by individuals with no training in counseling or dealing with troubled youth, but who are oriented toward rules and a regimented order. In the following chapters I describe how disciplinarians often fail to listen to students, and instead assert authority in non-empathetic, impatient ways. Though I cannot claim that being a current or past coach predisposes one to take this kind of no-nonsense, masculine approach to discipline, it certainly seems likely. At the very least, it's clear that the type of discipline one gets when hiring coaches to do discipline would likely vary sharply from what one would get if hiring counselors trained in adolescent development for the same position.

Like the other schools I studied, Unionville High makes frequent use of its in-school suspension (ISS) room. It is housed in a classroom, though according to the ISS supervisor little instruction goes on during ISS. Many students are sent to ISS by their dean of discipline after being removed from a class, and they stay there for the remainder of that period. Other students are assigned one or more days of ISS as punishment, so that they remain in the ISS room all day instead of attending their scheduled classes. As a result some students are there for long periods of time, while others come and go throughout the day. Though they are sent there as punishment, students talk casually with one another while there, and others use the room's computer to surf the web or listen to music.

Another similarity to the other schools is that Unionville High has one police officer who works there full-time. An African American male in his late forties, Officer Brandon is still in his first year working at a school. Most days he wears a traditional police uniform and carries a firearm, though he does occasionally wear street clothes, with his badge and firearm on a belt. Officer Brandon is also an assistant coach for Unionville High's football team, which gives him an opportunity to meet many students. I would often stand with him in the cafeteria during lunchtime, when he would banter with students. This conversation is usually friendly, and Officer Brandon makes clear attempts to mentor students and give helpful advice to those who he thinks need support. He makes a habit of lending books (novels) to students, particularly females. Yet he is also sarcastic and sometimes cruel. If a student shows bravado or teases Officer Brandon, he responds by putting the student in his or her place. For example, a black student who was hoping to play football the next season, Kevin, walked up to Officer Brandon and the football team head coach during lunch, and bragged about his ability to bench press 185 pounds fifteen times. Officer Brandon bet Kevin $25 dollars that he couldn't do it. When Kevin was unable to lift the weight, Officer Brandon bet him double or nothing, and Kevin again was unable to do it; he continued challenging the student to try again, for more money, and Kevin eventually owed Officer Brandon $125. Office Brandon later laughed about it with me and assured me he would collect his money. Indeed, though I do not know what became of the situation or whether he was being entirely serious, I saw him negotiate with Kevin and insist on the debt being repaid even when the student referred to the difference in financial means between them:

> OFFICER BRANDON: Well, why don't you just start paying me ten dollars a week then?
> KEVIN: OK, I can do that. I mean, you're a [police officer]—I work at Kmart. (FN)

Consider also the following note about a conversation among students serving ISS, each of whom relayed comments similar to statements I had heard Officer Brandon make to students:

> The students talked about Officer Brandon and how he cuts students down. [The ISS teacher, a black male] said he definitely agreed with that and thinks it's not right that Officer Brandon does that. One male student said Officer Brandon made a remark to him that he was on the six-year

plan for high school. Another student told of Officer Brandon making a sarcastic remark to a student implying that the student would never go to college. [The teacher] said, "Y'all don't need to hear that. Y'all need to hear that you can do whatever it is you set your mind to do." (FN)

Despite these comments, it would be unfair to simply think of Officer Brandon as mean. I watched him try to counsel, mentor, and befriend students often, and I suspect that some of these students' complaints were the result of his sarcastic (but well-intended) sense of humor. But it is important to realize that his comments and actions were sometimes inappropriate, regardless of his intent.

Unlike both southwestern schools but like Centerville High, there are no security guards at Unionville High. The school used to employ guards, but budget cuts forced them to eliminate these positions. There are two hall monitors who help escort students to the office or to a dean of discipline when necessary, but usually they sit outside of the boys' and girls' bathrooms with a sign-in sheet to monitor who enters and leaves the bathrooms. Teachers are assigned hall monitor shifts as well, though several respondents (including teachers) admitted that they rarely fulfill this duty. In then end, most duties once handled by security guards fall to the deans of discipline at Unionville High.

Despite its fiscal problems, there is a very sophisticated surveillance camera system in place at Unionville High. Cameras are mounted throughout the school, and the images that are recorded are saved electronically. These images are accessible on computers throughout the school. On several occasions I watched deans look through the surveillance footage to verify facts about an incident. For example, once I watched as a dean studied the tape of a fight in a hallway to determine which students were involved.

Centerville High School

Centerville High is a large school in the same mid-Atlantic state as Unionville High. Centerville High is in a community that has undergone tremendous growth recently, having been reshaped by the housing boom of the 1990s and early 2000s—in fact, the school was built during this boom, in 1997. Just ten years ago, the town of Centerville was mostly farmland, but now it is home to a vast array of commercial enterprises and luxury homes. The school itself sits immediately next to a housing development of 3,000–4,000 square foot houses on one side, and two strip malls (one on each side of the street) on the other side. Developers recognized the town as conveniently located and underdeveloped, and large houses began sprouting throughout town.

As a result of these housing shifts, there are a large number of wealthy students at Centerville. Staff members at Centerville High often describe their students as being privileged, using terms that are nearly opposite of how staff at Unionville High describe their students. For example, one black administrator, Ms. Doherty, stated:

I just feel that this is a school that's quite different. I just feel that there are a lot of, I feel, privileged students here. It's unlike any school that I've been [at]. I don't know if probably because the amount of money that our—let's put it this way, I don't know what the parents make, I can tell you what the price of the homes are, so based on the prices of the homes . . . I mean this is a place that's unlike any other . . . (I)

Despite the infusion of wealth brought about by the creation of large houses, remnants of the town's recent past are still visible. The school is located on a divided two-lane state highway, and there is an old family farm directly opposite the school. If one travels down this route two miles or so, one reaches the older portion of town, populated by older, smaller buildings built close together.

As one might expect, most of the students at Centerville are white, since there are relatively few African Americans or Latino/as among either the original residents of this formerly rural town or the relatively wealthy newcomers. The student body is 74% white and 21% African American, with only 9% eligible for free or reduced-price lunch (see table 2.1). Thus, though the student body is overwhelmingly white and middle-class, there are racial/ethnic minorities present.

Some staff noted class and racial tensions. For example, in the following statement a white assistant principal acknowledges his difficulty relating to students who come from different backgrounds than himself:

MR. MAJORS: As I grew into this role . . . I recognized that . . . my reactions to certain students in certain situations were different than my reactions would be to other students in those same situations. My reactions in particular to African American males [were] much more likely to end up in a confrontational situation than it was, than my reactions to white males. And you know, it took some independent help to, for me to see that I had some issues that I needed to address myself so that I could treat students equitably. There were cultural differences that I didn't appreciate, that I didn't understand, that meant that I shouldn't expect the same reaction from, if I were to approach one student in this way, and another student in this way, I could get very different reactions because they have different cultural systems. They have different norms, they have, I mean and it's not even just that the two students may be of different ethnicities, it could be you know two students of different socioeconomic [statuses], you know.

INTERVIEWER: What kinds of cultural differences?

MR. MAJORS: African American males in my experience here are more than likely to react angrily if confronted with anger. You know, if I were to come at somebody in a harsh way, for whatever reason, because I stayed up too late last night or because I'm having a rotten day or whatever, some students will get very quiet and understand that, "Wow, Mr. Majors is really serious and you know I better [back down]." And other students have a more oppositional approach to that. And only through working with my colleagues [have I come to] understand that you know, when you've been mistreated by white males in authority . . . white male authority figures fifty times, be they, you know, managers at stores or law enforcement, or fill-in-the-blank, then you have a different reaction to that, and it comes from your experience. (I)

One can also note social class tensions in the following statements from the school's police officer, about how poor youth have moved to the area:

Officer Malvern said that the boy who stole the iPod is like a growing number of kids here at Centerville who live in multiple-family homes. He talked about this phenomenon, and how other groups have done this before, especially Asian Americans and Mexicans. Since they can't afford to buy a five-hundred-thousand-dollar home, several families buy it together—they may be cousins, but they aren't in the same immediate family. He talked about how this is very interesting, and seems to be a growing problem. The problem is that you still have a poor kid, but he's in a rich environment. Officer Malvern stated, "He's still poor—financially and culturally—but he's living in a nice big house and in this school district," and described how now the student wants to steal so that he can have things everyone else has. (FN)

The recent changes to the school have resulted in some difficulties, the most apparent of which is overcrowding. Despite an intended capacity of 1,700 students, there are approximately 2,100 enrolled during my fieldwork, though this situation is scheduled to improve, as another high school in the district was soon to open. During the course of my research, though, overcrowding was clearly a problem. The hallways are clogged during breaks between classes, with the main hallway near the cafeteria often completely stopped due to the gridlock of students trying to go in many different directions at the same time. There are other, less apparent difficulties as well, such as the fact that students have to share lockers.

The overcrowding problem also has forced the use of a series of trailers for additional classroom space. The main building of Centerville High is a large structure with two wings of two stories each, a main area with the auditorium, cafeteria, and administrative offices, and a side wing with the gymnasium, shop classes, and other miscellaneous rooms. Past this side wing, one can leave the main building and enter a fenced-in area with several trailers that are temporary classrooms. The in-school suspension room, which I discuss below, is one of these.

Doors to Centerville High are locked to outsiders, and all visitors must enter through a waiting room outside the administrative offices. There visitors sign in, obtain a temporary badge, and get buzzed in through an electronically operated security door. But the town's library is located at one end of the school—it doubles as the school's library—and is open to the public. Though there are signs telling non-students that they are not allowed to enter the school through the library, school staff complained to us more than once that this is a security liability, in that anyone could enter the school through the library without signing in.

While walking down the hallways of Centerville High, one sees much less of the disorder that is evident at Unionville High: less litter, less cursing, and less physical play among students. There are motivational posters—the kind

FIGURE 2.3

Frequency of Recorded Incidents, by Category, at Centerville High

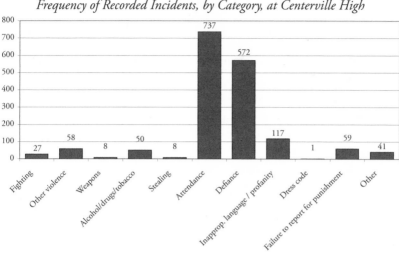

found in corporate lobbies, such as one with an image of an eagle and the caption, "Vision"—throughout the hallways, which are well-lit and appear to have been recently painted.

The district's statistics of offenses at Centerville High indicate that there are few serious incidents, with the bulk of misbehavior being related to either attendance or defiance of authority. Figure 2.3 shows the relative frequency of each type of misbehavior for the 2005–2006 school year. The majority of recorded incidents fall into two categories: attendance (including skipping class, tardiness, absence without permission, and loitering) and defiance (including defiance of school authority, disruption of the educational process, and inappropriate behavior). These two categories of misbehavior account for 78% of all recorded incidents in the 2005–2006 school year.

The most common type of rule enforcement I observed was for a rule newly instituted the year I visited the school: that students must have an ID badge displayed at all times. Most who follow the rule wear their ID badges on lanyards around their necks. This is a source of contention among students, especially returning students for whom it is a new requirement, and consequently the rule is not frequently followed. Once while waiting for an interview to begin I counted the number of students in line for lunch who had ID badges visible: only about one-third of them.

While walking with administrators down crowded hallways, it was common for me to watch them remind entire groups of students that they need to wear their ID badges. Some students ignore them (usually with no repercussions), while others respond by pulling their badges out from under their shirts (these students wear them, just not visibly). At other times, especially when passing students alone or in small groups, administrators stop the students if their badges are not visible and ask to see them. It is extremely rare to see any punishment result from this, since most administrators simply tell the students they need to show their ID badges but take no action, though I did observe a few students being given detention for an ID badge violation.

Academically, Centerville High is in good standing. It is listed as being under improvement, though below target for its annual yearly progress. Overall, the percentages of students who meet or exceed standards in English and math exceed state standards (77% vs. 68% goal for English; 68% vs. 50% goal for math), and the graduation rate is 95% (well beyond the state goal of 78%), though special education and low-income students are below the state standards for both English and math, as are African American and Hispanic students for English scores.

The administration at Centerville High is very stable, in that each assistant principal has been at the school for at least three years. The principal has been in that position for four years, and prior to that had served as the school's interim principal. In addition, the administrative staff is diverse: of the five primary administrators (one principal and four assistant principals), there is a black female, a black male, a white female, and two white males.

Discipline Policies and Practices

Despite the fact that serious offenses are rare at Centerville High, and that the school, overall, is very orderly, it is still common to see students suspended. The most common type of punishment I observed was in-school suspension, where students are sent for either multiple days, a day, or part of a day, and where they are supposed to sit quietly and do schoolwork. More serious offenses result in out-of-school suspension. According to data provided to us by district officials, in the 2005–2006 year there were 869 in-school suspension punishments served. Data from the school's profile state that 10.1% of the student body was suspended or expelled in 2005–2006, but because of multiple suspensions for some students the school has a rate of eighteen suspensions per hundred students.

The process of disciplining students is somewhat different at Centerville High than at the other schools studied. Rather than using security guards or deans, Centerville High employs two staff members with the title "interventionist," who perform duties similar to those of both security guards and deans of discipline at other schools. They are the first responders to misbehavior incidents; when a teacher sends a student out of the classroom, for example, the teacher will usually either radio to one of the interventionists to meet the student in the hallway or send the student to the interventionist directly. The interventionists supervise the in-school suspension room, and they handle referrals and assign punishments to students for minor misbehaviors (the majority of incidents). They also take all hard copies of referral forms—the forms recording student misbehavior—and enter them into the computer system.

Both interventionists are men. One is an African American, and is the coach of the school's varsity basketball team; the other is white, and previously worked in the physical education department of another school after spending twenty years in the navy. Similar to two of the deans at Unionville High, the interventionists both have backgrounds that would make one expect a masculine, non-empathetic approach to discipline, rather than backgrounds in counseling or adolescent development.

Since interventionists are authorized to assign punishments only for less serious incidents, any action that could result in a suspension goes to an assistant principal. Each of the four assistant principals is responsible for disciplining members of one grade (freshmen, sophomores, etc.). If the administrator assigned to a particular student's grade is unavailable (which is common), one of the other assistant principals will meet with the student and handle the discipline duties.

The police officer at Centerville High, Officer Malvern, is a white male in his thirties. Like Officer Brandon, he wears a traditional police uniform and carries a firearm on his belt. He has a great deal of experience in schools as a DARE (Drug Abuse Resistance Education) officer for three years and as an SRO for other schools. I began observing him during his first few months working at Centerville High.

Officer Malvern uses two very different styles in interacting with people: in his office he is very polite, inviting, and warm; in the hallways of the school he is more formal and businesslike. He is never rude while outside his office, but more alert to potential problems and less willing to engage in casual banter. His interactions with students in his office are very warm and fatherly. He encourages students to come to his office and talk to him about anything, and in response he praises them for their successes, encourages them to continue positive behaviors, and offers his assistance, such as giving positive referrals to potential employers. I often observed him listening to students and giving them advice. He interacts casually with students in the hallways as well, but the conversations are shorter and more formal. While in the hallway, he often stands quietly with a serious look on his face and watches students.

Officer Malvern stated to me more than once how he and the administrators have a good working relationship:

> They support me a hundred percent and I support them a hundred per-
> cent. Now, that's not to say we can't disagree . . . but the nice thing about,
> so far, here, is that we're all pretty much on the same page. (I)

This collaboration becomes evident at times, such as whenever students are caught fighting. The principal wants all students caught fighting arrested, and Officer Malvern has agreed to arrest both parties involved in fights under most circumstances. This means that students are arrested both for being aggressors and for defending themselves.

Monthly discipline team meetings are another example of disciplinary collaboration at Centerville High. These meetings are attended by Officer Malvern, administrators, interventionists, and a group of teachers appointed to serve on the committee; about six to eight participants attended each meeting I observed. The main purpose of the meetings is to discuss students who are serving "behavioral contracts"; these students have been disciplined before, and have signed a document agreeing to stay out of trouble or risk being sent to an alternative school. Prior to each meeting the head of the discipline committee sends an e-mail to each teacher of the students on behavioral contracts, asking for a report on the student's behavior. The participants then discuss these teacher reports, along with records of new infractions and the committee members' overall perceptions of the students. Though intended to collaboratively help at-risk students, these meetings sometimes devolve into complaining sessions about difficult students, such as in the following field notes:

> Mr. Klockars [the white male teacher who organizes and runs the sessions] mentioned the first student's name, and several people in the room groaned, commented, or raised their hands all at once (as if to say "I have a story about him"). The student had been at an alternative placement, but recently returned to Centerville High. Several people mentioned recent incidents of defiance, rudeness, tardiness, or skipping school from this student. Participants unanimously described the student as being difficult, causing problems, and not showing up for class. Officer Malvern said that he suspected that the alternative school sent this student back here not because the student was better, but because they were sick of him and needed a break from him. Mr. Klockars looked at his school records from the file, and reported on the student's grades, which were not good. After talking about him for five minutes or so, Ms. Hemlock [a white female teacher on the committee] blurted out, in response to others' descriptions of the student's behavior: "He's gone." Someone else said, "He's out of here." Ms. Hemlock then asked why they were still discussing him. She added, "He isn't worth the time." Mr. Klockars asked if the committee should recommend that this student be considered by the alternative placement committee, and everyone raised their hands in agreement. (FN)

Centerville High administrators have thought a great deal about their process for disciplining students, and have a system in place for doing so. Despite these plans, I observed the discipline process break down near the end of our visits to Centerville. During December, the administration discovered that the interventionists had failed to enter any referral data into the school's computer system. This means that students who were punished did not have a record of these punishments. But even more important, it means that most misbehavior went unpunished—teachers or other staff members wrote up referrals that received no response from anyone at the school, unless the infractions were severe enough to go directly to an assistant principal. In response to this large error, the assistant principals began assuming more discipline duties by talking to more students themselves.

Like at Unionville High, there is also a surveillance system in place, but a less extensive one. About a dozen cameras at Centerville High are placed near the exits and in main common areas, but not throughout the school. Like the system at Unionville High, images are stored electronically and available to designated people throughout the school.

Frontera High School

Frontera High School is in a poor area of a large city in the southwestern United States. Like other areas in the Southwest, the city is marked by a great deal of urban sprawl rather than concentrated development with multiple-story buildings. As a result, despite its location in a large city, it shares many characteristics with suburban schools: it is surrounded by single-family homes and businesses, and it is located on a large, fenced-in lot with school buildings and multiple athletic fields.

The community in which Frontera is located differs considerably from the other communities studied because it is a very poor area and predominantly Latino/a. There are graffiti on many nearby homes and businesses, the surrounding houses are very small, and the nearby businesses are characteristic of poor neighborhoods: a used-car dealership (with a broken sign out front), fast-food restaurants, and a convenience store. As one white male administrator stated:

> When we hire people, we take them for a drive. And we drive through our community and we show them. . . . There is not a mall around here. There is not a theater around here. . . . I can take you to areas that if you stood out and walked around and looked you would swear you're in Hermosillo, Mexico. I mean you would swear it. And there's industry and little houses. (I)

The church directly across the street from the school is boarded up and has graffiti on it, and there are often homeless people sleeping outside. There is a park with a public swimming pool (open in the summer only) across the street from the school; the principal told me that because of the many fights at the park after school, the city closed the park during after-school hours at his request.

The community is known as an area where many Mexican immigrants live. When I first visited the school and received a tour, Principal Ruiz told me that he estimates that about 80% of the students at Frontera High are undocumented immigrants. The student body is almost entirely Hispanic (92%), with 4% classified as white and 3% classified as African American. The students are mostly poor—94% are eligible for free or reduced-price lunch—and it is very common to hear Spanish being spoken on campus (see table 2.1).

School staff members often talk about the high crime rate in the community, with a particular focus on gangs. According to the police officer at Frontera High:

> Gangs have a big, a big portion of what goes on around here, and when you look at the families, there's a lot of families that are deep[ly] rooted in gangs, and it's just fermenting and passing on to the upcoming generation. So that has an effect on that big circle of negativity that's happening to the family, where they're not getting educated because they're believing more in the gang than they are in education. (I)

The fear of crime is so high in this community that there is an armed guard at the convenience store across the street from the school, where many students go before and after school. With this community problem in mind, the school administrators try to ensure that the school is a safe haven for students amid a violent community. For example, the dean of discipline, Ms. Flores, stated:

> All I can tell kids is, you know, "I can't help what goes on in your neighborhood, but at least I can stop you guys from bringing it to school for those few hours." And that's all I can promise them, is like I'll try to do my best to keep that stuff off the campus. You know I wish I could make their community safer for them, because I don't think any child should live in fear, but at least you know those six hours they're in school they should feel safe. (I)

Indeed, though I observed very little violence at the school, there was a great deal of concern over students' gang activities. Gang affiliation is often discussed when students are disciplined; students who misbehave are often questioned about their gang involvement, and administrators or security staff

FIGURE 2.4

Frequency of Incidents, by Category, at Frontera High

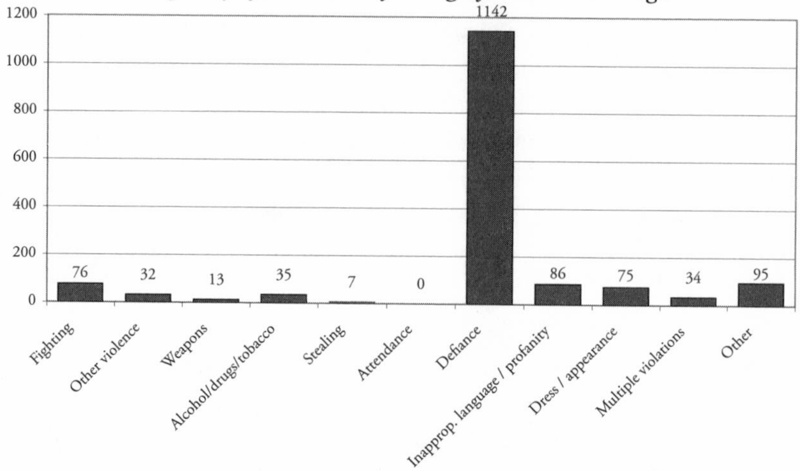

often question whether their clothing or drawings (on personal belongings such as notebooks) are gang symbols.

The overall rarity of violence was noted by several interview respondents, and is reflected by the school's discipline statistics, shown in figure 2.4. Two-thirds of all 2005–2006 discipline incidents involve "defiance," which includes disruption of class/campus, defiance of authority, and violation of school procedures. After defiance, the largest categories are "other," inappropriate language, dress code violations, and fights.

Approximately 2,500 students in grades 9–12 attend Frontera High. The school consists of multiple buildings forming a campus rather than a single enclosed building. Students walk outside through a central courtyard to travel between buildings for different classes. Given the warm weather most of the year, students often eat their lunches outside as well, in the central courtyard, where there are a number of picnic tables.

Academically, Frontera High is in good standing. It is categorized as a "performing" school, in that it has met its state standards and has met adequate yearly progress under federal (No Child Left Behind) standards as well. Almost 80% of students graduate within four years, despite the poverty among the student body. While I was conducting research at Frontera High the school's robotics team earned national recognition in an academic competition, where the robot constructed by Frontera students outperformed robots constructed by other high school and college teams, including a team from MIT (according to the school robotics teacher).

The administration at Frontera High is both stable and diverse. Among the principal and three assistant principals, two are Latino men and one is a white woman. The principal is in his sixth year leading Frontera High, and the assistant principals have each been there at least three years.

Discipline Policies and Practices

Students arrive at Frontera High each morning with a number of social deficits the school must deal with: the student body consists of many undocumented immigrants from Mexico who live in an impoverished community plagued by gangs and violence. Many of these students do not have well-educated parents, and they may be fearful of violence on their way to and from school. If there is indeed a crisis of school crime and violence that stems from community and family problems, one would expect to find it at Frontera High. Yet there is little violence in the school, with the majority of school misbehavior falling under the category of "defiance." Despite the rarity of violence, students are commonly suspended at Frontera: during the 2005–2006 school year there were 449 off-campus suspensions handed out (for a suspension rate of 17.8 per 100 students) and 1,251 in-school suspensions (49 per 100 students; see figure 2.2).

Clearly, in-school suspension is a common punishment at Frontera High. Students serve ISS in a windowless room filled with about twenty-five desks. Students sit quietly throughout the day. They are not allowed to talk, and they receive no curricular instruction. They are watched by a non-teacher staff member who gives them worksheets they can complete, though they are encouraged to obtain homework (on their own) from teachers to complete during this time.

There is a single dean of discipline at Frontera High: Ms. Flores, a Latina with a background in teaching, who handles most disciplinary duties with the aid of an administrative assistant. When a staff member writes a referral, a copy of the referral goes to Ms. Flores. She usually has a stack of at least 10–20 referrals on her desk waiting for a response. When she has time she sends for students to come to her office by either calling the teacher and requesting the student or asking the security staff to pick the student up. Once the student arrives, she discusses the incident with him or her and assigns a punishment. Students are also sent directly to her when teachers remove them from classes, or when security staff observe them breaking school rules. Though Ms. Flores assigns suspensions without any need for supervision, when cases involving violence or potential expulsion arise, she usually consults with an assistant principal or Principal Ruiz.

Frontera High also employs a group of security guards, who work in two shifts to ensure coverage both during and after school. There are eleven guards in total, with five to six usually working at any one time. The guards wear security uniforms and carry two-way radios but no weapons. One stays outside, in a guard shack by the front entrance, monitoring who enters and leaves the school. All visitors sign in on a clipboard and obtain a visitor pass. Other security guards roam the hallways and courtyards throughout the day; each has an assigned patrol area, though by my observation they rarely stick to these areas. Instead they walk around the building and chat casually with people they encounter. The security staff are the first responders to incidents; if a teacher or other staff member observes an incident that requires a response, he or she will alert the security guards, one of whom then brings the student to Ms. Flores or an administrator.

The police officer at Frontera High changed soon after I began fieldwork there; most of the discussions of the officer at Frontera throughout the book pertain to the new officer, Officer Martinez, since I had more time to observe him than his predecessor, Officer Bartol. Both officers are Latino men. Both wear a bulletproof vest under a full police uniform and carry a firearm; Officer Martinez carries an electronic Taser-brand stun gun as well. Both officers, and especially Officer Martinez, spend a good deal of time inside the SRO office with the door closed. I also observed them walk around campus, but neither one interacted a great deal with students while I observed them. For example, one day Officer Bartol and I walked around campus together during lunch, and he told me about the strong mentoring relationships he had with several students at the school. We entered the gym, and he pointed out several students within twenty feet of us whom he knew well—yet he never once said hello to any of them or interacted with them in any way I could see.

Officer Bartol and the school administration had what appeared to be a very good working relationship, though he accepted a new position within the police force soon after our fieldwork began. In contrast, several administrators and teachers complained to me about Officer Martinez soon after his arrival at Frontera High. Staff perceive him as being aloof, in that he is not sufficiently connected to the school, and the administrators are particularly upset that he doesn't spend enough time on campus. According to Officer Martinez, the source of the conflict is that Principal Ruiz wants to control his working schedule, even though he reports to the police department (with a supervisor who sets his working hours), not the school, highlighting the potential for conflict when schools incorporate nonschool employees into their community.

There is a surveillance camera system at Frontera High, though it goes unmonitored. When I asked about it, the security staff laughed at the system, telling me it was archaic and unusable. The images are not digital, so it is difficult to sort through tapes if one needs them; they are of poor quality; and they cover only a small proportion of the school grounds. This last issue is important, since the school is arranged in a campus layout with a great deal of ground for cameras to cover, rather than an enclosed series of corridors.

Fairway Estates High School

Fairway Estates High School is located in a mid-sized city of a southwestern state, just outside of the large city that houses Frontera High School. This city, Estateville, has expanded greatly in size and population in recent years, though it has expanded laterally in a sprawling way, preserving broad streets, strip malls, single-family houses (many on expansive properties), golf courses, and even some farmland. Ten or twenty years earlier, there was little in Estateville, but now it is home to over four hundred thousand residents spread over one hundred square miles. There are many distinct communities in Estateville; the one in which Fairway Estates High is located is a wealthy area, with many large houses worth over five hundred thousand dollars each. The school sits next to a scenic city park with tennis courts, and a gated community with large houses.

One aspect of Estateville that distinguishes it from other areas I studied is that it is home to a large Mormon population. The school is located near a Mormon temple, and I met several Mormon students while conducting my research. Some staff members complained to me about the political power yielded by Mormons at the school, and this is occasionally evident. For example, despite the fact that Fairway Estates High is a closed campus, meaning that students are not allowed to leave during the day, an exception is made for Mormon students to attend their temple during the school day.

Staff members also talk a great deal about the wealth among Fairway Estates High students, often in disparaging terms. A security guard, for example, repeatedly pointed out to me the expensive cars in the student parking lot, and complained about the sense of privilege these students demonstrate. A white male assistant principal in his first year at Fairway Estates High told me that working here has required an adjustment:

> I'm not used to being around people with money, and it rubs me the wrong way. I grew up on a farm, with other farmers. I'm not used to spoiled kids like some of these. When I have a student in my office, sometimes it's like "take that silver spoon out of your mouth when you're talking to me." (I)

Not surprisingly, only 18% of students at Fairway Estates High are eligible for free or reduced-price lunch.

Most of the students at Fairway Estates High (83%) are white, with 11% Latino/a and only 2% black, according to the Institute of Education Statistics. These numbers are not representative of the city's population, which is 73% white and 20% Latino/a, and they illustrate that the school is in a relatively wealthy, white portion of Estateville.

Few people at Fairway Estates High expressed much concern about violence. Instead, several staff members complained about students' attitudes, usually in reference to their high socioeconomic status. Principal Sutter discussed this with me a number of times, using recent academic work to support his observations. He mentioned the book *Generation Me* more than once, and how much he agrees with the book's conclusions: that the current generation of youth has become self-centered and narcissistic due to constant praise, whereby everybody has come to believe in how special and unique they are, leaving them unprepared for the job market or adult life.[6] According to him and others with whom I spoke, this translates into problems at Fairway Estates High because the students have little respect for rules that apply to everyone, instead thinking that they are above the rules; this attitude, in turn, causes minor-level behavior problems, such as defiance of authority.

FIGURE 2.5

Frequency of Incidents, by Category, at Fairway Estates High

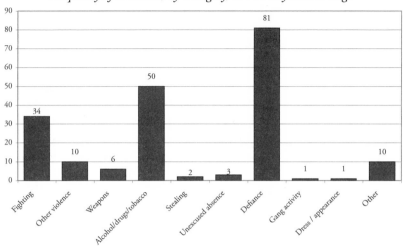

Indeed, as figure 2.5 shows, there are few suspensions handed out at Fairway Estates High (see also figure 2.2), and the most common reason for suspension is defiance or disorderly conduct. Drugs/alcohol/tobacco are the second most frequent, followed by fighting, with little violence other than fights. The rarity of behavior problems suggested by this figure matches my observations there. The hallways, classrooms, and courtyards are generally tidy and orderly, and I saw very little student aggressiveness, shouting, or other problematic behavior.

Fairway Estates High is a large school, with over 2,700 students in grades 10–12. The student population has grown recently along with the surrounding city. Just three years earlier the school served only 2,400 students. The school itself is a mix between the campus layout of Frontera High and the enclosed structures of both Centerville High and Unionville High. There is a single, large, two-story building that houses most classrooms, but other school activities take place in separate buildings. These other buildings include space for shop classes, the gym and locker rooms, and an auditorium. To accommodate the school's growth and to expand available classroom space, there is also a series of trailers that house about ten classrooms near the student parking lot.

Other than these trailers, the facilities at Fairway Estates High are impressive from an aesthetic perspective. The landscaping is neat, with several shrubs and other plants throughout a spacious courtyard that connects the main academic building and the school's other buildings. Students often walk through this large courtyard and eat their lunches in it. Part of the courtyard is taken up by a multilevel grass amphitheater that rises above a performance space.

The school is also impressive with regard to the resources available to students. During visits, I observed a TV studio room with many state-of-the-art cameras, where students film the daily announcements that are televised internally. Students in auto shop class work on actual cars, with several models available for their training.

A tall, black, iron fence encloses the school buildings and courtyard. This fence was new to the school the year I observed Fairway Estates High and a source of irritation for many of the students. There are gates through the fence at the front entrance to the school, at an infrequently used side street entrance, and at the student parking lot along another side, immediately off the main courtyard. This is the main entrance used by students, who must show ID to security guards (who monitor this gate) if they wish to enter or leave (visitors enter by the front door and sign in with a receptionist). The gate is intended to keep students in school during the day, and was built in response to a fatal car accident at another school in the district, involving a student who left during the school day. Certain students—seniors, Mormons going to temple, students who work off campus, and others—are allowed to leave the campus at certain times, though I rarely saw security staff prevent anyone from leaving, and the gates are occasionally left unlocked and unmonitored. Despite the porousness of this security device, I spoke to several students who were very upset about the gate's presence. One white female student stated:

> I think the gates are a big issue for the school. I mean, I understand why they did it, it's to help, like, with the accidents that are happening during lunch and stuff. But I just, it makes the students feel like they're trapped at school, you know, and it makes it harder for them to want to come. It makes students not wanna come to school because they feel like they're trapped in there and they can't get out until, you know, the day's over,

which is, which is why they have the gates so they can keep the students there. But I don't, I personally don't think that it was a good idea. (I)

Another white female student had more to say:

INTERVIEWER: Do you ever feel unsafe at school?
STUDENT: Nope, I don't think I've ever felt unsafe. I mean the gates are retarded.
INTERVIEWER: Why? Tell me a little bit about that.
STUDENT: I don't know, it's just like . . . it's worse than it was when the gates weren't in. . . . And I think that the gates shouldn't even be here, like our school had nothing to do with it. There's more car accidents after school and stuff, like, now that we have the gates rather than there was when there wasn't any.
INTERVIEWER: Why do you think that's so?
STUDENT: Because everyone's trying to rush to get out because they're, like, it's like you're caged in pretty much and so you're trying to get out, and you're trying to, you know. I think the school system, now that we have the gates, are a lot more stricter than they were when we didn't, and so a lot of people, like, don't like it anymore, and so they're just like trying to get out faster. (I)

Academically, the school is very well-regarded. It has earned its state's top performance label, "excelling," and has met federal standards under No Child Left Behind. It has an 84% graduation rate, and the vast majority of tested tenth graders have met the state's proficiency standards in math, reading, and writing (90%, 86%, and 87% respectively).[7] Additionally, there were three national merit scholarships awarded to Fairway Estates High students in 2005.

Principal Sutter, a white male, is in only his second year at the school, though he has several years of experience as a principal in another state. The three assistant principals are all men, one is Latino and the other two are white. Though one is in his first year at Fairway Estates High, the other two have four years and seven years of experience in the administration here. Three of the four administrators are former coaches or physical education teachers, much like the backgrounds of disciplinarians at Unionville High and Centerville High.

Discipline Policies and Practices

There are fewer suspensions issued at Fairway Estates High than at the other three schools observed: only 198 during the 2005–2006 school year, a ratio of 6.1 per 100 students (see figure 2.2). In part, this is because there are few problems at Fairway Estates High. Yet I also saw few problems at other schools, especially Centerville High and Frontera High, thus this is not a good explanation for why suspensions are rarely handed out. Moreover, despite its relatively orderly front, staff often talked about student disrespect, and I observed a fair amount of student defiance as well.

The lower suspension rate is due to the fact that staff at Fairway Estates High are more likely than staff at other schools to show restraint in punishing students. Rather than suspend students for showing disrespect to teachers or disrupting class, staff at Fairway Estates High are more likely to use less severe sanctions or none at all. An important influence on this might be the fact that the school has more white, high socioeconomic-status students than the other schools. When considering how suspensions are handed out at a rate sixteen times greater to the primarily black students at Unionville High, it is hard to deny the importance of race and socioeconomic status. Though prior research supports such a conclusion, in that it tells us that poor students and students of color are dealt with more harshly than middle-class white students, a comparison of only two schools is insufficient to make such a claim.[8] Instead, as I discuss in chapter 5, race and class shape discipline in complex ways. Further, though punishment is less frequent at Fairway Estates High, it shares qualities with the discipline used at the three other schools.

It is also important to note that though suspensions are not handed out often, the school does act punitively at times. When students are caught fighting, they receive a mandatory nine-day suspension, for example. And the school has a very tough policy for tardiness; if students are not in class by the time class begins, then teachers are instructed to not let them in. Instead, they must go to what the school calls "sweep," a section of the in-school suspension area, where they sit for the remainder of the period. Though I observed this enforced very rarely, the policy itself is more rigid than the tardy policies at the other schools.

Perhaps another reason why there are few suspensions at Fairway Estates High is because there is no dedicated disciplinary administrative staff. Unlike the other schools, which have one or more deans or interventionists, Fairway Estates High employs only security guards. There are five guards who all work during the school day; they enforce rules but have no authority to punish students. If they observe students violating school rules, the guards bring the student to an administrator to respond. The guards' other duties are to police the school gate, respond to teachers' and administrators' requests for assistance, and generally patrol the school. Thus, suspensions must be given out by one of the four administrators, even though they are constantly occupied by the business of running a school of over 2,700 students. In comparison to the other schools, each of which has at least one staff member dedicated to responding to discipline referrals, Fairway Estates High commits fewer person hours to this task. This likely has an institutional effect whereby school staff are subtly discouraged from writing referrals unless a case is serious enough to warrant an administrator's scarce time.

Each of the security guards at Fairway Estates High has experience either in the military, as a correctional officer, or as a police officer. One is even a retired elected sheriff from another state. The guards drive around campus in golf carts, spending much of their time either at the gate entrances or in the in-school suspension area.

Like the other schools, Fairway Estates High sends many students to in-school suspension. Instead of a dedicated room, however, the school uses a portion of the cafeteria for ISS. At one end of the cafeteria there is a desk and computer, which is used by a security guard. The long cafeteria tables directly in front of this security station are used for students who are sent to ISS for the day. Next to these tables, there are a few rows of plastic chairs, not at any tables; these chairs are for students who are sent out of class by teachers and told to go to ISS, or for tardy students who are sent to "sweep." There they wait for the rest of the period, while the teachers resume class in their absence, returning to their class schedule beginning with the next period. Though students in ISS for the day are encouraged to do work, students in the isolated chairs are not allowed to do anything but sit for the period. Both groups are supposed to be silent, though I usually observed students in both areas talking to other students; a security guard might scold them for this, but this seems to have only a short-lived effect, as the students often resume talking and the security guard usually leaves them alone.

The police officer at Fairway Estates High, Officer Frederick, is a white male in his forties. Officer Frederick wears a bulletproof vest under a short-sleeved uniform shirt every day, and carries a handgun and pepper spray on his weapon belt. I spent a good deal of time shadowing Officer Frederick, and I greatly enjoyed it; he is energetic and personable, and he displays these qualities when interacting with students. He often expresses himself through humor and sarcasm, though at times this comes across as inappropriate. For example, once when I was in his office he introduced me to a student he was questioning as "the ultimate fighting champion of New Jersey," and asked the student if he wanted to fight me. During his office another time he was showing off the weapons on his belt to a student who came to see him. He told the student that he couldn't wait to try out his new pepper spray, and that a new spray was needed because the old brand of spray would catch on fire when he sprayed someone and then "tasered" him. I was never sure whether students interpreted statements like this as threats or benign banter. I did, however, meet a teacher on campus, a former school administrator in another state who now teaches criminal justice at Fairway Estates High, who dislikes Officer Frederick because of these inappropriate interactions. This teacher explained her dislike by referencing his actions at a recent student talent show, when Officer Frederick performed break-dancing moves for the student body; in her view, acting silly like this is not appropriate for a school resource officer, and it reduces students' respect of him as a police officer.

Despite the fact that Fairway Estates High has sufficient funds to purchase a TV studio, outdoor amphitheater, and old cars for the auto shop, it is the only one of the four schools with no video surveillance system. Several staff members told me they wished the school would purchase one, though like Frontera High the spread-out campus layout is not conducive to efficient electronic monitoring.

Similarities Across Schools

Though these four schools are located in very different areas and house dramatically different student bodies, they share a great deal in common. One important similarity is that each one faces tensions and strains. The two schools with more low socioeconomic-status and minority students, Frontera High and Unionville High, must cope with the effects of poverty, crime and disorder, and gangs. Yet even in the wealthier schools, Fairway Estates High and Centerville High, the schools must find room for students despite overcrowding; both have responded by using trailers as temporary classrooms. Both of these two schools are in rapidly growing areas, which has led to overcrowding, but the space issue is fueled by the schools' (or districts' and states') own actions as well. Each state follows a school choice/open enrollment program, which means that students who live in a school's district but not within that school's residential boundaries can apply for admission to that school. Through these programs, both Fairway Estates High and Centerville High have enrolled additional students. This benefits them because it boosts their enrollment and therefore their per-pupil funding, but it also contributes to crowding.[9] The point is that even when we look at academically high-performing schools in middle-class white communities, they are still forced to cope with problems that stem from the politics of contemporary public schooling.

It is also interesting to see how these four schools have enacted very similar security and punishment practices. There are differences, of course, particularly with regard to the personnel who handle punishment: Frontera High uses a single dean and security guards, Fairway Estates High uses security guards and administrators, Centerville High uses interventionists and administrators, and Unionville High uses three deans. But all have similar processes for dealing with perceived misbehavior. In each school, a staff member writes a referral, which is then given to the point person for punishment, who decides on a "consequence." In each school, students removed from class are sent to in-school suspension to "cool out," as are students spared out-of-school suspension. Each school has partnered with a police officer to facilitate security and participate in school discipline.

Moreover, the punishments for misbehaviors listed in each school's code of conduct are fairly similar. In table 2.2 I list the prescribed punishments or punishment ranges for four offenses: defiance/insubordination, fighting, drug possession, and possession of a weapon. The differences in how schools list the punishments makes comparisons difficult (note the broad ranges given by Fairway Estates High, such as the range of a student conference to expulsion for defiance), but one can see that they share a great deal, especially for the more common offenses: defiance and fighting. Defiance generally results in a reprimand, conference with the student's parents, and detention or short sus-

TABLE 2.2

Comparison of Prescribed Punishments for Selected Offenses (Initial Infractions)

Behavior	Unionville High	Centerville High	Frontera High	Fairway Estates High
Defiance of authority/insubordination	Parent/guardian notification, 1-day detention to 1-day suspension.	Required: Teacher reprimand, parent/guardian notification, detention, or 1- to 3-day suspension.	Detention or suspension.	Range: Student conference to expulsion.
Fighting	Parent/guardian notification and conference, restitution (if necessary), referral to mediation, and 3-day suspension.	Required: Suspension (3 to 5 days), parent/guardian notification and conference, police notification (when nec.), and restitution (if applicable).	Suspension for 9 school days, referral to an alternative school, suspension for up to 2 semesters, or expulsion.	Range: Parent involvement to short suspension
Drug possession	Parent/guardian notification and conference, drug/alcohol assessment, notification of police, 5-day suspension, and recommendation for alternative placement.	Required: Suspension (5 to 10 days), police notification, parent/guardian notification, drug/alcohol screening and assessment, and recommendation to counseling. Option: Expulsion or referral to alternative program.	Suspension for 9 school days, suspension for 18 school days (student may be removed to alternative school), suspension for 2 semesters (student may be removed to alternative school).	Suspension for 2 semesters and alternative school assignment to expulsion.
Weapons	Parent/guardian notification and conference, notification of police, 5-day suspension, recommendation for expulsion; and mandatory 180+ day suspension for firearm.	Required: suspension (5 to 10 days), police notification, parent/guardian notification, and recommendation to counseling. Optional: Expulsion or referral to alternative program.	Suspension for up to 2 semesters, with loss of credits, expulsion.	Expulsion.

Note: For Frontera High, punishments are for first, second, or third infractions; each other school's punishments are for the first infraction.

pension; fighting generally results in suspension. There are larger discrepancies across schools for drug possession and weapon possession, though these offenses are rare. Ironically, the school that gives out the fewest suspensions, Fairway Estates High, has the toughest punishments on the books for these offenses, while Unionville High, the school with a suspension rate of ninety-six per hundred students, has the most lenient punishments on the books. In response to drug possession, both schools consider alternative placements, but students at Unionville High face five days of suspension compared to two semesters of suspension at Fairway Estates High.

Another important similarity across these schools is the distribution of different student misbehaviors. The common abundance of subjectively perceived, usually minor offenses such as defiance or insubordination says a great deal about how schools approach discipline as a way to enforce authority rather than correct problems, as I discuss at length in chapter 4. Further, since these misbehaviors are subjectively perceived, they allow greater opportunities for racial, class, or gender biases to shape disciplinary decision making.

The similar approach of these four schools is especially interesting given the vast differences in the schools, their communities, and their student bodies. Though the institutional dynamics, personalities, and challenges vary across schools, each has taken a comparable perspective on school discipline and security. All four schools govern through crime in a way that is amazingly consistent, given the distinctions one would expect to see among schools located in such very different areas.

3

A BLUE LINE ON
THE CHALKBOARD

Police Presence in Schools

with Nicole L. Bracy

Biko is a seventeen-year-old junior at Samuel J. Tilden High School. He plays center midfielder for the school soccer team and is active in school and community activities.

On the morning of January 12, 2007, Biko chatted for several minutes with his math teacher after class about additional work assignments. He then hurried to reach his next class, Chemistry Lab, when Val Lewis, the Assistant Principal for Security, stopped Biko in the hallway. Worried that he would be late to his Chemistry Lab, which has a strict attendance requirement, Biko pleaded with Mr. Lewis to allow him to continue walking to class. He explained to Mr. Lewis that he had been talking to his math teacher and was attempting to reach his chemistry class. Mr. Lewis refused to listen to Biko's explanation, and told Biko to go to the "focus room," the detention center at the school.

As Biko continued to talk with Mr. Lewis, Mr. Lewis grew angry and threatened to send Biko to the principal's office. Mr. Lewis then ordered Officer Rivera, a police officer stationed at the school, to arrest Biko. Officer Rivera then grabbed Biko and slammed him against a brick door divider, lacerating Biko's face and causing him to bleed. Officer Rivera then sprayed Mace at Biko's eyes and face, causing Biko's eyes to burn. Rather than treat the student, Officer Rivera then called for back-up on his radio, and proceeded to handcuff Biko.

After being escorted to the school security office by numerous police officers and school safety agents, Biko was taken to a hospital, where he spent approximately two hours being treated for his wounds, and spending most of his time in the hospital handcuffed to a chair. He was then transported to the local precinct, and then to central booking. Biko missed the rest of his classes that day, and spent more than 28 hours in police custody. He faces five criminal charges. The principal at the school suspended Biko for four days.

Biko's story is told in a report recently published by the New York Civil Liberties Union.[1] The report describes the growth in numbers of police officers and school safety agents (who are under the control of the New York City Police Department) in New York City public schools, and tells several stories—like Biko's—illustrating abuse of students and school staff at the hands of these officers. The report is disturbing. The abuses described include physical abuse and sexual harassment of students, retaliatory arrests of school staff who protect students from abuse at the hands of police, and other offenses.

Though I never witnessed such physical abuse at the hands of a school resource officer, Biko's story illustrates very dramatically some of the problems I observed firsthand with placing police officers in schools: relatively minor problems can escalate into larger problems as a result of police involvement, and students are unnecessarily sent to the criminal justice system rather than having their issues dealt with at the school level only. Consider, for example, the less dramatic story of how a student was arrested at Centerville High:

> A student was asked (by a school staff member) to remove his "do-rag" upon arriving at school prior to the start of the day. He resisted at first, but then removed it (unhappily). He then cussed out the assistant principal, who wrote him a referral for doing so. Then, he was sent to the office, and he wanted to leave, but Mr. Majors (another assistant principal) stood in his way and wouldn't let him leave. The student tried to push Mr. Majors aside, and as a result he was handcuffed by the school resource officer and arrested for pushing a staff member. (FN)

Though the officer at Centerville High is far more restrained than the officer who maced Biko, the two stories share an important theme: in both, a student gets in trouble with a school administrator for violating a school rule (Biko was late for class; the student at Centerville High violated the dress code), becomes upset, defies the administrator, and winds up in handcuffs.

We have no way of knowing for certain what would have happened had an officer not been there. Yet it is hard to imagine that either of these situations would have resulted in an arrest without an officer already on the scene. Neither case involves drugs, a weapon, or student-on-student violence. In both cases, the only action that could possibly be considered violent is the direct result of a school administrator blocking a student's passage: Biko is prevented from going to class, and the student at Centerville High is not allowed to walk away from an upsetting disciplinary situation (which is ironic, since students at Centerville High are told that instead of engaging in conflict, they should just walk away from it). But since an officer was there and observed at least the last part of each interaction, it was unnecessary to call 911, wait for the police, and explain the incident to an officer. Further, since the police and school administrators know each other well, they have working relationships that preclude the necessity to explain why an arrest is necessary despite no actual violence having taken place. The fact that an officer is stationed at the school makes it much easier to have the student arrested by removing the inconvenience, hassle, and uncertainty that the school would face if it called the police.

I begin this chapter by discussing these two cases because they illustrate some of the potential problems of placing police officers on school grounds full-time. Yet the issue is not so simple—there are also benefits to having police in schools. Police officers can be a powerful resource for school administrators, they can facilitate policing in the community, and they can be of benefit to students as well. Amazingly, there is no critical discussion among the public or policy-makers, and extremely little among academics, about whether police *ought* to be in public schools to begin with. Perhaps some schools—such as those in high-crime neighborhoods—need full-time officers. But are those officers necessary in low-crime areas as well? When we think about how much energy parents and policy-makers spend debating details of public schools—issues such as dress codes, school vouchers, prayer in school, the content of school lunches, testing, and even the necessity of recess—I am stunned by the fact that they are silent on whether uniformed, armed police officers should be stationed full-time in schools.

Take, for example, the New York Civil Liberties report that includes Biko's story. After illustrating the litany of problems associated with police in schools, the report concludes that these officers should be better trained and supervised, that there should be a process in place for reporting abuses by these officers, and that they should be under the control of the schools rather than reporting only to the police department. Though at times the report questions whether it is problematic to have police in school in general, it does so only in passing, and the recommendations avoid this fundamental question. Moreover, the report highlights exemplar districts with effective school resource officer programs that "create a symbiosis between the security officers and the schools," such as in Fairfax County, Virginia, and Orange County, Florida.[2] Chicago, as well, is praised for how principals can hire and evaluate the part-time law enforcement officers who work in the schools.[3] So long as they are properly supervised and trained, it appears that the New York Civil Liberties Union accepts their presence.

To a large extent, academics have also avoided critical thought about officers in schools. A classic example of this can be found in *Rampage*, by noted sociologist Katherine Newman and her colleagues. The book presents an in-depth study of school shootings in Kentucky and Arkansas, and considers ways to prevent such tragedies in the future. Despite the many thoughtful and sound suggestions, one that I find troubling is that all schools should have police officers. The reasoning for this is as follows: since there is a chance that a potential shooter's friends will tell an officer about the friend's plan, the officer could theoretically intervene and a shooting would be averted. This conclusion flows from two important discoveries in their research: (1) that although non-involved students know about most school shootings before they take place, the school does not have an effective way to obtain this information; and (2) that school shootings are acts against the school itself, toward which many other students are hostile as well, so an official outside the school may have a better chance to break the student code of silence that prohibits "snitching" on friends. Newman and colleagues continue by stating that "students seem to feel more comfortable confiding in an adult who does not have the same authoritative relationship over them as their teachers," and that "SROs make the daily process of maintaining order easier on the educational staff, and their presence is helpful in preventing school violence."[4] Newman and colleagues do note that there are potential unintended consequences of having police officers in schools, such as increases in arrests, involvement in the criminal justice system, and the creation of criminal records for students. Yet the book concludes that, "as with all interventions, the consequences of the change are mixed, and on balance we think the pros outweigh the cons."[5]

On the face of it these arguments seem reasonable. It's a classic trade-off: while increased police presence might lead to more intense monitoring and unnecessary involvement with the criminal justice system, the fact that we are less likely to have another Columbine on our hands justifies these measures. I am arguing the opposite. I find that the presence of police in schools is unlikely to prevent another school shooting, and that the potential for oppression of students—especially poor and racial/ethnic minority youth—is a more realistic and far more common threat than Columbine.

What Do Police Officers in Schools Do?

On the day I first met Officer Frederick, the school resource officer at Fairway Estates High, I followed him around as he:

- searched throughout the school for a student, whom he then talked to about when and from where (off school grounds) her car was stolen;
- called the front office to see if the student he suspected of stealing the car, Carter, was in school;
- visited the class of a teacher who had asked to see him because she was concerned about one of her students;
- visited another teacher to ask about Carter's recent attendance in her class;
- returned to his office at the school, where he used his computer to visit students' MySpace pages;
- went to the attendance office to find the location of a student;
- went to the automotive shop class where this student was at the time, so he could serve the student a citation for smoking on school grounds (he caught the student smoking the prior week);
- chatted with students in the hallway in between classes—he asked one student to find out who broke a teacher's window;
- met in his office with a student involved in a disagreement with other students (one student tipped him off that morning that the three of them might soon fight);
- went to the attendance office to find if any of three students suspended for smoking marijuana were back in school (they weren't);
- filled out a police report for an iPod that was stolen two weeks ago.

All of this occurred before noon.

Though Officer Frederick typically stays busy with tasks like these, Officer Martinez at Frontera High spends more time in his office and says that there is little for him to do. Thus, there is no typical school officer.[6] Each school is different and has different needs of its officer. That said, by observing officers at four different high schools, I was able to see what they do on a day-to-day basis, and come to a better understanding of what the job actually entails. The officers I observed spent the majority of their time watching the halls, investigating minor incidents, and conducting administrative police work. Some officers also try to counsel students and participate in (non-criminal) school discipline matters, and even get involved in extracurricular school activities.

Watching the Halls

All the officers I observed spend some part of their day patrolling; this includes making rounds in the hallways, supervising the cafeterias during lunchtime, and overseeing students as they board school buses at the end of the day. These patrolling activities serve two main functions—to remind students of the presence of the officer (i.e., it is a show of force), and to help school administrators watch over students.

Approaches to this task vary among the four officers, particularly with regard to whether they interact personally with students or silently observe them. In two of the schools, Frontera High School and Centerville High School, Officers Martinez and Malvern silently observe students more often than they interact with them. These officers quietly watch students during high-traffic times such as lunch, immediately after school, and during breaks between classes. Officer Martinez at Frontera High occasionally drives his police car onto the school's courtyard during lunch, parks it in the middle of the picnic table area where many of the students dine, and sits in his car throughout the period (this school is an open-air campus with a central outdoor courtyard). While these officers could respond quickly to a disruption if needed, their presence seems to be primarily a reminder (or a threat) to students and staff that the police are there.

In the other two schools, the officers have more frequent face-to-face interactions with students. At Unionville High, Officer Brandon periodically makes his way through all of the hallways of the school building, checking doors that lead outside to make sure they are not ajar, and demanding hall passes from students he encounters along the way. His more interactive approach in the hallways casts him in the role of a school administrator, in that he determines if students are following school rules that have no bearing on criminal laws, and sends them to an actual administrator when they violate these rules.

Investigations

Serious criminal offenses are very rare on school campuses, both nationwide and on the campuses I visited.[7] As a result the officers I observed spend most of their time investigating minor on-campus incidents such as suspected thefts, fights among students, or drug or alcohol possession. For example, Officer Malvern at Centerville High described how he investigated a case involving a stolen iPod:

> One student had her friend's iPod and a male student, Devin, took it away. The girl asked for it back, and Devin said, "No, you're not getting it back." The father of the girl who owns it called the school, and she came to Officer Malvern to complain. Officer Malvern looked up Devin on the computer and saw that he wasn't in school. Devin is a ninth grader, so Officer Malvern went to Mr. Morris [the assistant principal for ninth grade], during lunch, to tell him about this. Mr. Morris said, "Devin, he's right there." The boy was at the school even if he wasn't going to classes, and he was wearing headphones at the time. They talked to Devin, who denied stealing the iPod, and said it was his friend's. Officer Malvern said, "I told Mr. Morris—you better deal with this, because I'm going to lose it with him if he lies to me." Mr. Morris convinced Devin to turn in the iPod, and sure enough, it was the stolen iPod. [The girl who owns it] identified it and picked it up. I asked whether Devin would be arrested and Officer Malvern said no—because the family wanted their property returned, they can't press charges. Officer Malvern said, "But at least we know now that he's a thief. That boy is a thief, and we can keep an eye on him." (FN)

An officer's involvement in cases like this—where an arrest is not warranted and the school administrator actually does more than the officer to facilitate the return of stolen property—seems to be more of a formality than a necessity. The owner of the stolen property came to Officer Malvern, yet Mr. Morris is able to resolve the issue with minimal help.

At another school, Fairway Estates High, Officer Frederick responded to a teacher's complaint about a student driving recklessly out of the school parking lot by tracking down the license plate number and looking it up in the school's records to determine the car's owner:

> Officer Frederick had another license plate number written down, and he went to the bookstore to have the staff look up whose car it was [in the student parking records]. This was for a student who drove recklessly and took a left turn out of the school parking lot last week and almost hit a teacher. The bookstore worker told him what student it belonged to, and said that she was currently in class in the trailers, room 611. I recognized this as [Ms. Buford's] room, who Officer Frederick doesn't get along with. Officer Frederick said, "Oh, I'm not going over there—where is she fifth period?" He wrote that down, and said he'd visit her then. (FN)

Again, this is an incident that could be considered criminal, yet Officer Frederick's response to the situation clearly lacks urgency and suggests that the severity of the situation is minimal. Minor incidents like these arise with some regularity and compose the vast majority of the criminal offenses the officers handle.

Though I observed officers pursuing criminal investigations rigorously, their efforts sometimes appeared to be excessive relative to the actual offense. For example, it seems unlikely that a police officer at a precinct would respond to a complaint about a stolen cell phone by interrogating suspects, yet officers do this at school. Such actions are appropriate in the sense that this is what school resource officers are supposed to be doing, yet it also means that their presence in schools subjects students to tight scrutiny. The surveillance over students by the police is far greater than they face outside school. And school resource officers often look for ways to redefine misbehavior as criminal, even when the label doesn't apply, such as in the following field notes recorded at Centerville High:

> Officer Malvern was called to Ms. Doherty's office [Ms. Doherty is a black assistant principal]. I went with him there. We arrived and saw Ms. Doherty, Mr. Michaels [white male interventionist], and Principal Miller in the office, standing, with a white male student, who was seated. One of the school

nurses was kneeling by the student with a medical kit, tending to him (taking his pulse, looking in his eyes, etc.). Principal Miller told Officer Malvern that this student apparently took some drugs. He's unresponsive, can't talk, and is having trouble moving. He can't even make eye contact. An ambulance was on its way. . . . The nurse said that he's burning up, and has a pulse of 140. . . . The boy opened his mouth as if to say something, but no words came out. . . . The EMTs arrived with a stretcher. . . . A minute later, the . . . EMT helped the boy onto the stretcher. The boy was unable to move, and it took two people to ease him onto the stretcher. As he was wheeled out, I saw that Officer Malvern held a plastic bag with several red pills in it.

[I then spoke about the incident with one of the assistant principals, Mr. Bodley, and we went together to Officer Malvern's office.]

We entered Officer Malvern's office, and he told us that [the students who had just exited his office] . . . informed him that the student going to the hospital had drunk two bottles of Robitussin DM and took some pills. They didn't know what kind of pills, so Officer Malvern told them to try to find out and let him know. Mr. Bodley asked several other questions, such as where the boy got the drugs, how many he took, and if anyone else was a part of it. Officer Malvern said that he didn't ask any of that. If he asks too many questions right away, they'd stop telling him anything. He's concentrating on what this boy took to overdose—he'll try to get the rest of the information later.

Officer Malvern looked at a poster on his wall with pictures of different drugs, trying to determine what these pills were. He didn't find a match. We then went to the nurse's office to look through two pharmaceutical books for a match. He didn't find a match there either.

I then followed Officer Malvern to his office. He called the pharmacy across the street. Officer Malvern said to me, "This is a good opportunity for me to make a contact with the pharmacy." He spoke to the pharmacist and asked what the pills might be—red, coated pills with "411" stamped on them. The pharmacist asked that he come in and show him.

Officer Malvern said that he didn't have his squad car—it was in the shop—and that he needed a ride. I offered him a ride, and he accepted. We went out to my car and I drove him there. We went to the pharmacy, and the pharmacist looked at the pills. He said that these were not prescription pills—they looked homemade. The "411" stamp might just be something to throw off the police in identifying it. Officer Malvern asked if they could be ecstasy, and the pharmacist said that that might be it. Officer Malvern described the student's symptoms, and also that he took two bottles of Robitussin. The pharmacist said, "Well, that alone will do it. One bottle of that stuff will make you hallucinate for about six hours, the time that it lasts. Two bottles will really send you flying. And the fast pulse—that's probably the drugs."

We returned to the school and he thanked me. I walked back to his office with him. He told me that they wouldn't know for sure what the drugs were until he sent them to the medical examiner's office and they test the pills. He added, "But I'll tell you one thing—he's going to be locked up." I asked more about this, and how he could be sure before he knew what the drug was. Officer Malvern said, "Well, you've got possession, and you have possession in a school zone. You're talking a felony. He'll definitely be locked up." I asked about the timing of when the arrest would happen. Officer Malvern said it would wait until after the lab tested the pills—the boy would probably return to school for a couple of weeks and then later get arrested.

The following Monday I spoke to Officer Malvern and asked about the overdose incident, and how the student was doing. He said that the student is out of the hospital, but in a mental health facility for seventy-two hours. He said that he found that the pills were cold medication, but that the student had taken an [attention deficit disorder] medication as well. When I asked how he knew this, he said that other students told him. Since they knew the quantity of cold pills that he had, he thought their information was good. The student had only taken one of the ADD pills that day, plus the Robitussin.

Officer Malvern looked at me and said, "I don't know what I can charge him with now. I have it down as an investigation in process for now, until I can think of something. I can't charge him with having a controlled substance, since the cold medication isn't a controlled substance. And the ADD medication is a controlled substance, but he took the only one he had—so I can't charge him with possession, since he didn't have it any more. It might just be a school code violation." (FN)

In this incident the officer works hard to obtain information that could help in treating a child in clear danger of overdose. It was exciting to observe his investigation (and to participate in it by driving him to the pharmacy), as it was intense and executed with a sense of urgency. Given the intensity and the mystery I was surprised to learn that the elusive drug—not in the nurse's drug book or the officer's drug identification poster, and purported to be homemade with a stamp to "throw off the police in identifying it"—turned out to be over-the-counter cold medicine. It was also interesting how the effort I perceived to be therapeutic (the officer finding out what the student had taken so he could tell the doctors, who could then treat the student) became punitive, since in the end, the officer expressed frustration that he was unable to charge the student with a criminal offense.

This case illustrates another avenue (in addition to the escalation noted at the beginning of the chapter) for the presence of officers to lead to more arrests at school.[8] Though the incident only involves actions that could be defined as criminal under a very broad interpretation of the law, Officer Malvern actively considers various charges that might apply. On the one hand, this is appropriate—Officer Malvern is acting exactly how one would expect a police officer to act. On the other hand, cases like this illustrate how the presence of officers in schools is problematic because student misbehavior is interpreted not as a health problem or emotional problem, but instead as a criminal problem. In other words, though Officer Malvern acts appropriately, the fact that a police officer is the point person for responding to a case like this means that students are at risk of arrest even when counseling or less severe punishment is probably a better strategy.

In addition to responding immediately to relatively minor on-campus incidents, officers also perform investigations over time, collecting evidence against students for more serious offenses committed both on and off campus. For example, for much of the time that I observed Officer Frederick at Fairway Estates High, he was building a case against a student, Carter, for a series of severe offenses (an exception to the observation that most school offenses are minor). When I first shadowed Officer Frederick, he talked to a female student about her car being stolen by Carter:

The first issue that we dealt with was a stolen car. He told me that one of the students there, a female, had a car stolen. This student's mother had died, and she was living with her twenty-two-year-old sister. She had a car that has a bad transmission, and [the parking gear] doesn't work. She has to leave it in neutral and put on the emergency brake—but this means you can't remove the keys. And she has only one key, so she has to leave it unlocked with the keys in the ignition. Somebody stole the car, and he knows who did it [I later find out it's Carter].

I asked how he knows who stole the car, and he said that students tell him things. He develops a rapport with the students, and they tell him all sorts of things that go on. The person who stole the car was a kid who's been in trouble recently. He sells cocaine on campus. Officer Frederick said that he's a good kid, and he likes him, but he's stupid. He said he recently called Carter into his office and told him that with only five and a half weeks left in the school year, he didn't want any problems. He told Carter that he knows he's selling drugs and doing other stuff, and to just keep it off the school's property. Carter said, "OK," which Officer Frederick took to be an admission of his guilt.

I asked why Carter was still in school, and Officer Frederick said that they're still building a case against him, for the drugs and now for the car. Officer Frederick said that he just collected DNA evidence from Carter yesterday [by saving a Pepsi can from which he had drunk]. (FN)

Carter's name would surface during conversations between Officer Frederick and other school staff for the rest of the school year. During this time, Carter committed an armed robbery of a store and even robbed a bank. The evidence against Carter for the bank robbery was strong: Officer Frederick showed me the bank surveillance photograph clearly showing Carter at the teller window, a classmate and friend of the student's informed on him, and Officer Frederick elicited a confession—on audiotape—of the armed robbery. Yet Carter wasn't arrested for an entire month after the stolen car and three weeks after the armed robbery, as the police continued collecting evidence. Officer Frederick told me that the delay was because he was waiting for Carter to turn eighteen, though this seems unlikely since what matters for prosecution is his age at time of offense, not at time of arrest.

Other Police Work

When the officers were not patrolling the halls or responding to a particular incident that occurred on campus, I would often find them in their offices (usually with the door closed) working on administrative issues. This typically includes reviewing incident reports, following up on previous cases, and completing arrest reports after a student has been arrested at school. This administrative police work demands a significant amount of time, up to half of each day, according to some officers.

Occasionally the officers are gone from the schools for a day or longer when they attend meetings or conferences. In some cases, their absence seems to put school administrators and other staff on high alert. For example, the following field notes describe a day when Officer Brandon was off campus:

> I turned left to see if Officer Brandon was in his office—his door was closed and I knocked. There was no answer. [The principal's] secretary saw me and said, "He isn't here. I don't like to tell that to too many people." (FN)

The secretary's reaction implies a feeling of uneasiness when Officer Brandon is not around and suggests that the administrators and staff really do come to rely on officers in their schools, at the very least for a sense of security.

Officers in these four schools are occasionally involved in community police work in addition to their school responsibilities. At Unionville High School, Officer Brandon is responsible for performing "victim services duty" on a rotating basis. At Frontera High School, if Officer Martinez is not too busy, he occasionally responds to calls about something going on in the community; however, he pointed out that the school does not like it when he does this. Officer Frederick regularly responds to calls from a school down the street (to which he is not assigned) that does not have its own officer.

Teaching

Law-related education is a key component of most school resource officer programs. Indeed, the funding for officers in the southwestern state requires that they spend 180 hours in class on law-related education each school year. Despite this requirement, I very rarely observed officers in classrooms. When

I asked Officer Frederick how he fulfills his teaching requirement, he smirked and said that he tries to teach more, but he is too busy and it is lower on his priority list than his other duties. He told me that he is listed as co-teaching courses on law or government with teachers, and that he goes to these classes when he can.

The one time that I did observe Officer Frederick teach a class, he was a guest instructor in a driver's education course (as described in my field notes):

Officer Frederick begins by introducing himself, and telling the students that he's a regular cop, but that he works at the school. . . . He then shows them a PowerPoint slide show he says he stole from someone. It begins with a picture of a teenage girl, who Officer Frederick points out as attractive. Pictures then show the car that this girl was in when it was hit by a drunk driver and caught on fire, and what the girl looked like after. She survived, but was severely burned to the point where she is not recognizable—her face is completely deformed, and she lost an eye and most of her fingers. The slide show then includes pictures of the girl with her father before and after—it is really a gruesome sight, and the class looks on silently. Officer Frederick concludes this portion of his presentation by stating how innocent victims of drinking and driving always seem to be the worst off—they aren't always killed, sometimes they are maimed—but the drunk always seems to be either killed or not hurt at all.

The class continued with more pictures of alcohol-related crashes and dead bodies of the crash victims. Officer Frederick then discussed field sobriety tests, and demonstrated how even a sober person could be perceived as failing a sobriety test.

Officer Frederick asked for a volunteer. When nobody volunteered, he asked, "Who's the biggest class clown?" Students said a name and pointed to one student, a male Latino student sitting near the front. Officer Frederick looked at him and said, "Come on down." Officer Frederick then made the student walk heel-to-toe along a straight line, and stand on one foot. After the student performed these tasks, Officer Frederick announced that he did well, but even sober there were inaccuracies that would have allowed him to test his breath. The point, he tells them, is that these sobriety tests are so tricky that any amount of alcohol can impair your ability to perform them.

To further reinforce his point that drunk driving can get you arrested, Officer Frederick told the class that police can almost always find some justification for pulling over a motorist: "[He tells them that] the police can find several different reasons for pulling them over to begin with. One that is common is a license plate bulb that doesn't work. Or young drivers often take wide right turns, by not staying in their lane with making a right turn, and for which they can be pulled over." For the remainder of the class, Officer Frederick then showed the students his uniform: the bulletproof vest he wears daily, and what weapons he carries on his belt. Throughout the period he is friendly, approachable, makes jokes, and seeks students' involvement. (FN)

Though Officer Frederick clearly made efforts to relate to students and be likeable to them, there are many aspects of his lesson that made me uncomfortable: he began by telling them that his presentation was stolen intellectual property; he then commented on how attractive a female teenager was before her accident; and he showed gruesome *Blood on the Highway*–esque slides. But what I thought was least appropriate was how he made police work seem illegitimate, in that even a sober person could fail a sobriety test, and virtually any motorist can be pulled over by an officer at any time. Subtle lessons like these reinforce students' powerlessness at the hands of authorities, especially when coupled with their experiences with school discipline (which I discuss in detail in chapter 4). My point is that by having a police officer teach a course, the resulting lesson is of questionable content, yet it expands the ways in which students are taught about the ubiquity of social control and that they are powerless relative to authorities (in this case the police; in other cases, school administrators).

Counseling

Counseling students is a key part of the school resource officer program. Many such programs across the United States explicitly state that being a counselor, mentor, or role model is an important task for police in schools, and I heard several staff members at each school I visited talk about the importance of having them as counselors and role models. In describing the role of school resource officers for an issue of *American School and University*, journalist Connie Mulqueen states, "They develop mentor relationships with students as a proactive measure to prevent crime and tragedies by identifying and solving problems before they erupt into violence."[9] Indeed, most of the officers at the schools I observed make at least some attempt to counsel students, and do so in a variety of ways. For example, Officer Brandon at Unionville High is an assistant coach for the school's football team; he told us that he hoped this role would give students a chance to see him as a real person and not just a cop. The following field note illustrates how Officer Brandon attempted to counsel a student:

> Officer Brandon approached a student whom he described to me as "troubled," and who was attending his first [mainstream] school. He talked to the student for a few minutes, and asked the student why he was not in class earlier. The student said that because he has ADD he can't sit through a whole class, and he has to get up sometimes. Officer Brandon encouraged the student to come to his martial arts class again. They seemed to have a good rapport. He later explained to me that he teaches a martial arts class, and he gave the student some passes to come to it. (FN)

Conversations like this are common for Officer Brandon, despite the fact that he can also be sarcastic and sometimes even mean.

Not all the officers feel the same way about counseling, and some encounter difficulty with the mentoring process. Officer Frederick said he avoids counseling because he doesn't feel qualified to do so:

> INTERVIEWER: Do you ever try to mentor them or counsel them in any way?
>
> OFFICER FREDERICK: No, I don't try. I mean sometimes they come to me and then I've had kids come in here and say, "Look I'm having problems with this," or "I wanna be a cop," or whatever and I'll shoot them in the right direction. One of the officers who's a little weird, he mentors young ladies, and that usually, that kind of concerns me, so I try to stay away from the mentoring, because I'm not qualified to mentor. So I mean, not to be a counselor or anything: I'm a cop. (I)

At Frontera High, Officer Martinez expressed interest in counseling, but feels the administrators are resistant to it. He talked about wanting to get students to open up and feel comfortable talking to him, but then said:

That's kind of been shot down because of the adminisiation here, and they see things differently so . . . I guess you could probably say they wouldn't want me to be more, I guess you could look at it as being touchy-feely. They don't want that, they want me to just have visibility and do my job. (I)

One issue that may facilitate counseling is that the officers in both schools with mostly nonwhite students, Frontera High and Unionville High, are racial/ethnic minorities as well. Officer Martinez at Frontera High is Latino, and Officer Brandon at Unionville High is black. The fact that each of them is of the same racial/ethnic background as many of their students might help reduce the social distance between officers and student at least somewhat, and make it more likely that students will seek their advice or counsel.[10]

Helping with School Discipline

While some officers are resolute that they only enforce criminal laws and not get involved in school discipline matters, others frequently insert themselves in situations that are clearly school discipline matters rather than legal violations, and that have little or no impact on overall school safety (e.g., dress code violations or attendance policies). Both police jurisdictions in the southwestern state requested that their officers only enforce criminal laws, and the officers in these two schools usually follow this direction, which means that most of our observations of officers enforcing school discipline are from the mid-Atlantic schools.

One of the more troubling findings of this research is that the officers' involvement in these matters often escalates minor disciplinary situations. For example, at Unionville High, Officer Brandon overheard a student in the halls cursing and told her to watch her language. The student responded by repeating the curse word several times. Officer Brandon turned the situation over to a dean of discipline, Mr. Compton, who instructed the student to write an apology letter to Officer Brandon and planned to give the student one day of in-school suspension as punishment. When Mr. Compton brought the apology letter to Officer Brandon, however, he called for a more severe punishment:

Mr. Compton called over to Officer Brandon and handed him an apology letter. . . . He told Officer Brandon he had her rewrite it several times until it was good enough. Officer Brandon took the letter and asked what [the student's] punishment was going to be. Mr. Compton said that because she wrote the apology letter, he was just going to give her one day of in-school suspension. Officer Brandon said he thinks her punishment needs to be more severe than that. He said because of the circumstances of this particular situation, he wanted her suspended out of school. Mr. Compton said, "OK," that he would give her a day of out-of-school suspension. Officer Brandon repeated that he thinks this is necessary because of "the way it went down." (FN)

Officer Brandon's call for harsher punishment of this student is outside the realm of his job. Moreover, the student received a harsher punishment than she would have otherwise received, only because the adult involved in the situation was the school's officer.

Police officers are in a very difficult position when forced to decide whether to help enforce school rules. When they enforce school rules, there is a lot of room for small problems to escalate into larger ones, especially if students become upset at the rule enforcement. But if an officer does not enforce school rules, it could easily send students the message that the school rules are unimportant.

Benefits and Dangers of Police in Schools

There is no question that having a police officer benefits school administrators.[11] The principals at the schools I studied each rely on their officer as a legal adviser of sorts. Today's school officials must know the relevant rules of law, since state laws mandate that schools report certain criminal offenses to the police or the state, though without legal training it is often difficult to classify such behavior. For example, a principal may be uncertain whether a Swiss Army knife qualifies as a "deadly weapon," or whether a student found with somebody else's prescription drugs should be reported as a drug offender. Police officers, on the other hand, are accustomed to making decisions about whether a crime has been committed, thus school administrators often seek their advice on these matters.

Similarly, school administrators use officers to advise them on security matters. For example, during one visit to Centerville High administrators responded to a bomb threat:

> A student had reported graffiti in the girls' bathroom that said: "Bomb. You better get out, cuz there in the school." I am told that there was also a similar message written in the boys' bathroom the day before. To help determine whether these messages should be considered legitimate threats, Principal Miller consulted with Officer Malvern. Officer Malvern examined the messages written on the stalls and together the principal and Officer Malvern determined that not only were the two messages written by different people, but that each message was written at a different time—this suggested to them that a benign message was successively reshaped by multiple students, rather than representing a legitimate threat made by a single student. Principal Miller decided not to evacuate the building or end the school day early. (FN)

In this case, a difficult decision for Principal Miller was made easier by the fact that she had a trusted, well-trained security expert at her disposal.

Police officers also help school administrators by lending legitimacy to their school safety initiatives. If questioned by a concerned parent, schools can highlight the presence of an officer as evidence of how seriously they take school security threats. When students are caught violating school rules in ways that the school and officer together define as criminal, the officer can explain to parents why their child is being arrested, and absolve an administrator from having to defend this harsh response; I observed this in cases when students were arrested for fighting on school grounds, for example. Further, by outsourcing part of the job of school security to an officer, school administrators are somewhat insulated from public indignation, accusations of incompetence, and lawsuits if a violent incident does occur on campus.

Finally, the presence of an officer helps administrators if they wish to target certain behaviors for particularly harsh consequences. Administrators know that they can implement policies that may be unpopular and coercive because they have recourse to a police officer if students rebel. For example, the school in our study with the highest suspension rate, Unionville High, demands that a parent accompany a student on his or her return to school following a suspension, per school district rules. When students and parents disobey, the school asks that Officer Brandon arrest these students for trespassing, since technically they are still suspended until a parent accompanies them. The presence of an officer allows the school to follow a very strict policy, since Officer Brandon, not a school administrator, is responsible for dealing with students who violate the rules.

Despite these advantages to the school administration, the presence of an officer can be problematic for the school administrators as well, since it may result in administrative role confusion. Because school resource officers typically are not supervised or evaluated formally by anyone at the school, there may be questions as to whose authority is greater—the officer's or the principal's—and who should prevail in a conflict over school discipline.[12] The New York Civil Liberties report illustrates extreme examples of this, as in the case of teachers who were actually arrested because of a disagreement with police about school discipline, one of which is as follows:

On March 8, 2005, at least seven NYPD officers arrived at the New School for Arts and Sciences after teachers called 911 to ask for medical assistance for a student who had been involved in a fight.

Several teachers had successfully stopped the fight and controlled the situation before the police responded, and Cara Wolfson-Kronen, a social studies teacher, informed the 911 operator that the fight had been defused. Despite this, one of the officers demanded that the teachers identify the students who had been involved in the fight and said that they would be handcuffed.

Quinn Kronen, an English teacher, pointed out that those students were now peacefully sitting in the classroom. Officer Bowen responded by yelling: "You fucking teachers need to get your shit together. These kids are running crazy. You need to get rid of them." When Mr. Kronen objected to such language, Sergeant Walter told Mr. Kronen that he had "better shut the fuck up" or she would arrest him. When Ms. Wolfson-Kronen objected, Sergeant Walter said: "That is it; cuff the bitch." Officers arrested Ms. Wolfson-Kronen, paraded her out of school in handcuffs and forced her to stand outside in sub-freezing temperature without a jacket. They also arrested Mr. Kronen.

The teachers were detained at the 41st Precinct for approximately two hours before being released. The charges against them—disorderly conduct—were dismissed at their initial court hearing, because their alleged wrongdoing did not constitute unlawful activity.[13]

Conflicts between the school and the police can come in more subtle forms, especially when their interests diverge. Though the officers I observed all talk about the importance of working with the school administrators as part of a team, they leave no doubt that they are ultimately police officers, not school employees. When the interests of the two organizations diverge, officers prioritize their policing duties. This is clear in the aforementioned case of Carter at Fairway Estates High, who steals a car, robs a store, sells drugs, and robs a bank before being arrested. Officer Frederick frequently updated me on his ongoing efforts to build a case against Carter, including DNA evidence, a confession, and statements from the student's friend. Yet despite this strong evidence and a growing list of offenses, Carter was not arrested for nearly a month after I began following the case (and according to Officer Frederick, he knew of Carter's drug selling even before then). Waiting to build an unimpeachable case against an offender may be in the police department's interests, but it is entirely opposed to one of the school's fundamental interests in having an officer: being able to remove potentially violent students without delay. I suspect the principal at Fairway Estates High would have been outraged to know that this student was allowed to continue attending school during this time, exposing the rest of the school to risks of violence and drugs at the hands of someone on a crime spree.

Moreover, some research suggests that police power in schools may be overtaking that of teachers, administrators, and other school staff, undermining the school's authority, and shifting discipline responsibilities away from teachers and administrators.[14] As a result, teachers' jobs are becoming increasingly segmented; what was once considered routine classroom management is now outsourced to security guards and school police officers. This routine then becomes a self-fulfilling prophecy—the less teachers are expected to manage student behavior in their classrooms, they less they will do so and the more they will come to rely on external support. In a classic ethnography of school security, anthropologist John Devine describes this process as one where roles within schools become more restrictive and hierarchical. Because of the buildup of security in schools, teachers now see their roles in more limited terms than in years past, where teachers now deal exclusively with students' minds and security forces with students' bodies.[15]

Aside from evaluative judgments of whether the presence of an officer helps or hinders the school administration, it is important to note how their presence can alter the way the school relates to students. In allowing the officer to help deal with potential and actual problems, the school is complicit in redefining behavioral problems as criminal problems. As an example, consider a note that Officer Malvern at Centerville High showed me, which was written by a student and taped to a classroom door. This note, which was given to Officer Malvern to handle, read as follows (with all errors intact):

> The puppies would love this. It was a 3rd of the left nut when blue and red elephants swung from trees like man eating oders ate away at the flesh of an unborn baby like a regular old pork chop And then we put puppies in a bag and threw them in a river to marinate them and the rocks would brutaly pound on their flesh like salt and pepper on a fuckin grilled chees with bacon. (FN)

Officer Malvern used student informants to find out the identity of the note's author. He told me that it was a skateboarder, and that these students are "a little off." He had decided that the student was weird, but not violent or threatening. Officer Malvern noted that now that he knew about this student, however, he would keep a close eye on him. Though the note is certainly odd, it does not mention any interpersonal violence or threat to any individual or the school. Perhaps it is an attempt at abstract poetry or possibly even a sign of mental instability, but if it is the latter, the fact that it is referred to the officer rather than a counselor or psychologist is important. In this example, and many others I observed in all four schools, the school resource officer is the primary contact for a wide range of misbehaviors, rather than non-police professionals who may be able to discuss with a student his or her problems and help the student in ways unrelated to enforcing laws or school rules.

Relatedly, a school resource officer may know only about students' offenses, not their personal backgrounds, which can influence them to treat students as criminals more than as troubled teens. This is evident in the following field notes from Frontera High, in which I talk with Officer Martinez about a Latino male student, Victor, who apparently threatened to shoot another student:

> I later learn more about Victor from the school's intervention specialist and counselor, who says, "Oh, not Victor! He's got nothing to lose!" [when

Ms. Flores, the dean, tells her about Victor's threats]. She explains that two weeks ago his mother died, and Victor was the one who found her. He doesn't know CPR, but he tried to perform it, and she was already cold. Now, his teachers say that he keeps talking about death. The intervention specialist and Ms. Flores both say that he already had problems—he had a quick temper and was a class clown. They're concerned more about his behavior now.

Later that day as I was leaving campus I chat with Officer Martinez, who had been involved with the case earlier (talking to Victor):

AARON: That's a tough case you guys are dealing with.

OFFICER MARTINEZ: What case?

AARON: With Victor, making threats.

OFFICER MARTINEZ: Oh, that. Yeah, he's got what's coming to him. He's a real hothead, and those two have been having problems since middle school.

AARON: I guess his mother died two weeks ago, too.

OFFICER MARTINEZ: Oh. (FN)

The recent trauma preceding Victor's current misbehavior is not an excuse for threatening to shoot someone, but it is certainly relevant in responding to his behavior. Yet even after questioning Victor and the other students involved, and having dealt with this case for at least an hour, Officer Martinez had no knowledge of Victor's situation.

Though this was not a focus of my research (i.e., I did not interview police command staff or other officers who do not work in schools), it is apparent from my work within schools that having a representative in the school benefits the police department as well as school administrators. Police organizations view school-embedded officers as opportunities to build relationships with youth; this view presumes that through regular and casual interaction with school police officers, students will gain a better understanding of and greater respect for law enforcement.[16] Ultimately the hope is that they will view police officers as resources or allies rather than adversaries.[17]

School resource officers facilitate community policing because they are constant fixtures within one of the most important community institutions. They get to know many of the students and learn about these students' families (and their families' problems), as well as the needs and problems the community faces. Since these officers are still members of police precincts and report to these precincts regularly, they can easily share this information with other officers, who can act on their tips. For example, at Frontera High, which was located in a community purported to have a lot of gang activity, both Officer Bartol and Officer Martinez studied gang affiliation and activity by watching students (looking out for gang colors or signs, and talking to students about gang loyalties) and shared this intelligence with other officers working in the community.

Additionally, to the extent that the officers can befriend some students and reduce fears of police, they may help lower the boundaries that separate community members from the police department, and thereby facilitate future police investigations. Importantly, recent research questions the effectiveness of school resource officer programs at improving students' perceptions of police.[18] Though student bodies overall may not shift their thinking about officers, it is clear from my research that at least some students do befriend officers and provide them with information that assists police work. Officer Frederick at Fairway Estates High stated:

> I don't enforce the school rules, because I don't wanna be the bad guy, but I hold them accountable when they break the laws. And if anyone needs anything I'm here for them, and I'm supposed to teach classes, and every time I teach a class I've got thirty new best friends, well probably about twenty-seven and then three of them still just hate cops, but people that were, are more apt to [know] me than [to] just say "hi." . . . It's cool because I'm creating informants for later on. (I)

Some of the officers' efforts to enlist student informants, however, can alienate students. At Centerville High, there had been a theft of a large amount of property from the girls' locker room. One girl in particular was identified as one of the thieves. Officer Malvern described to me how he brought her into his office and got her to admit her part in the theft and then to inform on her friends:

> As Officer Malvern described it, "I told her that she had to tell her friend that we were suspicious, and that she should bring the stuff back now so they didn't get into trouble. She said, 'You won't let her know that I told you, will

you?' I said, 'No.' So she called her friend, and as soon as the friend answered, I grabbed the phone [away from her] and told the girl, 'This is Officer Malvern. Your friend just told me you were involved in the theft. You have ten minutes to get back to the school with everything you stole.' She came back, then I had them tell me who the third girl was. The second one told me and agreed to call her and tell her that I suspected them, and that she should come in. She asked, 'You won't let her know that I told you, right?' I said, 'No.' So she called the third girl, and as soon as she answered, I told her, 'This is Officer Malvern. I know you were involved, so bring all the stuff you stole and get in here right now.'" He laughs as he tells me this story. (FN)

While this type of procedure is a common police technique (lying to suspects to get them to admit guilt, inform on coconspirators, etc.), it does very little to build rapport between youth and police.

Officers also help gather information that can be used by the police department to detect and respond to crimes occurring outside of school. At Fairway Estates High, for example, Officer Frederick commonly views students' MySpace pages. When I asked what he learns from this, he said that he often finds out about parties that are planned for the weekends; he then tells other officers, who break up the parties if alcohol is being served. Here, the officer uses his knowledge about the students (who they are, and that they have MySpace accounts) to expand the police department's surveillance of youth, thereby facilitating police work that occurs during the weekend and off school grounds.

Enhanced surveillance can also occur in a more open way. At Frontera High early during my fieldwork, a current student and a recent student were both murdered, execution style, while working together at a local fast-food restaurant. This horrific incident was covered extensively by the local news. The case did not occur at school and the individuals who were later arrested were not students at Frontera High. But because the victims were a current and recent member of the school community, it affected the students and staff considerably. Since Officer Bartol knew the victims and many of their friends, and since he had a great deal of knowledge about the community generally, he was in a good position to help solve the crime.[19] He spoke to students about what they knew, and, according to school administrators, his investigative work helped the police department solve the case.

Though the presence of officers clearly benefits administrators, teachers, and the police department, it is less clear whether it benefits students. Some studies have shown some support for the argument that police in schools can prevent crime, but these studies are relatively inconclusive and methodologically weak.[20] Yet there are other potential advantages to having school resource officers, such as whether students feel safer because an officer is present, and whether officers can effectively counsel students.

When I began this research, I expected students to feel alienated by officers and hostile to their presence. I was surprised to find that this is largely not the case. When I asked students to reflect on what it is like to have a police officer in their school, I received many ambivalent responses and many positive responses. The ambivalent students tended to express either no opinion, or the opinion that it doesn't really matter one way or another whether their school has an officer. Several stated that the officer is not an effective deterrent to crime on campus because he is only one person and so cannot be at all places at all times. For example, when asked if having a school resource officer made him feel safer, a student replied,

It does, yeah, a little bit. I mean it's only one and there's, like, way more kids than there is cops, but . . . (I)

Just over half the students, however, offered a positive response, in that they like having an officer at their school. Most of these positive responses were based on the belief that having an officer deters crime, or because students take comfort knowing that in case of a crisis (such as a shooting), an officer is available for immediate response. Others stated that it's good to have an officer because he is someone to talk to or to consult in case of legal or personal problems. Interestingly, though, when students offered these comments, they tended to concern their particular officer, rather than officers in school generally. These comments suggest that though these students liked the personality of their particular school officers, the benefits of having an officer at school in general are still unclear.

I received few negative responses to our questions about having school resource officers. The most common complaints are either that an officer on campus is unnecessary because the school is safe, that having a police car out front or an officer in the building makes it seem as if there is more violence than there really is, or that they dislike the individual officer at their school. Yet most students who offered negative views—all but one student—also expressed ambivalence, as if to say that they don't like it, but that it also has some advantages, doesn't matter, or isn't so bad. For example, one Latina student said:

> An officer at school, at times one feels like, like he's looking at you in a bad way and one feels, like, under scrutiny or bad, but one also has to realize that it's for our own safety, it's for our security that in case there is an accident or a person that has a gun. Then in that sense it is good. (I)

Overall, students report being either pleased or ambivalent about the fact that their schools have a police officer. This result is important, regardless of its empirical basis. That is, even if officers do not make schools safer, if students *feel* safer, this has positive consequences on its own.[21] Students who feel safer will be less distracted in the classroom and may be more likely than others to regularly attend school and school functions.[22]

Yet the students' comments raise more questions than they answer. When I considered the students' comments, and particularly the ambivalence many feel, as well as the fact that many positive and negative comments are based on individual officers' personalities rather than the institutional practice of putting police in schools, it caused me to question how deeply students think about the issue. In other words, students in today's high schools are conditioned to not see any alternatives to having a school resource officer. Asking them if they like having a police officer in school might make as much sense to them as asking whether they like having a principal; neither one makes much sense if it is all one knows and there are no apparent alternatives. Students have been socialized to expect a school resource officer, thus police have become a part of the fabric of schools. Nonetheless, it is very rare for them to express disapproval, a result I take seriously and which suggests that students do benefit in some ways from the police presence.

The advantages to students of having a school resource officer also became apparent during the only fight I observed during the field research. (That my research assistants and I saw only one fight during hundreds of hours of fieldwork across four schools is important in and of itself.) According to my field notes:

[During an interview with a teacher], we heard a commotion out in the cafeteria. [The teacher] looked out the window, then ran outside. When we got out into the cafeteria, we saw Mr. Brook restraining a student by lying down on top of him. . . . Mr. Brook was yelling at the student, "Stay down! Just stay there!" as he lay on top of him, pinning the student to the ground. The student was struggling, clearly trying to get up. Another student, much smaller than the one on the ground, was out of breath and sitting at a table next to me.

Mr. Brook told the student he had to stay down until Officer Brandon arrived. He then turned to the teacher on hall duty (who was standing next to them) and asked him to radio for Officer Brandon. The teacher said, "Officer Brandon, we need you here," and he arrived within about twenty seconds. Mr. Brook got up, and Officer Brandon calmly grabbed the student and walked away with him. I noted that Officer Brandon looked very calm, did not at all yell, but was quick and firm: he took the student by the arm and walked him away quickly. (FN)

Immediately after Officer Brandon arrived the incident ended. If this incident is representative of other crises, then officers are indeed helpful at ending violent or potentially violent situations.

Officers seem less successful at helping students when it comes to mentoring or counseling. Most school staff members and parents I interviewed believe that the officer at their school is a good counselor or role model to students, but the students themselves are somewhat less positive about this aspect of the school resource officer program. I found nobody who had actually gone to the officer to discuss a serious problem. Instead, when asked about how their officer interacts with students, most discussed how he might be friendly in the hallways, how they feel comfortable bantering with him, or how he can give helpful advice for things like arguing traffic tickets. For example, according to one white male student at Fairway Estates High:

STUDENT: He's a really nice guy. He goes to classes, like driver's ed, and teaches us about how it's a bad thing to drink while driving, DUI. And if you ever need help . . . like [advice on buying a car] . . . he'll be happy to help you out.

INTERVIEWER: OK, does he talk to students a lot or just stand around and watch everyone?

STUDENT: He talks to them and he goes to assemblies and talks to the student body. Again, he goes to classes and teaches what the teachers ask him if he can do it. (I)

This doesn't mean that students never come to the officer in their school to discuss serious issues, because certainly some do; but it does suggest that this happens somewhat rarely.

A minority of students voice uneasiness or dislike for their officer, mainly because of reasons like "being mean" or "being suspicious of students." One black female student talked about how Officer Brandon is nice unless a student gets "on his bad side," and then he watches them suspiciously and strictly. Though she said that she gets along with him, she added:

A lot of boys in this school probably don't get along with him. The boys who actually do stuff don't get along with him because he's nice until a certain point, and if you get on his bad side, he will follow you if he sees you in the hallways he will ask for passes and if you don't have them, he'll immediately take you to the office. (I)

Another student, a black male at Centerville High, said that he would not talk to Officer Malvern about a problem because he believed that Officer Malvern would only consider safety threats and was not willing to discuss other issues, and as a result might be suspicious of students. These negative voices are few, however, and relatively tame, as most students spoke about the officer at their school as friendly and helpful.

Based on my observations, I see several ways that police officers are limited in their capacity to effectively counsel students. Despite some notable instances, overall the officers I observed sincerely try to help students by being a positive, supportive influence, something that is reflected by the students' positive appraisals. But the role of counselor can conflict with their obligations as police officers. This is especially apparent when a student confides in the officer about illegal actions that either they or their friends may have committed— here the officer has an obligation to take legal action, even if it means betraying the student's trust and subjecting the student to arrest or ridicule (for betraying peers). This is particularly acute at Frontera High, which is located in an area with a large number of Mexican immigrants, many of whom are undocumented (according to the principal). For example, one student there said that he would not talk to his school's officer about a problem she was having:

> Because of legal matters. I've heard that police officers also have the right to call immigration and so, no. (I)

More commonly, though, officers are in the position to interact with students in an informal counseling role rather than act as confidants. Yet here, too, the role of police officer can conflict with the role of counselor/role model. Police officers are trained in conflict and deal with it on a daily basis—shifting gears and adopting a "softer side" is not a strength of the officers I observed. Consider, for example, the following interaction with a student at Centerville High, as described by Officer Brandon:

> The other day a student on the football team [for which Officer Brandon helped coach] was messing around during practice, so Officer Brandon made him run two laps. Instead of running, the student walked the two laps. Officer Brandon said he told him to leave practice; the student said he wasn't going to leave and that he couldn't make him. They got into an argument and the student called Officer Brandon "a bitch." Officer Brandon told me that in his training as a police officer he is taught to not back down from situations or to walk away. He said they are supposed to go toward problems and do what needs to be done to resolve them. Officer Brandon then said he told the student that if he had something to say to him to "be a man" and say it to his face instead of mumble it under his breath. The student said to him, "What are you going to do—hit me?" Officer Brandon replied, "Why would I need to hit you?" The student said if Officer Brandon hit him he would sue him. Officer Brandon told me that this let him know that the student was just running his mouth and didn't really want to engage in a confrontation with him. He said he kicked the student off of the team. (FN)

Here the officer seemed proud of the fact that he "put a student in his place" by asserting his own authority, eventually kicking the student off the football team for being disobedient. The training one receives as a police officer—to assert authority and not back down—conflicts in this case with a conflict resolution approach to dealing with a student's behavior problem. Though Officer Brandon may have wanted to help—he was generously volunteering his spare time to be an assistant coach for the team, after all—his role and training as an officer made him a less than ideal counselor in this case. In a national assessment of SRO programs conducted for the National Institute of Justice, criminologists Peter Finn and Jack McDevitt find this as well. They state: "Program coordinators, SROs, and school administrators all recognize the difficulty SROs experience trying to maintain authority as enforcers of the law while at the same time preserving a helping relationship with students as teachers and mentors. *Walking this line plays itself out in two particular areas: counseling and familiarity with students.*"[23]

The mismatch between one's training as a police officer and the difficulty of working with students is noted by one of the deans at Unionville High as well, though in more negative terms:

MR. COMPTON: The biggest problem that I see with a school resource officer is that police officers are trained to deal with adults. . . . They're not
trained to deal with children and they have maybe [only] a class or two
[for training].

INTERVIEWER: So how does that come into play?

MR. COMPTON: They deal with them terribly. In their day-to-day interactions, the SROs that I have witnessed deal with children, they deal with
them like criminals, they do not trust anything they say, they assume
they're lying before they open their mouths. And it's not their fault,
they've been trained to do that. That's what they have been trained to
do and they're usually the type of people that take training very well.
You can't become a police officer if you can't follow orders. I can't follow
orders. I do what I think is best in any given situation. I can't do what
the person above me tells me, "just do it." That's the way it is, I can't do
that. Police officers from what I've seen are those types of people. You
have to be, it's like a military position, you have to be able to follow
instruction. So what I see is them not understanding that you have to
work with kids, you have to give them respect if you want respect back,
that's the way, you have to [to] work on an equal playing field. (I)

It would be a mistake to blame individual officers for responding in negative or counterproductive ways, since they may be responding in a way that is consistent with police training and socialization—this is clear in the above example of Officer Brandon and the football player. During the course of my research I met with senior officials in my home state's Department of Education, including the secretary of education, about ways to improve school discipline. When I discussed this observation that police training leaves officers ill-prepared to counsel and mentor students, I received an interesting response from the person in charge of statewide school discipline programs. A former police officer who had worked in a school as a juvenile officer (before the school resource officer program was implemented in the state), she told me that she agreed with me, and that when she began working in schools she had to go back to college for a master's degree in secondary school guidance in order to learn how to relate in meaningful ways with students.

One would think that if any police officers would be able to effectively counsel students, it would be school resource officers. Though the process of selecting school resource officers varies, usually they are a self-selected group who volunteer for the assignment because they are skilled at interacting with youth and they sincerely want to work with and help children. They also receive training in dealing with students, since police practices in the streets and school hallways can vary considerably. Some of this training includes "verbal de-escalation," where officers are taught how to diffuse confrontations and avoid physical confrontation. According to Officer Malvern, however, school resource officers are also trained to approach conflict more violently than would officers on the streets; since a school officer is always vastly outnumbered, the officer must respond to conflict swiftly and with force in order to immediately end the problem. He discussed how a street officer's job is to use as little force as necessary, and to physically control someone while waiting for assistance—but if a school resource officer tried to do this during a group fight, he could easily find himself swarmed by dozens of angry students. His argument makes sense and seems to represent sound police tactics. But this also highlights one of the central problems of putting police in schools: their training and experiences in dealing with conflict and negative situations on a daily basis leave them ill-prepared to respond to challenging youth in ways that avoid further conflict.

Occasionally, the officers' attempts to mentor or counsel students result in inappropriate interactions. For example, I observed Officer Malvern advise a white female student on how to talk to her probation officer. This student came to Officer Malvern's office to update him on her case, during which

> Officer Malvern chatted with the student a bit, and gave her a lot of encouraging feedback (e.g., "that's terrific," "good for you") when she said that she was going to take extra classes to graduate early, work for a year, then go to college to be a veterinarian. He said to her, "I think this is going to be a good year for you." Then, when she was leaving, he called out to her, "I love you," in a very fatherly way. (FN)

Officer Malvern was clearly trying to counsel the student by advising her with regard to her probation case, giving positive feedback to her future plans, and letting her know that he cares. Though well-intentioned and kind, telling her that he loves her seems inappropriate. Clearly, counseling students is a challenge to some police officers for which they are not prepared.

Police presence in schools also disadvantages students by criminalizing behaviors that are not actually threatening to school safety.[24] This is evident in the examples I use to begin this chapter. Police involvement in school punishment means that some behaviors that would have led only to school punishment (had an officer not been present) now result in arrest.[25] At Unionville High, for example, there were two girls who did not get along and had a history of ongoing disagreements and minor incidents between them. Most recently, one of the girls, Tamara, had reportedly thrown an open can of soda at the other girl, Sierra, on the school bus. When Officer Brandon caught wind of this, he got involved:

> I followed Officer Brandon down to Ms. Calhoun's [an African American administrator] office where there was an African American female, Tamara, seated, slouched over with her head down on Ms. Calhoun's desk. Ms. Calhoun greeted Officer Brandon and me. Ms. Calhoun said that she just finished telling Tamara that she thinks they are going to have to refer her for alternative placement because of the continuing problems she is having. Officer Brandon told Tamara that he thought they had talked about this issue with Sierra and that [Tamara] told him it was squashed. Tamara

stayed slouched over and didn't say anything. Ms. Calhoun told her to sit up several times before she actually sat up slightly. She never turned around to face Officer Brandon while he was speaking to her. Tamara said it is squashed and she hasn't done anything. Officer Brandon said he just talked to Sierra right now and she just told him that she and [another female student] are still bothering her. Tamara didn't say anything but just sort of shook her head. Officer Brandon told her to stay away from Sierra and that he didn't want any of her friends bothering her either.

Officer Brandon then asked Ms. Calhoun if someone was going to come pick Tamara up so that she didn't ride the bus today. Ms. Calhoun said she had already called her grandmother but that her grandmother couldn't come pick her up. Officer Brandon said that he would give Tamara a ride to [the police station]. He said if he hears that she bothers Sierra again he was going to lock her up for harassment. He said what she was doing to Sierra was harassment and she was going to get locked up for it if she continued. Tamara didn't reply. (FN)

Here Officer Brandon involves himself in a situation that was already being taken care of by an administrator. Ms. Calhoun makes it clear that she is going to discipline Tamara for the incident on the bus by suggesting she be placed in an alternative school. Officer Brandon then escalates the situation by threatening to arrest Tamara for harassment and take her down to the police station.

Some studies have found that students prefer to talk to officers rather than school officials because the officer is external to the school's authority over students.[26] Given adolescent angst about schools, and the fact that the school controls their every movement for hours a day, it is understandable why students would feel this way. Yet it is also an unfortunately naive belief, since the authority of the police extends well beyond that of the school, and the potential punishments for misbehaviors given out by the criminal justice system are far more severe than those given out by schools (the most severe punishment available to the school is expulsion).

The ability of officers to help students is also limited by the fact that the presence of a police officer can infringe on students' rights. When it comes to questioning students about a crime or searching students, school administrators and officers are bound to different standards under the law. School administrators can search a student with "reasonable suspicion," for example, while police must meet the higher legal standard of "probable cause." In their partnership, however, schools and school resource officers find ways to get around this legal impediment to police control. For example, at one school a student was sent to an administrator's office to be searched because she was caught reentering the school building during school hours, which is a violation of the school's closed-campus policy. The student's rule violation constitutes reasonable suspicion for an administrator to search, yet falls short of probable cause that a criminal offense has been committed; thus the officer had no legal authority to search the student. The administrator, however, asked the officer to observe the search, which was physically conducted by the administrator. Had the administrator found any contraband, such as drugs or alcohol, then only at that point would there have been probable cause for the officer to directly intervene, continue the search, and arrest the student. Thus, though the officer was legally prohibited from conducting the search, his presence meant that the student did not receive the protections the law intended. With the infusion of police into public schools, it is increasingly likely that schools and police will partner in ways that put students' rights in jeopardy.

In another incident, Officer Martinez at Frontera High violated a student's rights by ignoring the fact that she invoked her Miranda right to not be interrogated:

> Officer Martinez reads Miranda rights to the student. When he finishes, he asks the student if she wishes to talk to him. The student, a Latina female, says that she does not want to talk to him.
> OFFICER MARTINEZ: That's fine with me.
> (Officer Martinez gets a call in between regarding something that had happened over the weekend. He speaks briefly to the person on the line and then returns to the proceedings with the student.)
> OFFICER MARTINEZ: Have you ever been arrested before?
> STUDENT: No.
> Officer Martinez calls in the student's name to the police station and verifies her name and that of the mother, which he gets wrong, and the student rather impatiently spells it out for him as he also corrects it on his report.

OFFICER MARTINEZ: I need to run a report on subject [student's name]. . . . [They wait, then he continues to talk to the student.] . . . OK, you won't talk to me, but let's see what you will do in front of the judge because he doesn't mess around.

(At this point, for the first time I see a dramatic change in the student's face. He goes on to tell her that she is facing a "class 6 felony.")

Officer Martinez continues to write the report as he asks the dean, Ms. Flores, what happened. Ms. Flores explains how the school security guards found the student and some other students smoking on campus. All of them had run away from the security guards, but the guards had been able to catch them and the first thing they did was to take away their backpacks.

MS. FLORES: I had them come in one by one and identify their backpacks and she chose this one. [Officer Martinez takes out a small plastic bag about an inch in size with marijuana inside of it. Ms. Flores proudly states with a smirk on her face:] I went through the backpack and found that black little bag and when I looked inside of it, I found that in one of the side pockets was that pouch.

(Tears begin to surface on the student's face.)

MS. FLORES: How much do you think it is?

OFFICER MARTINEZ, LOOKING THE POUCH OVER: Oh, about a gram at most. [He walks over to the backpack and asks the student:] Is this yours?

STUDENT: Yes, it is. [She wipes the tears with her hand.]

Officer Martinez asks if there is anything that has her name on it as he proceeds to go through the materials inside the student's backpack. He finds a notebook with her name, and says, "I guess this does make it yours." (FN)

Finally, the presence of officers negatively affects students by socializing them to expect a law enforcement presence in their lives. One white male student said that he does not object to the penalties at his school for possessing drugs or alcohol, or for fighting (each of which is automatic arrest and suspension or expulsion), because:

I mean, it's like, if you, in order to have freedom you have to have restrictions. So, in order to be able to do whatever you want in this school basically, to do whatever club you want, to choose your classes, you have to have the restrictions of: no, you can't get in a fight, and if you do, these are the consequences, and everyone knows that. So you signed the code of conduct, if you don't sign the code of conduct you don't have to go here, transfer to another school. The security's fine here. (I)

The fact that growing numbers of children will go to schools that have full-time police officers on campus is likely to make views like this even more common. In his book *Being Down: Challenging Violence in Urban Schools*, education scholar Ronnie Casella suggests that:

> for a majority of students, the police officer was a built-in part of school-ing—a taken-for-granted part of education. Some were critical of the apparent need for the officer but most students seemed to think that the officer and guards made the school safer. These were students who were born in the 1980s and have been raised during two decades of panic about crime, of increased police power, of prison expansion and soaring rates of incarceration, and during the rise of "get tough" policies. Many can hardly remember a time when there was not a police officer in their school.[27]

My research—completed several years after Casella's—leads me to agree com-pletely. Though my study was not able to measure changing student attitudes over time, I am shocked at the lack of critical thought students give to the pres-ence of a police officer—that they view police as a normal part of high school rather than a historically exceptional security strategy. Though I find it shock-ing, based on my own notions of what high schools should look like (formed through my own non-police public school experiences), this acceptance and expectation of police involvement is precisely what one should expect, given what we know about how schools socialize students into a set of expectations about social roles. Further, this growing normalization of law enforcement is consistent with the trends toward increasing punitiveness and centrality of law enforcement in everyday affairs (as noted by scholars such as David Garland and Jonathan Simon), and contributes to problems like mass incarceration.[28]

Police and School Climate

It is clear that police help school administrators run the school and help the police department regulate communities, enhancing the school's control over students and the police department's surveillance of communities. Yet it is not at all clear whether they help students, the school's primary constituents. Some limited benefits are apparent, particularly reduced fears and greater comfort among students knowing that an officer is there. And, as some have argued, their presence means there are additional adults who are outside the school authority system to whom students can confide about a potential school shooting. Yet there are also serious potential harms. Importantly, these are an institutional rather than individual problem; they stem from the official role, obligations, and training of police officers, not from deficits of individual officers.

It is tempting to argue—as did several of the students with whom I spoke—that the presence of police should only bother the students who get in trouble. This way of thinking mirrors how citizens often talk about public surveillance and other invasive security or criminal justice policies, and supports the idea that discipline practices only affect a small group of citizens (or students).[29] But this is not true—these practices subtly shape how citizens relate to the state, and how students relate to the school. As I illustrate throughout this chapter, having SROs in school affects how school administrators govern all students, not only those caught committing criminal offenses. In fact, this is perhaps the most important conclusion from this chapter: that officers affect the overall school climate. Having an officer can escalate disciplinary situations; increase the likelihood that students are arrested at school; redefine situations as criminal justice problems rather than social, psychological, or academic problems; introduce a criminal justice orientation to how administrators prevent and respond to problems; and socialize students to expect a police presence in their lives.

For all but the most violent areas, it is a bad idea to keep police in schools. The potential harms to students are serious and widespread. Perhaps the most troubling consequence is how a police officer can shape the school discipline climate. As I illustrate in this chapter, police officers, though well-intentioned, can influence the school discipline climate in ways that could contribute to students' sense of alienation from the school, thus making a school shooting even *more* likely. Further, I find that when students feel comfortable confiding in officers (because the officers do not have the same authoritative relationship over them as their teachers, and because they believe the officers will maintain their confidence better than will school officials), the students are being naive in ways that can hurt them. Finally, though I agree that an additional adult in the school whom students can confide in and who is separate from the school authority would be helpful, it is not clear to me why that person should be a police officer, as opposed to a counselor, social worker, or other individual trained in how to talk to and help adolescents.

But arguing this point is problematic, because it would be elitist to ignore the fact that most people with whom I spoke are happy to have police in their schools. The desire to welcome police into the school is important, since if the presence of officers makes students and staff feel more comfortable, then it has positive effects too. An alternative is possible, whereby schools and police seek to achieve the same ends but without such potential harms. Schools can still establish relationships with police departments, whereby certain officers can be designated as school responders even if they do not work in the schools. These officers can visit the schools occasionally, can be available to the schools for legal consultation, and can be first responders in case of crisis. At the same time, instead of having full-time police officers schools could hire community-based adolescent counselors. Currently, guidance counselors at most schools spend their time scheduling classes, helping with college applications, and performing other administrative duties, with little time left for actual counseling. Counselors who do not work for the school (like school resource officers) and who have training in dealing with adolescents would be in a better position than police officers to counsel students and help them with their problems. Further, these counselors would still be outside of the school's authority system, and thus might also be good protection against school shootings.

4   TEACHING TO THE RULES

I could hear Mr. Wade talking loudly outside the ISS room: "You don't have to like her but you have to respect her enough to let her teach the rest of the class." His tone was very firm. I could hear a female voice arguing with him (it was Jade).

MR. WADE: If she tells you to stand on one leg, you stand on one leg.

JADE: No I don't!

They continued to argue back and forth.

MR. WADE: Well, who is right then? She's right.

JADE: She's wrong!

MR. WADE: You're the one that's going to suffer, you're the one that's going to fail.

Jade said something about not liking the teacher, to which Mr. Wade replied, "It's not about who you like and don't like, it's about what you do and don't do."

MR. WADE: She has the final say. She's the *only one* that has a say.

JADE: I hate her . . . I hate her guts. (FN)

This conversation between Jade, a black female freshman at Centerville High, and Mr. Wade, a black interventionist, illustrates an important dynamic I observed regularly at each school: that following school rules and reinforcing the school's authority are themselves the primary achievement of school discipline, not inducing behavioral changes in students or solving students' problems. These may not be the goals that are laid out in the schools' mission statements or codes of conduct, and school staff may not be aware that this is how they enforce school rules, but these goals were clear in most rule-enforcement situations I observed throughout my research. Contemporary school discipline puts such a high priority on the school rules that they often are pursued above even pedagogic goals when the two compete for attention.[1]

This pursuit of rule adherence and maintenance of authority mirrors what others have called "teaching to the test," when schools structure their curricula to prepare students for standardized exams. In extreme cases, this means teaching only courses directly related to the tests (often only English and math), at the expense of other subjects (e.g., social studies, physical education, science). Critics of teaching to the test argue that by teaching only material likely to appear on the exams, schools encourage rote memorization and fail to teach students critical-thinking skills.[2] School discipline follows a similar pattern, since rules are enforced in a way that teaches students only how to abide by rules but not how to resolve conflict, solve their own problems, or correct their behaviors. Jade, for example, is taught that she needs to stop arguing because she can't win, with no discussion about what actually happened that made her upset or how she could resolve her conflict with her teacher. She apparently feels that she is treated unfairly and wants to be listened to, but instead she is taught that she must follow school rules and obey the teacher's authority—end of story. Given the parallel between school discipline and "teaching to the test," I call this "teaching to the rules."[3]

When considering the powerful socializing function of schools, the importance of teaching to the rules is apparent. Students do learn from this process, but the content of what they learn is disconcerting: they learn a model of citizenship that is at odds with a democratic ethos, as they become socialized to accept authority and to follow rules uncritically. Teaching to the rules also means that we miss out on opportunities to teach children conflict resolution and behavior management skills.

Actual Problems Go Unaddressed

Teaching to the rules happens in a variety of different ways, but it characterizes rule enforcement in most situations across the four schools in this study, despite the differences between them. One important characteristic of teaching to the rules is that students' actual problems go unaddressed, since these problems are secondary to rule enforcement.[4] For example, consider the following field notes, describing how a black student, Heather, enters the office of a black male administrator at Centerville High to ask for a tissue. It is clear that she has been crying, but instead of discussing her problem the administrator lectures her on the dress code:

> Heather entered Mr. Morris's office and asked if he had a tissue. He said,
> "Sure, come on in. Here you are, help yourself" (and held out a box of tis
> sues that was on his desk). Heather took a tissue, said thank you, and turned
> to walk out. As she did, Mr. Morris said, "Hold on there, what are you wear
> ing? That shirt is a bit too short." Heather was wearing a tight shirt that
> revealed her navel and the small of her back. She pulled it down and said,
> "No, it's OK." She turned to leave again, and when Mr. Morris saw that the
> back of the shirt was still about three inches over her waist, he said, "No,
> it's not. Do you want me to take a picture of it with my camera phone to
> show you? You can't wear that to school." Heather mumbled something and
> slowly turned, again, toward the door. As she did she sniffed, and put the tis
> sue to her eye, as if she had been crying. She left, and Mr. Morris said to me,
> "I hate to have to do that, getting on students for how they dress." (FN)

It is important to note that this administrator perceives himself to be a mentor to students, especially the school's black students, and often encourages
them to come talk to him if they are having any problems. Yet when this
student approaches him, she receives only a reprimand for how she is dressed.
Even when it is obvious that the student has been crying, Mr. Morris does
not ask why or even how she is doing.

The following, from Fairway Estates High, is another example of how a
student drops a hint that he might be having a serious problem, which is
completely ignored in favor of punishment for a minor rule infraction:

> Brian, a black student wearing shorts, a T-shirt, and a camouflage-colored
> baseball cap, is called to the office of Mr. Alameda (a Latino assistant prin
> cipal). Mr. Alameda reads a referral from last Thursday (today is Monday)
> stating that Brian was at the gate and trying to leave campus. Brian was
> excused from class to go use the bathroom, and the teacher thought he was
> going to the nurse too. But he was in neither place. Brian apologizes, says
> that he wasn't trying to leave campus, but he knows he shouldn't have been
> there. He says that it won't happen again. Then he says, "Please, can I get
> a second chance? It won't happen again. I wasn't trying to leave the school,

and I can't get in trouble. I'm having a lot of trouble at home, family issues, and we're moving on Thursday." Mr. Alameda asks if he's moving back to Texas, where he's from, and Brian says, "Yes." Brian repeats his request—pleading this time—to get a second chance. Mr. Alameda never asks what his family problems are.

Mr. Alameda calls Christine, a bus driver who often helps with security tasks. He asks her if she was the one who [wrote the referral about the incident], and she says, "No." Mr. Alameda then calls a teacher, apologizes for interrupting her class, and asks if she knows about this, and she says, "No." He then asks Brian to wait outside, and he calls in the next student waiting to see him.

[After dealing with another student] Mr. Alameda calls Christine back to his office. He asks her again if she saw this student trying to leave, or by the fence. She reads the referral, and then walks outside of the office to look at Brian, and says, "Yes." She tells Mr. Alameda that she now remembers what she saw: another student got his truck from the visitor lot and drove up to the gate, where Brian was. She didn't see the other student, but she wrote down the license plate. Brian was talking to him, and she drove up in her cart. As she did, the truck drove away. She asked Brian what was going on, and he said that the other kid was going to give him lunch money. She then saw in her rearview mirror that the truck pulled back around, and the driver motioned to Brian to meet him around the side. She said that she didn't believe him, since if he was just getting lunch money there was no reason to be secretive. She told Mr. Alameda that she called it in, and was told to escort him to [ISS], which she did.

Mr. Alameda thanked her, and then called Brian's mother. He told her what happened, and said that though her son never left the school grounds, he wasn't where he was supposed to be. And he looked "suspicious." He repeated this: "Even if they believed him, he wasn't where he was supposed to be and he looked suspicious. . . . I know this isn't the worst crime in the world, but he did break school rules. I'm going to give him a detention."

Mr. Alameda then called Brian back in. Brian's demeanor was much different now, after Mr. Alameda had told him he called his mother. Brian just glared, and barely answered Mr. Alameda. Mr. Alameda told him that he was giving him detention on Wednesday, from one to three (it's a half day), and also during any periods of the day when he wasn't taking a final [exam].

Brian said, "I didn't do anything." Mr. Alameda responded, "I understand, you were still inside the gate. But I think you would agree with me that you weren't where you were supposed to be." Mr. Alameda then offered for him to work the detention off by picking up trash during lunch. Mr. Alameda asked if he'd do that instead, and Brian grunted. Mr. Alameda said, "Fine, you can just do that for an hour, and that will be good." He excused Brian, who said, "This sucks!" when he got up. Mr. Alameda said after him, "Don't give me any attitudes, Brian." (FN)

That Brian mentioned problems at home while pleading for leniency, and that he was visibly upset at having his mother informed of the incident, are clear warning signs that Brian is having trouble at home-but they all were ignored.

The problem of overlooking underlying problems happens not just when students interact with disciplinarians—it is a part of everyday school rule enforcement. Many school punishment incidents begin when students misbehave in class and are given a referral by a teacher; often, the teacher sends the student out of class to in-school suspension, to a dean of discipline, or to an interventionist. But when I spoke to teachers, most of them told me that a primary cause of student misbehavior is academic trouble, since students act up in class when they do not understand the course material.[5] This gives the student an opportunity to get attention on his or her own terms, rather than being shown up for not understanding the material, and it gives the student an escape (being kicked out of class) from an uncomfortable and potentially embarrassing situation.[6] In other words, even though teachers acknowledge that students act up because of academic trouble, many respond to misbehavior by kicking students out of class, forcing the students to miss class time and putting the students further behind. Not only does this response ignore the students' actual problems, but it actually makes their problems worse. Certainly not every teacher takes this strategy, as some pride themselves on being able to manage their classrooms so as to prevent the need for referrals or removing students from class. But I observed this to be a very common practice for most teachers at all four schools.

Over thirty-five years ago, education researcher Ray Rist also observed discipline that was prioritized over pedagogy in a way that hurt students' academic experiences.[7] Rist observed young black children from kindergarten to second grade in an urban school, and found that socioeconomic status shapes how teachers treat students even at this young age. In particular, he found that when students used "street talk" instead of proper English, they were scolded by their kindergarten teacher and admonished to not speak up unless they could do so properly. The response, Rist observed, was that these students became more reticent and participated less in lessons, thus limiting their opportunities to learn (including learning how to speak in a way that would be rewarded in school). Limiting their exchanges with the teacher for the sake of discipline hampered their academic training from day one.

More recently, in her book about how schools teach racial identity and reproduce racial inequalities, *Race in the Schoolyard*, sociologist Amanda Lewis notes a similar problem when schools punish students, particularly African Americans. She discusses how school disturbances are often the result of miscommunication or cultural clashes, but that teachers respond to these disturbances only by removing students, leaving the root problem unaddressed: "Generally, when a teacher responds to 'disruption' by removing a student from the class . . . an important message is conveyed—specifically, a lack of commitment to having that child participate as an equally important learner or member of the class. . . . As the student advisors noted, underlying issues are avoided when teachers call someone else to handle the 'disturbance' so they can get on with their job—teaching—and the 'the issue of race or any other issues aren't addressed.'"[8] By removing students from class, teachers assume that the problem lies only in the individual student perceived as disruptive, leaving more fundamental problems unresolved.

Of course, it often makes sense to remove a misbehaving student from class, especially if the student is getting in the way of the rest of the students learning. Teaching in public high schools is difficult enough when everyone behaves, but when a student disrupts class and takes a teacher out of his or her lesson plan, it is even harder. Thus, the problem isn't that teachers kick students out of class, it's that for many of them it's the only thing they tend to do. In the four schools I studied, I saw no efforts to tutor the students on the subjects they were missing or to keep them on task (working on the academic subject they were missing) while being punished. Students are supposed to do work while serving in-school suspension, but they rarely do, and there are no instructors present who can help them with the material they might already be struggling with. There are several ways that schools might address this problem without overburdening already-busy teachers and administrators, such as more classroom management training, or group tutoring after school for students removed from class. The point is that removing the student from class and assigning a punishment is the end of the line—the student's academic or personal trouble is never addressed.[9]

After being sent out of class, disciplinarians ask students what happened. But these conversations usually do not address the real reasons why students misbehave. Instead, they generally focus on the rule violation, and the disciplinarian forces the student to accept responsibility. Consider, for example, the following field notes from Frontera High, where a student was caught cursing after being accused (falsely, he claims) of cheating on an assignment:

> A small Latino male student walks in to Ms. Flores' office [the Latina dean of discipline]. The student, Hector, is fourteen, and acts very contrite to Ms. Flores. He answers her questions and gives his side of the story, but doesn't argue or act disrespectfully to her in any way. She begins the meeting by saying, "You called your teacher a 'motherfucker.' Why did you call your teacher a motherfucker?" Hector then tells his story: he completed an assignment and looked at his friend's paper to see if he got the right answers. The teacher saw him and scolded Hector for cheating, saying he is always cheating and this time he caught him. The teacher then told Hector that he is giving him a detention, so Hector put his head down on the desk and cursed to himself. The teacher thought the curse was directed at him, so he gave Hector a referral. Ms. Flores listens to the story, and then reminds Hector that he cannot curse at a teacher. She tells him that nobody should have to work in an environment like that, with others cursing at you, and that you can't talk like that to a teacher. She tells him that the mandatory punishment is five days of suspension, but that if he goes to anger management class, it will be only a two-day suspension. She tells him that they would rather he take the class, so he agrees to do so.

Ms. Flores never addresses whether Hector actually cheated, whether he actually swore at the teacher, or why he might have done either of these actions. Hector at least perceives the teacher as out to get him (reporting that the teacher said Hector is always cheating, and now he caught him), which suggests that a meeting between Hector and the teacher might help improve their relationship. But instead he receives a lecture on not cursing at a teacher and an out-of-school suspension (to a student who might have been cheating because he was behind on his course material to begin with).

Perhaps teaching to the rules would not be bad if it were only a part of the punishment process, with school psychologists or other trained counselors also intervening to address students' underlying problems. But this largely does not happen. Deans of discipline, assistant principals, and interventions do not seek involvement of counseling professionals. Each school has counseling professionals on staff, but unless the disciplinarian knows that a student is already working closely with a counselor, the disciplinarian does not involve the counseling staff in punishment decisions. With few exceptions that I observed, the two departments remain entirely separated. For example, when I asked Mr. Sussex, a white dean of discipline at Unionville High, whether he ever has the opportunity to send a misbehaving youth to a counselor or psychologist, he answered:

> You know, I don't know. Yeah, I don't know. I mean, I guess I could always contact one of the counselors and say, "Hey, you know, I'm working with so and so and something's not right, maybe you can take some time [to talk to him or her]." You know, but I've never done that. Maybe I could ask. I'm sure I could, I mean. (I)

In fact, when Mr. Compton, the new dean of discipline, arrived at Unionville High, I asked where his office would be and Mr. Sussex told me that Mr. Compton would be housed in the office that was recently occupied by the school psychologist. Mr. Sussex said that as far as he knows she stopped showing up one day, and nobody knows where she is. He shrugged, and said that he doesn't think there is a psychologist on staff anymore. I found it disturbing that although Mr. Sussex assigns punishments for students who misbehave, possibly due to emotional or mental health problems, he isn't even sure if there is a psychologist at the school.

In addition to focusing on the rule rather than the problem that led to the misbehavior, school officials' responses to students offer only the school's authority system and potential punishments as reasons for following school rules. This was clear in Jade's story, when she is told that she must obey her teacher in all circumstances, or she will be the one to suffer. Similarly, in the following field notes, the principal at Centerville High explains to a student and his parent why he is in trouble for fighting, even though the student claims that he defended himself. I observed this interaction while shadowing Officer Malvern, who received a call to come to the office and talk to a student involved in a fight. In the end, the circumstances of the fight don't matter, only that the student violated school rules:

Officer Malvern and I entered an office that Mr. Bodley [a white assistant principal] was in, along with a black student, Philip, and his mother. Philip was sniffling and drying his face with his hand. Officer Malvern introduced himself, and explained to the mother that her son would receive a summons to appear in court. He said that this was the school's policy: that in all fights both people get arrested. When the mother said that her son had never been in trouble before, Officer Malvern told her to tell that to the judge, and that nothing [bad] would happen.

Principal Miller [a white female] entered and introduced herself. The mother asked Philip why he fought, and he said that the other boy hit him, so he defended himself. She turned to Philip and said, "This is just at school—you're not in trouble at home." The mother asked Principal Miller why her son was in trouble for defending himself, and Principal Miller explained that they don't tolerate any fighting. Principal Miller asked Philip, "Did you hit him back?" He responded, somewhat hostilely, "Yeah, why shouldn't I?" Principal Miller quickly responded, "Because we tell you not to, that's why." (FN)

In her book about social power in schools, *De-facing Power*, political scientist Clarissa Hayward notes a similar orientation to rules in an urban elementary school. She finds that when rules are enforced, teachers give no reference to a purpose for the rule or a reason why one should obey the rule, other than the need to avoid punishment.[10] Like a parent who tells her child to obey her because "I'm the parent, that's why," school officials tend to justify rules and punishments only by citing their own power and the consequences of violating the school rules.

Teaching to the rules also resembles a problem noted by philosopher Ivan Illich in *Deschooling Society*. Illich discusses how schools teach students to "confuse process and substance"—that is, students believe that simply by being in school they are learning, regardless of the actual substance of what they learn. Thus, they begin to value the process of schooling even if it has little productive outcome. This protects the school's monopoly, since it assumes that only in a formal school can one properly learn. It also makes the school seem legitimate, since the public assumes that if someone is in school then he or she is learning.[11] I am arguing that school discipline is very similar, in that it also confuses process and substance—when schools teach to the rules they enforce the rules for the sake of those rules themselves and the authority structure on which they are based, not to pursue actual behavioral objectives. Thus, schools teach the value of the discipline process, regardless of behavioral outcomes.[12]

Teaching to the rules is a way of invoking and strengthening the school's power and its authority over students. Linguist James Gee notes how institutions like school maintain their power by making their version of meaning seem like the only possible one.[13] This process is clear when rules are enforced, since the school rules are presented as inevitable and inviolable. Again, when considering Jade's case, one can clearly see how power and authority are maintained by teaching to the rules. Jade's questioning of authority is not seen as legitimate, since Mr. Wade never even bothers to consider whether she has a point; such a discussion is not one that students are able to have, since the school's authority to punish goes unquestioned when schools teach to the rules. Or, in the words of the following white male teacher at Unionville High, who is describing what he says to misbehaving students:

> MR. LANGLEY: "Here's where you're going with this, here's where it's gonna end up. I don't care how right you think you are, and even if you are, in this situation I'm always gonna be right. You need to learn that and that's the way it is." And usually I am right, but these are kids that usually have problems with every other teacher in the school and I've had students where they give them to me because I end up getting along with them. And I say, "Look, this is why you're here because you think you're right all the time, and you know what? You're not right now. You might be with your other situations with your teachers, but even if you are right, you're wrong, so you've got to learn that in this situation."
> INTERVIEWER: Even if you're right, you're wrong?

MR. LANGLEY: Yeah, yeah, well, even if you are right, you're wrong in this situation because the teacher's always right and you've gotta get used to that. (I)

Though Mr. Langley is trying to help students learn how to navigate the school authority structure and protect themselves, he is also teaching students that they have no right to question authority, even if their complaint is legitimate, since "the teacher's always right."

Occasionally, teachers or disciplinarians noted to me how schools teach to the rules, such as in the following incident at Unionville High:

The bell rang for lunch, and [Mr. Compton, a white dean of discipline, and I] walked into the hall leading to [one of the cafeterias]. He saw a black male student, James, and called James over to him. Mr. Compton told James that he needed to talk to Mr. Sussex [another dean of discipline] to sort out his problem. From their conversation, I found out that James had been suspended by Mr. Sussex earlier in the school year, but Mr. Sussex didn't enter the suspension into the computer. James stayed home for three days as instructed, then returned, but found that he was marked absent without an excuse, and now he had too many unexcused absences to pass his classes [meaning he would fail his classes and not graduate]. He was clearly upset at Mr. Sussex for suspending him over [what he perceived to be] nothing, and then for not entering in the suspension as he was supposed to. James said that he had been accepted into college, and planned on going. He said that he was already appealing, and would win—he noted that he wouldn't let something stupid stop him from going to college. Mr. Compton tried to convince James to talk to Mr. Sussex, and respectfully ask him to make the absences excused. James didn't want to talk to Mr. Sussex, saying, "No, I don't like him, he doesn't like me, and I don't want to deal with him." Mr. Compton told him Mr. Sussex made a mistake, but people make mistakes. He added that in life there will be people he won't like and who won't like him, but he'll have to deal with them and make the best of things, and this is a good lesson on that. James seemed content to let his appeal process handle this, noting that it's going forward and that he's going to win, but Mr. Compton encouraged him to talk to Mr. Sussex and not let it get to an appeal. James added (passionately), "[Mr. Sussex] told me I should leave school—I should drop out, just because I had a cell phone! He doesn't know me, he doesn't know anything about me! He told me to leave school just for that! I'm not talking to him." Mr. Compton responded, "I can't talk negatively about a colleague, so I can't discuss whether he was right or wrong. I'm just saying that you should go talk to him and try to resolve this." James said he might go talk to Mr. Sussex.

After James walked away, Mr. Compton told me that James's problem was frustrating for him. He said, "Here's a kid where I basically have to tell him to follow the rules, even if they don't make sense. But you follow the rules because they're the rules. The rules here don't make any sense for him, but he has to follow them." To clarify, I asked, "He has to follow rules just for the sake of following the rules?" And Mr. Compton said, "Yes, exactly." (FN)

Of course it's important to teach youth that rules must be followed. But in a case like this, the rule takes priority over fairness and substance. James was treated unfairly, as Mr. Compton subtly acknowledges, but it doesn't matter. The deeper lesson he learns is that he must accept the school's authority without complaint, even if it is unfair.

In the following transcript, Principal Miller at Centerville High notes how the school enforces rules without addressing the causes of student misbehavior:

> We automatically think that it's the child's fault, that it's the child's problem, fix the child and everything will be OK. That's why when a child gets thrown out of class the first conversation I have with them was, "What were you working on?" And I don't think we do enough of that. We automatically go to the code of conduct when the kid says, "This is f-ing stupid!" and we put them out of school for inappropriate language or abusive language, and we never have the conversation, or we rarely have the conversation, about "What were you doing?" And [it might be the case that] the child was really working on something that he was struggling with for two weeks, and he's been asking for help and hasn't gotten any help, and there's the root of the problem. We're not solving the problem, we're just putting a Band-Aid on an amputated leg. (I)

Though it is encouraging that Principal Miller understands this deficiency of teaching to the rules, the problem is as bad at Centerville High as at the other schools I observed.

Students, as well, note the fact that school punishments fail to address underlying problems and reasons for misbehavior. This is evident in the following statement of Gerald, a white student at Fairway Estates High:

> INTERVIEWER: If you could change anything about how your school prevents crime and punishes students, what would it be?
>
> GERALD: Um, let me think about this one . . . I would say instead of just having, like you know, how kids get in trouble for something real bad and will get suspended for a period of time and then come back to school and it'll just be all over with? I think they should do something that'll make the kids think of more of what they've done and actually have them have to interact in some way to make up for what they've actually done and the problem they've caused. Because when they're going away from school and just sitting at home all day and not having to deal with it and not hearing from anyone, they're just sort of forgetting about it and it'll probably happen again.
>
> INTERVIEWER: OK. So you're not, you feel that that's, they're not really dealing with . . .
>
> GERALD: They're not really, no they're not really dealing with the problem, they're just, well at school the immediate problem, they're getting the kid out of there that caused the problem, but when that student returns, the student probably won't have any change of mind or the way they think about what they've done. (I)

This quote is important because it shows that teaching to the rules is apparent to students. If many of them recognize this problem, the school's authority becomes less legitimate.

Not Listening

A key component of teaching to the rules is that students' problems, issues, and complaints are rarely taken seriously when they conflict with the school's rules or authority. When the school prioritizes the rules and the school's authority, it matters little how students perceive their situations—only whether they broke the rules. As a result, school staff often fail to listen to students when the students try to talk about perceived unfairness or why they broke the rules.

At its worst, not listening to students is active and intentional, such as in the following field notes:

A tall, thin, black male student came in the office and sat down next to a female student who had been waiting to see Mr. Brook. Mr. Brook (a white dean of discipline) continued to work on his computer during the following conversation:

MR. BROOK: Why are you here Mark?

MARK: I want to file a complaint.

MR. BROOK: Against who?

MARK: Against a teacher—she told me to shut up. [The female student laughed.]

Mr. Brook turned to look at Mark and said, "Mark, I'm gonna put it to you like this—shut up!"

MARK: Naw man, if I had said that to her, I would have been in trouble, so she shouldn't be able to say that to me.

MR. BROOK: Mark, it's funny that you mention that. [Mr. Brook dug through a pile of paperwork.] Because I have a referral for you here that says that you told a teacher to leave you the f- alone.

MARK: Naw man, I didn't say that. I just told her to go do her job somewhere else.

Mr. Brook didn't respond to this; he turned his back to Mark and kept working on his computer. (FN)

Additionally, I observed some deans of discipline or interventionists routinely decide on students' punishments before ever talking to the student about the incident. More than once, for example, I saw deans at Unionville High decide on punishment for a student who received a referral (based strictly on the punishment prescribed in the code of conduct), write the punishment on the referral form, and only then meet with the student about the incident. When this happens the student has absolutely no opportunity to deny or justify the behavior, a clear violation of any due process safeguard and, when the punishment involves removal from school (such as a suspension), it is a violation of the student's constitutional rights.[14]

In his analysis of an urban high school, Ronnie Casella describes a similar dynamic during screening committee meetings for students seeking reinstatement after suspension or expulsion.[15] Though the meetings are (rhetorically) intended to help decide whether a student should continue at the school or instead attend an after-school GED preparation or other alternative institution, there is little decided during the hearings Casella describes. Instead, decisions are made in advance, usually that the student should attend the alternative program, and the meetings are rituals in which the hearing officers convince the student and his or her parent to accept the preformed decision. The students he describes often raise viable issues, but these issues are ignored; when students disagree with the committee's decision, they are treated as defiant.

More common than deciding on responses to student misbehavior before actually meeting with them, school staff members listen to students but discount their issues and complaints, especially if these complaints are voiced against another school employee. Students' complaints about mistreatment by teachers usually fall on deaf ears, and when their perception of an incident varies from that of a teacher or administrator, the student's version is ignored. Regardless of whether the teacher has acted unfairly, or whether the student's version of events is plausible, by resisting the teacher's authority the student has violated the rules. In the following incident at Frontera High, a teacher calls the dean of discipline, Ms. Flores, about a conflict between two students. Ms. Flores and her assistant believe at first that one of the students is a special education student, then find out from his file that he is not; Mr. Flores nevertheless asks the teacher to send only the other student:

> The student doesn't show up in Mr. Flores's office, so after about twenty minutes she radios to security to pick the student up. Jose, an eighteen-year-old Latino, arrives in her office ten minutes after that. Irene thanks the security officer who brings the student in, and notes that this student was supposed to report in on his own twenty minutes ago, but instead has been cruising around.
>
> MS. FLORES: What's going on?
> JOSE: I wasn't doing nothing. [The teacher] is lying.
> MS. FLORES: Wait, first we have to talk about why you didn't come here, and how I had to go get you. You were told to come here, right? [Student mumbles.] So what were you doing? Why didn't you come in here? That wasn't good—now you'll get a referral for not coming in, when before it wasn't even a referral.

JOSE: [The teacher] said she was writing up a referral.

MS. FLORES: She didn't. You were going to just fill out a behavior change form, which isn't a big deal at all. A behavior change form just takes you out of class for a little while and lets me talk to you. Now you're going to have a referral, when you wouldn't have if you'd just come in like you were supposed to. Here, look at this . . . where is my book? The rules say you have to come in when we tell you to. Why didn't you?

Ms. Flores's assistant walks behind the student to look for Ms. Flores's rule book. While she passes, she intentionally hits Jose on the head and says, mockingly, "Oh, excuse me." She does the same thing five seconds later as she walks back.

Ms. Flores finds her student handbook and reads from it how students must follow the orders of teachers and staff. She shows it to the student and again reprimands him for not showing up. Ms. Flores then asks him about bullying the other student, and Jose denies it. He states: "I'm just a humorous guy, and he doesn't like it." After a lot of prodding, Jose described today's incident: "I was holding the glue, and pretended like I was going to squirt it on him, but I wasn't. He kicked me. He yelled and said something about [getting glue on] his jacket, and he kicked me."

Ms. Flores then lectures Jose for several minutes about bullying. She reads from the student handbook again, this time the section about student bullying and harassment. She repeats certain segments of it. She also tells him: "You're eighteen now, so you can be arrested. You can't do this. . . . There's a reason for this. Do you know what happened at Columbine High?"

JOSE: No.

MS. FLORES: Were you born in the U.S.?

JOSE: Yes.

MS. FLORES: You don't remember that? There was a school shooting five years ago—no, it'll be the sixth anniversary in April. Fourteen students were killed, and it was the bullying victims who did it. Have you lived in the U.S. your whole life?

JOSE (WHO IS VISIBLY IRRITATED BY THIS QUESTION ABOUT LIVING IN THE UNITED STATES): Yes ma'am, [city in] Nebraska. I just don't know everything.

MS. FLORES: Well, this shows how important it is to not bully other kids.

As they continue Jose protests verbally at first by saying that he wasn't bullying the other student, he is just "a humorous guy" and doesn't do anything [harmful]. Ms. Flores tells him several times that it doesn't matter what he thinks, it's only about the victim and how the victim interprets it. If the other student thinks it's bullying, then it is. It's like sexual assault. It doesn't matter what you think, only what the victim thinks of it. After a while Jose stops saying anything, and just stays quiet, but rolls his eyes often. He is clearly annoyed, but just answers "yes ma'am" and "no ma'am" in response to questions. Jose then asks: "Can you bring in [the other student] so you can talk to him too?"

MS. FLORES: No. Never. I would never, never bring in the bullying victim in a situation like this.

Mr. Flores asks more questions about the incident and the history between the two students. Jose still insists that he just jokes around and isn't causing problems, but the teacher can't handle it. Ms. Flores asks if the teacher has said something before about these two students, and he says yes, that this is the third time. At this Ms. Flores again reads from the student handbook, this time about how harassment is something that occurs over time. Jose mumbles something, so Ms. Flores scolds him.

MS. FLORES: Don't give me that. I don't take that "yeah, yeah, yeah" stuff.

JOSE: You've already read it to me.

Ms. Flores' proposed solution is for this student to completely avoid the victim. He shouldn't joke with him or talk to him.

JOSE: Fine. I won't talk to him at all. I'll have nothing to do with him.

MS. FLORES: Good. Are you friends?

JOSE: We're not enemies. I guess. We talk sometimes. The other day I noticed he wasn't wearing his hat. He always wears a Cowboys hat, and he wasn't wearing it. He told me he didn't feel like wearing it. We talk—stuff like that. But I won't talk to him again. (FN)

Throughout the discussion, Jose insists that he is "a humorous guy" who is just playing with the other student. Ms. Flores refuses to even entertain the notion that this is true, or to offer to talk to the "victim," even without Jose present. Moreover, by reading the rule against harassment to Jose multiple times, Ms. Flores maintains the focus on the rule, not on the context in which Jose may have broken the rule. It is heartening to see that Ms. Flores takes bullying so seriously, since bullying is a serious problem that schools often fail to take seriously.[16] Yet the way that she deals with the problem fails to address the underlying issues, such as why Jose might be aggressive or what his relationship with the other student is really like, and as a result it isn't likely to help the situation.

But this is not always the case; sometimes school staff do listen to students' complaints, even about teachers. Even in these circumstances, however, the end result is the same—the student is reminded of his or her powerlessness as the school rules are prioritized. According to my field notes:

> A Latino student, Renaldo, came into [the cafeteria] and told Mr. Compton he didn't want to go to class because he was having problems with the teacher. Mr. Compton asked him what was going on and Renaldo said that the teacher singles him out and picks on him in class. Mr. Compton said, "OK, he singles you out. That's his right to do that. You have to defend yourself. You have to go there and sit in your seat and not say a word. If you don't do anything to give him any reason to single you out, that's how you can protect yourself. You know what I'm sayin'"? Mr. Compton told Renaldo to give it a chance and go to class. (FN)

Here the dean is sympathetic to Renaldo, but tells him that the only thing that might come of his protest is punishment, thus it would be better to quietly accept the unfair situation.

Moreover, only some students—those seen as "good students"—receive the benefit of this limited receptiveness to complaints. Upon my first visit to Unionville High I observed the following:

> Mr. Brook spent about ten minutes explaining how school punishment works at Unionville High. He showed us some referral forms, and said that a few things can happen when a student acts up. One, the teacher might send the student directly to ISS and then write up a referral. The teacher sends the referral to Mr. Brook, and he reads it. He said that the punishments for violating rules are cut-and-dry, and leave little room for interpretation. So, if the teacher's description is straightforward, he will assign a punishment on the referral form and then give a copy of the form to the

student. However, he described times when it isn't so straightforward, like if a student has received several referrals in the same day, if it's from a teacher who gives out a lot of referrals, or if it's a student who is never in trouble. In such a case, he'll talk to the student before assigning a punishment, and ask the student what happened. He described how the student always says right away, "I didn't do it," and they're lying. But, if he sees a referral from a teacher who never gives referrals, and it's a student who gets in trouble a lot—a "frequent flyer"—then he knows it's a legitimate complaint. (FN)

"Good students" are those who are high academic achievers or who rarely get in trouble. Students who are often in trouble, especially the "frequent flyers," are usually dismissed outright when they express concerns or complain about unfairness.

My point is not that disciplinarians need to take students at their word when they contest punishments, for it would be a problem if school disciplinarians begin trusting adolescents over the school staff. If this were the case students would always deny wrongdoing, staff would refuse to enforce any school rules, and it would be difficult to maintain a level of trust among staff necessary for running a school.[17] Rather, it is important to listen to students because doing so can help one learn a lot about their needs. If disciplinarians listened to students, they would have an opportunity to help students make better choices and to learn more about students' personal and academic troubles, so that they can either help students with these problems or refer them to the appropriate resources. Disciplinary incidents are also an opportunity to learn more about weaknesses in how the school enforces discipline, such as which teachers need help with classroom management, or what kinds of student interactions are likely to lead to conflict. Students' complaints, justifications, and explanations are packed with information that could help the school and the students, but they are usually ignored. By paying attention only to rule violations and not to students' explanations or descriptions of the events, these opportunities are missed.

Students' Efforts to Resist

High school students are a demographic group that is known for rebellion and challenging authority, not passive acceptance of discipline.[18] Consistent with this image, I did observe students resist efforts to teach to the rules, though their avenues for resistance are limited and usually counterproductive.

The most common form of resistance I observed once students are referred to a disciplinarian is very passive: eye rolling, refusing to admit wrongdoing, sarcasm, or silence in the face of questioning. The example above of Jose being punished by Ms. Flores for bullying a student illustrates this—Jose denies wrongdoing throughout their encounter and his body language and sarcasm show he is unhappy with the interaction. Jose demonstrates a contained anger—he was visibly perturbed, but had little room for expressing it. This type of passive resistance is explained by the following black female student at Unionville High as a product of students learning that they are powerless to shape disciplinary situations, since deans and administrators have already decided what punishments they will assign before they speak to students:

> STUDENT: I've seen students get mad, I've seen students cry, and I've seen students act like, "Oh well."
> INTERVIEWER: So they just kind of accept it?
> STUDENT: There's not much you can do about anything in this school.
> INTERVIEWER: Yeah? Tell me.
> STUDENT: Their mind's made up or whatever. (I)

As I describe above, there is some merit to the perception that decisions about punishments are made in advance, and that students are powerless to change the outcome of these decisions. That students usually show only passive resistance illustrates the depth of powerlessness that many feel.

Students also resist authority in active but somewhat mundane forms, such as when students refuse to listen, pretend they don't hear a school official, or continually test the boundaries of what they are allowed to do. For example, consider the following field notes from Frontera High, which describe my interaction with a Latino security guard, Juan, at the security booth by the school's front entrance:

> While Juan and I are talking, several students congregate near the security booth. There were already four there when I arrived, and about six to eight more arrive while we talk. One starts to walk by Juan, and he says, "Please

wait here a few minutes until the end of first period." I ask Juan if this is because students aren't allowed to walk around during class time, and he says, "Yes," but even more so that these students have already been marked absent for their first period classes, so they would only be a distraction if they walked in now—they need to wait until the period is over. As he and I are talking about this, another student just walks right in—I presume that Juan just didn't notice.

At about 9:05, before the bell rings, all of the students by the booth begin walking slowly toward the school. The bell then rings a few seconds later. I said to Juan: "Wow, they really know the schedule," and he responds: "These kids will try to get over with whatever they can." (FN)

We also see this in the following notes, where I describe being with Henry, a white male security guard at Fairway Estates High, as he tries to drive his golf cart through a crowded courtyard passageway in between classes:

Henry checked his schedule, and saw that he is supposed to be in the study hall/ISS room for the next period. He invites me to go with him, so I get in the cart as the bell rings and the break between classes begins. We start driving to the east side of campus, but it is slow going because the courtyard is filled with students. Henry drives slowly, and repeatedly yells, "Hello!" and "Excuse me!" to the students in his way. The students don't seem to move out of his way. Some walk right toward him, rather than adjusting their course to avoid the cart. And when he needs to pass by, they are reluctant to step aside. I comment on this to Henry, who agrees, saying that they just don't care. (FN)

At other times, however, students respond by becoming angry and challenging the school's authority, either by walking away or fighting back. These responses usually just make the situation worse for the student. Such resistance is more likely to happen in classrooms than when meeting with a dean of discipline, interventionist, or administrator, such as the incident described below at Unionville High:

Mr. Compton looked at a referral that he had on his desk from a teacher, Mr. West. He read parts of it aloud to me. The referral said that someone put a big glob of lotion on Mr. West's chair and he sat down in it. The female student being written up was standing nearby and was laughing when it happened. The referral said he started to write her up and then she stormed out of the room cursing.

We arrived at the student's classroom and Mr. Compton called for her. A black female with a short bob-style haircut, Carol, came to the door. Mr. Compton walked with her down the hall. Carol immediately started saying that she "didn't do it," and she has witnesses to back her up. "So you know why I'm here?" Mr. Compton said to her. Carol said, "Yes," she knew Mr. West was writing her up.

Mr. Compton asked her to tell him what happened. Carol said she was in class and was asking another student if she could borrow a dollar. She said then she heard other students saying, "Oh look, he's going to sit down," and so she stood up and looked, and then started laughing. She said then Mr. West said he was going to write her up, and she said she didn't do anything, and so she felt like if he was going to write her up and she didn't do anything, why should she stay in his class? So she left. She said she didn't put the lotion on his chair—she said she didn't even have any lotion at school. . . .

[After trying unsuccessfully to find out who did put the lotion on Mr. West's chair,] Mr. Compton told Carol that he believed her version of the story, but that she just can't walk out of class because she is frustrated. He said she should have waited for him to get the referral, and then she could have told her side of the story to him. He asked, "Have I ever been unfair with you? Have I ever been rude to you and not given you a chance to tell your side of the story?" Carol said no. He asked her, "What if I had gotten a referral from Mr. West that said you flew out of the window?" The student looked puzzled. He said for her to hear him out, and asked the question again. He answered: "Then I would meet with you and tell you that Mr. West said you flew out the window and you would say to me, 'Mr. Compton, I don't even have any fuckin' wings.'" Carol laughed.

He said the point was that a referral doesn't necessarily mean that she would get in trouble. He told her that she shouldn't have walked out of class and she was wrong for doing that, so for that there has to be a consequence. [She was given a day of in-school suspension.]

In this example Carol claims to be unfairly targeted by her teacher, and leaves the class out of frustration. But in the end, though he empathizes with Carol and listens to her, Mr. Compton scolds her for leaving the class and punishes her for this—not for the action of which she was initially accused.

Students who respond negatively to the school's authority become marked for further surveillance, making it even more likely that they will have future discipline encounters. Consider the following field note from Fairway Estates High:

> The bell rings, so [the white security guard, Beth, and I] go over to the gate. When students approach the gate, Beth asks them for their IDs. Some complain, and ask why she needs it. Many of them have to pause while they fish for their ID. Some say that they don't have it, so Beth gives them a hard time and then lets them go. One student approached without her ID, so Beth asked to see it. The student kept walking, so Beth walked after her, shouting, "Hey, where are you going? I need your ID!" The student stopped and said, "Why, what do you care? This is stupid." The student then fished out her ID from her bag and shoved it right in Beth's face (probably only two inches from her face), yelling, "Here! OK?!" Beth then walked back to the gate.
>
> I asked her about the situation, and she said: "Yeah, I don't like her, that's why I needed to see her ID. She always gives me attitude." (FN)

Because this student has "given her an attitude" in the past, Beth presses the issue and does not allow her to walk by without showing an ID, which she let other students do.

These negative responses to student resistance—either further surveillance or additional punishment—are common. Recall from chapter 2 that student resistance to authority is the most common offense at each of the four schools I studied.[19] This is vitally important for understanding what happens when schools teach to the rules: rules become enforced to cover failures in school discipline.

Why Teach to the Rules?

To understand why schools teach to the rules, I want to first discuss potential explanations that do not seem to hold water. One such explanation is to view the individual disciplinarians as cruel, ill-tempered, or hostile to youth. This explanation is not at all helpful. Given the difficulty of the work and the relatively low pay, it's hard to imagine anyone working in a public school unless he or she wants to help children (or at least did want to help children earlier in his or her career). At each school, throughout this entire research project, I was repeatedly impressed by the extent to which school staff visibly care about youth and want to help them learn and grow. Consider, for example, the following interaction I observed between Henry (a security guard at Fairway Estates High) and a student, Trevor:

> Henry and I sit in a parked security golf cart near the west gate. A white male student walks up to us. He is somewhat heavy set, is trying to grow facial hair, and is wearing a baseball hat cocked to one side. He comes up cursing about a teacher.
>
> TREVOR: I wanted to hit that teacher but I didn't.
>
> HENRY: You can't do that, you'll just go to jail.
>
> TREVOR: Yeah, I didn't. He wanted me to fill out these worksheets—nobody else has to do that. So I just put my head down to nap. Then he comes over to me and says, "What are you doing?" So I said, "Nothing," and he sends me outside. He told me I have to finish these by the end of the period. Whatever.
>
> HENRY: Let me see those. [He looks at the worksheets, which are about the Korean War and other history topics.] You have ten minutes before the end of the period. Finish these. [He hasn't even started on them.]
>
> TREVOR: Why? Why do I care about the Korean War? Why do I care about what happened, like, forty million years ago. It doesn't matter to me.
>
> HENRY: We care because we learn from our mistakes.
>
> TREVOR: So what? What does it matter?
>
> HENRY: So we don't make the same mistakes.
>
> TREVOR: It doesn't matter. I'm not in charge. The government is in charge, I can't do anything.
>
> HENRY: Sure you can.
>
> Trevor leaves, and we see him later in his car, in the parking lot, listening to music. (FN)

Henry takes the time to sit and talk to Trevor, and seems to want to help him. But his vision of helpful advice is to follow the rules. Henry does give the student an actual justification for why he should learn history—to avoid repeating others' mistakes—which is somewhat unusual, since even this level of justification for why rules ought to be obeyed is rare. But he stops short of asking the student about what subjects he likes and why, how he gets along with the teacher usually, why he is the only one doing the worksheet, or talking to the student about the usefulness of education generally. Instead, he encourages the student to do what he is told.

At times, teaching to the rules happens because teachers and administrators *care* about youth. Many teachers and other school officials talked to me about strict enforcement of rules as a way of helping students by teaching them life lessons that will serve them as adults in the "real world." This "tough love" approach clearly has some truth to it, since being an adult does mean that one has responsibilities and faces consequences for not meeting them. Further, there certainly are parallels between school and the future workplace, as schools socialize students into the workforce by preparing them for the demands that will be placed on them, such as constant monitoring and bearing responsibility for executing decisions made by one's supervisors; one can liken, for example, a Wal-Mart employee held responsible for all idle time to the student whose schedule is rigorously managed.[20] Yet the presumption that school rules help students prepare for future life is misleading too, since the rigid schedule, lack of autonomy, and inability to rise in social status that students find at schools are unlike anything most adults face in life outside of a prison or other "total institution."[21]

Another unsatisfying explanation is that school staff respond this way to youth who lack social capital due to their class status or race/ethnicity. This explanation comes directly from prior research on social reproduction in education. Moreover, as might be clear from the above field notes, many of the disciplinary incidents I observed in the four schools involve racial/ethnic minorities, even in the mostly white Fairway Estates High and Centerville High. Yet I observed teaching to the rules at all four schools, and for all sorts of students—not just racial/ethnic minorities or those at Frontera High and Unionville High. Though race/ethnicity is an important element of school punishment—since it shapes school officials' perceptions of threat and because racial/ethnic minority youth are more likely to be punished in school than are white youth—teaching to the rules still occurs in each of the four schools, during interactions with both white and nonwhite youth.

Social capital does matter, but not in the ways that prior research might lead one to expect, with poor youth and youth of color being the primary targets of negative treatment. A large component of teaching to the rules is the assertion of the authority of adults in the school over *all* children—it reinforces the lesson of who is in charge. The dominance of adults over children is based on the power differential within the school between all adults and all children, even those who come from wealthy homes. This does not mean that race and class do not matter, because they absolutely do—but that teaching to the rules reproduces a different type of inequality, and one that is legally protected: the inequality between legal minors and adults.

A third explanation for why schools teach to the rules is that the practice is based on the spate of new security and discipline practices that have spread across the United States recently. In their book *Punishing Schools*, William Lyons and Julie Drew analyze how a "zero-tolerance culture" has eroded democratic dialogue in schools.[22] They argue that such practices undermine problem solving, since problem solving requires cooperation and negotiation, both of which are antithetical to a zero-tolerance approach.[23] I agree entirely with the end result (their concept of "zero-tolerance culture" is very similar to "teaching to the rules"), though I disagree somewhat with their emphasis on how a zero-tolerance approach has caused the problem.[24]

To be fair, without longitudinal data I cannot determine what has caused schools to teach to the rules. Yet as I illustrate by referencing prior research throughout this chapter, schools have been teaching to the rules for decades, long before the phrase "zero tolerance" was coined or police officers were placed in schools across the country. Moreover, prioritizing rules and authority over critical thought and problem solving directly responds to the struggle for adults to maintain authority and power over youth in schools, a struggle that certainly predates contemporary school discipline policies.[25] Teaching to the rules is about deeper issues than zero-tolerance approaches to discipline—it is a response to insecurities about school disorder and to the challenge of controlling difficult students.

That said, contemporary punishment and security do exacerbate the problem of teaching to the rules, even if they don't cause it. The spread of harsh punishment and tight security policies across the United States is a clear indicator that protecting against and responding to student misbehavior is now a top priority of schools. Within this climate, it is no surprise that rules have become more central.

Given the current emphasis on school discipline and security, school administrators face pressure to focus on the rules and the school's authority. Recently I attended an open forum held by the superintendent of a nearby school district (not one of the districts that participated in my research) on school discipline. I sat in the auditorium of a local high school as the meeting began, at 5:00 p.m. on a weekday, with about one hundred other attendees. For the first thirty minutes of this meeting, the superintendent discussed how the district is working hard to prevent behavior problems at all schools. He focused entirely on proactive, preventive, and counseling-based approaches, such as classroom management training, conflict de-escalation training for teachers, and better recognition of students' emotional and behavioral problems. He barely mentioned reactive punishment during this period, and then opened the meeting up to questions. The tone of the meeting shifted with the first question, asked by a man seated directly behind me, who wanted to know why the district spends so much time and resources on persistent problem students who don't want to be there anyway. Throughout the rest of the meeting, other attendees repeated this theme by asking why the schools couldn't do more to remove problem students from the schools. Almost every question or comment focused on either punishment for students or holding adults in the building accountable for properly punishing misbehaving students. I raise this example because it clearly illustrates the pressure administrators face to rigidly enforce rules against student misbehavior. Parents and citizens hold much insecurity about school and particularly about crime in schools, and requests for rigid rule enforcement and harsh punishments are common ways of voicing these insecurities. Thus, school punishment and security are self-propelling: they are fueled by insecurities, but school punishment policies also provide an outlet for the insecurities to be voiced. Given the demands of accountability for misbehavior among parents and other citizens, it is hardly surprising that school administrators focus centrally on school rules.

Contemporary punishment and security can also reinforce the trend of teaching to the rules because it leads to greater specialization. With more adults in the school specifically devoted to dealing with misbehavior, teachers may view their function as being academic instructors only, with no discipline duties. This was one of the primary findings of John Devine's ethnography in New York City public schools: that staff developed the assumption that teachers deal with students' minds and security staff deal with their bodies.[26] This is also consistent with Lyons and Drew's study of zero-tolerance culture in schools, at least among some teachers (who wish only to teach, and let security staff handle all discipline matters).[27] If teachers see student misbehavior as somebody else's job, then they will write referrals for even minor misbehaviors that they might otherwise have dealt with themselves. As result, there are more referrals; more students visiting a dean, interventionist, or assistant principal; more students going to in-school suspension for at least a class period; and more out-of-class punishments overall. If teachers stop handling discipline, then they escalate minor situations by creating a recorded incident instead of having a talk with a student or some other informal response.

Moments where school staff teach to the rules resemble a phenomenon the social psychologist Michelle Fine describes as "silencing," which she observed in a New York City high school during the 1980s.[28] For Fine, silencing happens when students' voices, especially critical voices that challenge social injustice and unfairness, are criticized or punished, while uncritical acceptance of the school's authority and curriculum are rewarded. Though silencing covers a broader range of interactions, silencing and teaching to the rules are similar: both are expressions of school authority and student powerlessness, both seek to conceal ways the school perpetuates inequalities, and both place responsibility for ineffective school governance and other school problems solely on students. Silencing happens when students' statements and behaviors come into conflict with school needs, be they the need to run a classroom or the need to pretend that dropout rates aren't at epidemic proportions (as was the case in the school Fine studied).

If we understand teaching to the rules in this framework, then it becomes clearer how contemporary rules and punishment practices make this problem worse. By creating more rules, placing more pressure on all school staff to enforce the rules, posting the rules in classrooms and throughout the schools, and raising the stakes for rule violations, schools have fertilized the seeds of conflict within the school. With rules and punishments now center stage within the school, more misbehaviors will be detected and reported. This means that there are more student-school conflicts about student behavior than before, and therefore more opportunities for silencing.

It would also be a mistake to assume that the presence of police officers alone causes schools to teach to the rules. Again, schools have been teaching to the rules for more years than police have been in schools. Yet officers do influence this problem. The presence of an officer introduces a law-and-order perspective and redefines counseling or behavioral problems as potentially criminal problems. These shifts in perspective distract school staff away from students' actual problems and toward rule violations, consistent with teaching to the rules.

Though some of these potential causes do reinforce teaching to the rules, the practice itself has deeper roots. It stems from the difficulties of maintaining order over sometimes-unruly adolescents who defy authority. Given this difficulty, schools assert their authority as a blanket solution, rather than attempting to uncover real reasons for misbehavior. Investigating these real reasons may pose a threat to the school, since it might uncover teachers or other staff who have acted inappropriately; schools are justified in hesitating to address this issue, because it would be problematic to undermine teachers' authority and make the school's teachers feel unsupported.[29]

Investigating real reasons for misbehavior is also less stable ground than teaching to the rules, since it requires disciplinarians to depart from a concrete set of rules, expectations, and responses, and instead to act like social workers. Yet the disciplinarians who have the most contact with students in the four schools I studied have no real training in how to address students' problems. Most are former (and current) coaches or teachers, and none has a social work or counseling background, or any official training in counseling or adolescent psychology.

Given the pressures placed on the schools—and especially on disciplinarians such as deans—to do so much, it is not surprising that they seek patterns of responding to misbehavior that are stable and secure, and that rest on a set of rules and expectations rather than investigations into emotional issues (for which they have no real training). The high caseloads that disciplinarians often face, especially at Unionville High, certainly reinforce this tendency.

As a parent of little children who are learning to assert their wills and defy my authority, I am all too well aware of how frustrating it can be to discipline a disobedient child, and how tempting it is to tell my children that they must obey me because I'm their father, rather than calmly explaining (repeatedly) why I'm asking them to do something. Though teenagers are very different from preschoolers, they present a similar frustration when they refuse to let teachers teach, or refuse to follow school rules. Given the pressures and frustrations they face, it is normal and understandable that disciplinarians save time and resort to reinforcing the school rules and the school's authority (analogous to "because I'm your father").

Indeed, contemporary schools face enormous challenges, and the sources of these challenges extend beyond the school, to parents and courts as well. School officials often talk about the difficulty of dealing with uncooperative parents and challenging parents; parents who are too involved in school and those who are insufficiently involved; parents who enable their students' misbehaviors and those who ignore it. Others discuss the fear of litigation. Consider, for example, a pamphlet distributed to all parents of Arizona public school students in 2004 (and which is still on the state Department of Education's website as of October 2009), which includes the following letter from the Arizona superintendent of public instruction, Tom Horne:

> Dear Parents:
>
> Our society has experienced a significant reduction in the extent to which parents support schools in the maintenance of classroom discipline. Parents used to support schools in making students understand that actions have consequences. Now, some parents become advocates for their children, and in some cases even threaten to "call a lawyer" if the school insists on enforcing discipline for student behavior.
>
> When schools defer to parents' demands, it severely interferes with classroom discipline and the ability to raise academic achievement.[30]

Schools are also constrained by students' legal right to an education. Richard Arum argues in *Judging School Discipline* that by siding with students over schools, U.S. courts have helped undermine the school's moral authority.[31] He describes several court cases that were primarily waged by liberal groups during the 1960s and 1970s over school punishment incidents perceived as unfair. Perhaps the most famous of these, *Goss v. Lopez,* was a challenge of the suspension of several black students who protested that their school (in Columbus, Ohio, in 1971) did not observe Black History Week. In response to these students' protests, which included refusing to return to class following a school assembly, dozens of students were suspended without any hearing, formal notification of charges against them, or opportunity to contest the charges. The students and their families, along with the NAACP and the OEO, challenged the suspensions up to the Supreme Court and won. Arum argues that as a result of cases like this, schools are now less likely to enforce rules strictly and students are less likely than before to accept the school's authority as legitimate, since the court decisions taught students that school rules are indeed violable. Many school officials with whom I spoke echoed this, complaining that their hands are tied because it is very difficult to expel students who chronically misbehave. More important than whether a loss of legitimacy is due to students being allowed the civil rights granted to other citizens (as Arum contends), or instead to the unfairness and procedural injustice of teaching to the rules, his argument rightly highlights the fact that school officials feel burdened being an open, public institution guaranteed to all comers and in which students possess rights restricting how they are punished. This burden, along with the many other pressures placed on them, makes teachers, deans, and administrators more susceptible to teaching to the rules.

Teaching to the Rules and School Climate

Again, my research is not intended to measure causes and effects, but instead to describe what schools do and how they do it. But there is a great deal of prior research that does look at what factors shape the school climate, and there are several parallels between what these studies find and my concept of teaching to the rules. For example, one of the classic sociological studies of schools that I discuss in chapter 1, Paul Willis's *Learning to Labor*, unveils how working-class British youth reject the school's authority in response to the school imposing its rules on them. This rejection involves criminal activity and a rejection of education, closing off future career opportunities and ensuring they remain on the low end of the socioeconomic ladder.

Michelle Fine makes a similar argument when analyzing causes of high dropout rates. She finds that an important reason for students dropping out is that schools disrespect students, largely through punishments and authoritative actions like "silencing," which I have argued is analogous to teaching to the rules. Like Willis, Fine states that when the school's authority is forced on students in ways perceived as unfair, students reject both the school's authority and the school itself. Teaching to the rules alienates some students from the school and (by extension) might increase the likelihood that they will dropout.

Importantly, teaching to the rules runs counter to what criminologists have found to be best practices in preventing school delinquency. Perhaps the most consistent and powerful factor shaping school delinquency is the perceived legitimacy of school rules: whether the rules are clearly communicated and enforced fairly.[32] But research shows that one of the best ways to ensure that subjects of authority perceive that authority to be fair and just is to communicate openly with them and allow them an opportunity to present their case—exactly what teaching to the rules denies students.[33] This style of school discipline leaves students feeling powerless and frustrated, believing that they have no say in what happens, which erodes perceptions of legitimate authority.

Teaching to the rules is also likely to increase bullying, one of the most significant and harmful problems many students face. In a recent study, sociologists Shoko Yoneyama and Asao Naito review the Japanese literature on bullying; they find that although most anti-bullying prevention initiatives focus on individual students and their relationships with peers or parents, school factors also contribute to bullying. Schools that are authoritarian—where power is rigidly expressed through school discipline, and where students do not feel they are listened to—have more bullying problems than others.[34] These risk factors—which are exactly what teaching to the rules produces—lead to bullying because they provide a model of aggressive, power-dominant behavior that students mimic in their relations with one another. Anti-bullying strategies that assume the problem only lies within individual students and not with how the school relates to students are much like a parent who smokes cigarettes yet lectures his or her child not to smoke.

Ironically, teaching to the rules does not even ensure consistency, another important aspect of perceived legitimacy of authority. With the ever-expanding rules and punishments in schools, consistency becomes problematic; it is normal for school staff to hesitate from enforcing minor rules consistently, since they would have to do it all day long. For example, in chapter 2 I describe the inconsistent enforcement of the new rule for wearing ID badges at Centerville High. Not enforcing the rule makes sense, since a staff member who consistently did so would do little else all day long—but it also makes instances of being reprimanded for not wearing an ID badge seem very unfair to students. Petty rules are of course less likely to be enforced consistently than rules against serious misconduct. But this means that the buildup of punishment and security in schools increases the inconsistency of rule enforcement; this was clearly the case in all four schools I studied, and was mentioned by several students, teachers, and administrators with whom I spoke.

When disciplinarians deny students an opportunity to talk about what happened or why they misbehaved, make decisions about punishments before even meeting with students, or rigidly follow rules that may seem arbitrary to students, they risk making school punishment seem illegitimate and unjust. As one black female student at Unionville High stated:

> STUDENT: If a student gets in trouble and a teacher goes to [a dean], the teacher will make up so many stories, and I had it from experience and I [didn't] do nothing and they will believe them. They will believe them even if they don't want to, they will still believe them, even if they have a slight chance that it don't sound right, they will still write you up or do some type of, or give you in-school suspension, or one day out-of-school [suspension], they'll find some way to punish you just because that's the rules, I guess, I don't know.
>
> INTERVIEWER: Would a student get a chance to at least tell their side of the story?
>
> STUDENT: Most times no.
>
> INTERVIEWER: Really?
>
> STUDENT: Not in this school. Now you get suspended, out of school, for every little thing, and then they will get in your face about missing too many days, but like you'll get suspended for being late to class now. And not even late, like, if the bell would ring, but you would see me walking down the hall, they will still shut the door. And I'm like, like you could be like two seconds away from the door and as soon as that bell rings, they shut it right in your face. Like they do that now and they know what's gonna happen, you have suspension and these teachers don't care. (I)

Perceptions of unfairness or illegitimate authority are likely to increase problems with disorder, not, as intended, to solve them.

Uphill Battles

It would be naive and overly critical for me to argue that no teacher, administrator, or school is aware of how schools teach to the rules, or that there are no efforts within schools to combat the tendency to do so. Certainly, I did observe teachers and administrators who notice both the lack of attention to students' problems and the authoritarian nature of school punishment, and who try to address these problems. Unfortunately, these efforts are uphill battles. They contradict the fabric of school discipline—the commonly accepted, or institutionalized, ways of doing school security and punishment. They also complicate efforts to prevent disorder in a potentially unruly place.

Conflict Mediations at Frontera High

When I began research at Frontera High, I was introduced to the sole dean of discipline there, Ms. Flores. As she described how she handles student misbehavior, Ms. Flores discussed the school's conflict mediation policy, which she was clearly proud of. When students engage in any conflict, they face suspension; the length of the suspension is reduced if they agree to participate in a mediation session, during which the students sit with a trained staff member and discuss the conflict.[35] For them to receive credit for the session they must verbally participate and the session must end with a handshake and the students' agreement to end their conflict.

I was impressed when I heard about this policy. It shows that the administration at Frontera High realizes that teaching to the rules alone is insufficient for reducing student violence, and that one must actually engage students in solving their conflicts. It also means that staff are being trained in how to talk to students about their problems, or at least about student conflicts.

But when I observed mediation sessions, I was surprised by how shallow they are—how they are an alternative way of teaching to the rules. The following are my field notes from one such session, conducted by two of the school's security guards, in response to a minor fight between two male Latino students (Javier and Angelo) in which neither was hurt:

Javier and Angelo sit opposite one another, and are asked to describe what happened by the two security officers running the mediation—Robert, a black male, and Donna, a Latina.

The guards turn to Javier. He has nothing to say and tells them repeatedly that nothing happened. For about ten minutes, the guards try to elicit information from him, but he resists. They try two tactics: (1) explaining that this is his chance to tell his side of the story, and (2) that if he doesn't follow through with this mediation, then he gets the full punishment for fighting and might be expelled if he has prior referrals. He finally relents and tells them that somebody (he didn't know who) told him that Angelo was going to jump him. When Angelo gets his turn, his story is almost identical. . . . This continues for a long time before any new information comes out. Both state that they have no prior relationship, don't even know each other well, and never received threats directly from each other, only from third parties. . . . Finally, we learn that they do have a prior history. Javier says that their [disagreement] began last spring, after a softball game. We then learn that he was upset because Angelo called Javier's sister "a bitch." Angelo says that she kept calling their house looking for his little brother and wouldn't leave him alone, so Angelo told her to stop calling. As soon as this information comes out the officers stop digging for information and wrap up the hearing. Their approach to solving the conflict is a lecture on how one can't react to gossip. One of the guards, Robert, also spoke, directly at Javier, on how one can't react to disrespect by fighting.

ROBERT: Trust me, I know about disrespect. I grew up in the 'hood, I know how important respect is. But you can't fight whenever you're disrespected. If you do, you're wrong. You need to come to authorities—to me, to another security, to a teacher.

JAVIER: That's "bitch shit." I can't do that.

ROBERT: It may be bitch shit, but it's what you got to do . . .

After a long time of this lecturing on not reacting to disrespect or listening to gossip, and on the importance of reporting trouble rather than fighting (because this is the rule), the two students sign a statement of mediation, shake hands, and leave. (FN)

Though the policy requiring mediation hearings is designed to unearth and resolve the sources of student conflict, this does not happen. Instead of teaching strategies for dealing with interpersonal conflict, discussing how each student feels about the incident, or considering behavioral solutions to this and future conflicts, the security guards only discuss the school rules and how one must conform to them. They teach to the rules. This is the only resolution they present—that the students must follow the rules, or they are wrong. At one point Javier even presents a valid normative reason for disobeying the instructions of telling an authority when a conflict is brewing, yet he is told that he has no other option.

Positive Behavioral Supports at Centerville High

Before conducting research at Centerville High, I met with the principal and assistant principals to discuss my research. During this meeting one assistant principal told me (and the others agreed) that I might be very interested in their positive behavioral support (PBS) program. I assumed that they mentioned this both because they were interested in evaluating the program, and also because they wanted to direct my attention to what they thought I would find favorable. Positive behavioral support programs have received very favorable attention lately as a way of reducing student misbehavior, and I was indeed impressed.[36]

The PBS program at Centerville High seeks to reinforce students' positive behaviors. The main way they do this is for school staff to give students raffle tickets as rewards for good behavior. With the tickets, students are entered into a raffle where they can win prizes such as MP3 players or school merchandise (T-shirts, key chains, etc.). There is a group of students who meet weekly before school (at 7:00 a.m.) to discuss the PBS program and strategize about how to improve the incentives given to students.

My initial meeting with the administrative team was in late August, just prior to the start of the 2006 school year. I began the research with the beginning of the school year that September. Yet neither member of the research team observed the program in action or even heard a reference to it until mid-November. Clearly, the program is not well-used. In fact, one administrator spoke to me about the fact that few teachers actually use it. She said what ends up happening is that when teachers do follow the program, they give tickets to students who usually misbehave but who are behaving on a particular day, and as a result "the bad kids end up winning all of the prizes."

She said there are plenty of kids who do the right thing all the time but go unnoticed. In response, the director of the program was trying to make it easier on teachers by giving them a list of their students and asking that they review this list every day to highlight all students who did something positive. But this, too, was problematic, because it resulted in a flood of tickets being distributed and a very small chance of any student winning a prize.

Centerville High uses other preventive approaches in addition to the PBS program. The school was in the process of developing both an instructional support team to help teachers improve classroom management and a mentoring program for youth who frequently receive referrals. Further, the principal meets regularly with randomly chosen groups of students to hear and respond to their concerns about the school. Like the mediation hearings at Frontera High, it is encouraging to know that these programs are in place, regardless of their success. It shows that administrators at these schools are aware of research-driven understandings about school behavior: that fights become less frequent when students learn how to resolve their conflicts, that positive reinforcements are effective at shaping behaviors, that mentoring helps students avoid trouble, and that listening to students will enhance their perceptions of the school's authority as legitimate. But the school is not designed to do these things well—the programs contradict accepted ways of managing student behaviors. As a result they have relatively little influence on everyday school discipline practices.

Individuals' Efforts

Some school staff clearly try hard to avoid teaching to the rules, such as one of the deans of discipline at Unionville High, Mr. Compton. Mr. Compton arrived at Unionville High midway through the school year and (given the district's budget shortfall) was not offered a contract for the following year. Perhaps because he realized he would not be at the school long-term as one of the deans of discipline, he strays from common punishment approaches and tries to address students' problems. He described this to me in an interview by referencing how he recently responded to a group of students:

I've caught them smoking cigarettes on campus several times. The last time I caught them smoking cigarettes on campus, I put gloves on them,

I walked outside, and they sat there and they picked up cigarette butts. That's what they did when I caught them smoking. I called their parents, I told them that they got caught smoking, the mom said, "I'm not buying you cigarettes anymore" to [one of the students], so that's another chicken's nest altogether. But you know, giving somebody ISS for smoking cigarettes is not gonna address the problem. The problem is cigarettes, you know? Make them write an essay on cigarettes, make them write an essay on cancer, make them go to [the local hospital] and talk to somebody with a trach tube, you know what I mean? Don't show them pictures, don't talk to them, let's go, me and you, right now [student's name]. Let's go over to [the local hospital]. Even better yet, why don't you watch Mr. Compton run up a flight of stairs and see what happens to Mr. Compton, and that's exactly what I did with her. Because I ran up the stairs as fast as I could and I let them sit there and look at their watches until I caught my breath and it was about twelve minutes. And I'm like is this what you want at twenty-four [years old]? Is this what you want because you made a bad decision at fifteen? Because I made a bad decision at fifteen and eight years later, as strong as I am, I can't do it, I just can't quit. You know, you need to address the problems as they are. You know, fighting, that's a tough one. I think out-of-school suspension for a day is good, let them go home, let them cool down, let the gossip go for a day without them there. Out-of-school suspension shouldn't be done without [anger management training]. You know, but anger management training should not be something that you can get out of the wellness center if you get a form, parents' consent, and you have to stay after school. Anger management should be a class we teach. (I)

Mr. Compton is not alone. I also saw other individuals at the four schools who make efforts to avoid teaching to the rules. Most commonly, a teacher may refuse to initiate the punishment process for all but serious misbehavior. I met some teachers who said that they never give referrals or remove students from class, because they view formal school punishment (e.g., referrals) as a failure of classroom management. These teachers said that when a student misbehaves, they pull the student aside and ask what's going on. Usually, a brief conversation and a request from the teacher to behave prevent a larger problem.

So why doesn't the school have alternative, constructive punishments like the ones Mr. Compton seeks? He describes above how he fashioned his own punishment for smoking: having students pick up cigarette butts. At one point he also began having students write essays describing why their behaviors were wrong. But these efforts are limited, and often amount to shaming rituals (such as being forced to write an apology to an offended teacher). Because the school has no programs set up that address the source of students' problems, there is little Mr. Compton can do in this regard.

Mr. Compton has no choice but to uphold the school's rules, even if he thinks they are unfairly applied. This is clear in one of the field notes included earlier in this chapter, when he counsels a student to be quiet when confronted with an unfair teacher. Mr. Compton told the student, Renaldo, that if he is being unfairly targeted by a teacher he must defend himself by sitting in his seat and not saying a word. Mr. Compton realizes that students will face punishments regardless of whether it is justified, and he counsels them on how to minimize the trouble they get into, not on how to confront their problems. In his interview he said that when a student complains to him about unfair treatment:

> I usually tell them that this is bullshit, but this is what the district is asking and you're part of the district. And I tell their parents the same thing, that I disagree with the rule and I completely respect their perspective, but they read the code of conduct or were supplied the code of conduct before their child came to Unionville High School and sometimes in life you gotta do things you don't agree with. I do things everyday that I disagree with. . . . High school is a great time to learn that lesson, high school is a lot, a great time to learn that life is full with shit you disagree with, you don't like, that's unfair, that to get what you want you gotta do, you just gotta. (I)

Additionally, a different dean at Unionville High, Mr. Sussex (a white male), once talked about how he has no choice but to support a teacher's request for punishment, even if he disagrees:

> Mr. Sussex said that he has a student who is a "good kid" and is on the football team. The student was written up for not handing over his cell phone when asked by a teacher. This is a mandatory three-day suspension. So he went to the student and asked what happened. The student's version of the events was that he checked the time on his phone, and the teacher

asked if he was using it, he said no and put it away, and the teacher walked away. He thought that was it, and was surprised that he was written up. Mr. Sussex told the student that he'd talk to the teacher and try to get him to drop it or work something out short of the full punishment, but that if the teacher wanted him to pursue it he'd have to. Mr. Sussex then reiterated this as a general approach: if a teacher is overreacting but wants him to pursue something, he has to do it. (FN)

Thus, there is little room in the system to avoid teaching to the rules. One can counsel students about their problems, but these discussions return to the rules, the misbehavior, and the punishment—they are only a temporary break from teaching to the rules, not avoidance of it.

These three examples—mediation hearings at Frontera High, the PBS program at Centerville High, and individual efforts such as those of Mr. Compton—illustrate that good intentions are not sufficient. Despite these intentions, schools still teach to the rules. In this way, schools are no different than other large institutions: it is difficult to implement practices that run contrary to how things are normally done. The anthropologist Mary Douglas discusses this tendency in *How Institutions Think*, and argues that answers to problems are interpreted according to existing institutional thinking; whether a solution to a problem is perceived to be a good one depends on whether it confirms the institutional thinking already in individuals' minds.[37] Thus, the logic held within schools is constantly refreshed, since potential new ideas are reinterpreted within the existing framework of institutional authority and thinking. Efforts to go beyond teaching to the rules may sound good, but in practice they are enacted with the same old ideas, strategies, and motives. The mediation hearing at Frontera High is a perfect example of this, since it is a strategy that in theory departs from the normal discipline but in practice aligns closely with it.

The stubbornness of teaching to the rules is precisely what proponents of a neo-institutional perspective would predict. In a series of essays rooted in Weber's studies of bureaucracy, sociologists such as John Meyer and Brian Rowan, as well as Paul DiMaggio and Walter Powell, discuss how institutions pursue legitimacy more so than efficiency, and they do so in ways that display what they call "isomorphism": similarity across different organizations. Regardless of whether harsh rules, the presence of police, and other school discipline practices are effective, schools rely on them because they are believed to work and they illustrate the school's commitment to discipline, and thus they convey legitimacy: "Organizations such as schools and colleges, the Stanford argument went, are held together more by shared beliefs—'myths'—than by technical exigencies or a logic of efficiency. Thus, the key constraint for educational institutions in this view is the need to maintain the trust and confidence of the public at large—in short, to maintain legitimacy by conforming to institutionalized norms, values, and technical lore."[38]

One reason for the similarity across organizations is coercive authority, whereby organizations respond to similar formal and informal pressures such as laws and cultural expectations.[39] This is very clear in the case of school rule enforcement, since schools respond both to laws (federal laws that provide funding for schools with zero-tolerance laws) and to cultural sentiments (the "culture of control" that shapes public demand for harsh punishments for offenders). A second reason for similarity across organizations is mimetic processes, whereby uncertainty encourages organizations to model themselves on other organizations. Given the anxiety surrounding school crime, schools model discipline and security practices that are seen as effective elsewhere, leading schools all over to use similar policies. An institutional perspective thus shows us how schools can become entrapped by the "iron cage" of school punishment practices, which helps explain why teaching to the rules happens at very different schools all across the country, despite efforts to avoid it.[40]

Conclusion

The goal of this chapter is to illustrate the logic that guides rule enforcement in the four schools I studied. In these schools, rules are so prominent that their enforcement is seen as an end unto itself: schools teach to the rules. In doing so, school staff often fail to listen to students, and students' actual problems go unaddressed.

This does not mean that *all* teachers and administrators teach to the rules. On the contrary, it is not difficult to find individuals and school-wide programs that seek to avoid this practice. But teaching to the rules is difficult to avoid. There are few resources or alternative paths available to individuals who want to avoid it. It is so deeply embedded in accepted school practices that school-wide programs often miss the mark as well. Teaching to the rules is the result of the practical problems schools face, especially the threat of disorder, lack of external support from parents and communities, and pressure to strictly punish misbehavers. As a result schools rely heavily on the school rules, and the rules become a central feature of how schools work.

When schools teach to the rules, they communicate to students the priority and centrality of school rules and punishments. This teaches students a great deal about how powerless they are relative to the school's authority. Students are taught how to passively accept power, they are taught that their individual needs and problems are unimportant relative to the rules that apply to them, and they are taught that they have no ability to shape how power is exercised. Given the powerful socializing effect of schools, whereby students are socialized into their future life roles, these lessons are very important because they shape how students will approach their future relations with authorities. These lessons make it very likely that the coming cohort of young adults will internalize the discipline that will be imposed on them in the postindustrial workplace, participate less in civic life, and avoid critical reflection on social control generally.

5

UNEQUAL DISCIPLINE

The following appeared in a 2004 article in the *Arizona Republic*:

By most accounts, Marlon Morgan is a great kid. The soft-spoken junior plays basketball for Saguaro High School. He was nominated for Youth of the Year last year by a branch of the Boys and Girls Clubs of Scottsdale.

So why were his classmates wearing "Free Marlon" T-shirts last week?

The 17-year-old had just been arrested on campus during lunch for wearing his baseball cap sideways instead of to the front and refusing to turn it the other way.

Morgan, who is Black, believes he was singled out. Other teens in the same room were wearing their hats that way. . . .

Morgan was having lunch when Saguaro security guards approached him about his hat. It is against school policy to wear hats sideways because it can be a sign of disrespect for authority, the police report said, but Morgan said that the rule is enforced selectively. According to a police report, he pointed to several white students whose hats were on sideways.[1]

A mountain of prior research demonstrates that youth of color, especially African Americans, are more likely than white youth to be punished in schools, and that working-class and lower-class youth are subject to harsher punishments than middle-class youth. What is less clear is *why* this is the case, and whether poor and minority youth are selectively targeted for school punishment. Most school employees I met readily acknowledged that some students are punished more often than others, but many stated that those students are more likely to misbehave, and thus their rates of punishment are the result of race- and class-neutral rule enforcement. Others echoed what some prior sociological analyses have found: that poor and minority youth are perceived as more threatening than middle-class or white youth, and as a result they are more likely to be punished, even when they behave similarly.

Evidence of differences between boys' and girls' experiences is less clear. Some prior studies show that males (especially black males) are perceived as threatening and punished more harshly than female students; yet others suggest that teachers and administrators are quicker to punish female students in an effort to maintain their "purity," or to uphold standards of femininity that contradict unruly behavior.[2]

These considerations of whether one group of students is more or less likely to be punished than another typically rely on *within-school* comparisons. Though necessary, this type of analysis is insufficient for understanding the effects of student characteristics on school punishment. We also need to consider differences *between schools*. School punishment and security might look entirely different across different schools hosting different types of students, which is why I studied two schools hosting mostly middle-class white students and two schools hosting mostly lower-income nonwhite students.

Most prior research, and particularly those studies informed by social reproduction theory, suggests that we should see substantial distinctions between schools. This theory states that schools help create and maintain social inequalities between dominant and subordinate groups, such as early twentieth-century schools preparing lower-class youth to be factory workers and middle-class youth to be white-collar workers. Moreover, the theory suggests that schools hide social inequality by making it appear that one's success in life is the result only of how hard one works in school and beyond, not because of different opportunities.[3] Applying this theory to school discipline, we would expect that schools with mostly lower-income youth and youth of color prepare students to expect close surveillance from the state, a heavy police presence in their lives, and harsh punishments for when they do violate laws; in contrast, we would expect that schools with mostly wealthier, white students teach skills that help them avoid, manage, and control such risks, or to use these elements of control to their social, professional, and economic advantage. Lyons and Drew state this hypothesis in their study of school punishments: "Zero tolerance approaches to conflict and ongoing struggles over identity teach us to reproduce the social stratifications in school culture that are predicated on race, class, and gender subordination."[4]

Similarly, when I began this research I expected to find that the two sets of schools vary considerably in how they approach school punishment and security. I expected that Fairway Estates High and Unionville High (with mostly middle-class white students) would be less punitive and would view school security efforts as ways to protect their vulnerable youth from outside influences, and that Frontera High and Centerville High (with mostly lower-income nonwhite students) would use their security efforts as ways to police the potential criminals inside their walls. Though I find some support for this expectation, I also find that both groups of students have a similar, but negative, experience—both groups of schools teach to the rules, as I describe in chapter 4. Practices that were once reserved primarily for schools hosting poor students and students of color are now implemented in white middle-class schools as well.[5] As Jonathan Simon states, "The very real violence of a few schools concentrated in zones of hardened poverty and social disadvantage has provided a 'truth' of school crime that circulates across whole school systems."[6] As a result, students in these different schools receive more similar treatment than one would expect—the contemporary discipline regime negatively affects the school social climate for *all* students. Although the four schools have implemented similar policies, however, these courses of action still have unequal effects within schools. That is, race/ethnicity, class, and sex still matter, and in ways that marginalize students who were at risk of academic failure and behavioral problems to begin with.

Comparisons Across Schools

When comparing the two sets of high schools I studied, some important distinctions emerge. One distinction is in how schools perceive and define threats of violence, with these threats resembling racial/ethnic stereotypes. In Frontera High, for example, almost all students are Latino/a and come from a very poor neighborhood. Employees here clearly indicate that their concern about violence centers on gangs, a social problem often associated with Latino/a youth. When I asked whether there are certain behaviors he had particularly targeted for enforcement, Principal Ruiz responded:

Gang bangers, we went after real hard the first two years because they were running the school, at least they thought they were running the school. They were very active, very violent, very—they would walk around campus in groups and try to intimidate people, and it's like anything [else]: you go after the leaders, you make examples of them, you break them up, and once they don't have that person to lead them, things quieted down. (I)

School employees constantly watch for indicators of gang membership such as gang signs, gang colors, and other markers of affiliation, and this concern is reflected in their policies. For example, the student dress code that was distributed in writing to students at the beginning of the 2005–2006 school year stated, "[Students] shall not wear shirts with numbers 13, 15, 24, 27, 28, 31, 35, 36 (subject to change)." When I asked the dean of discipline, Ms. Flores, about this, she said that these numbers are used as gang signs, though they often change; I then asked how students know if the numbers change, and she told me that "they just know." In other words, not only has the school prohibited a set of numbers, but it is an often-changing set of numbers and nobody tells students what the changes are. A student could get punished for wearing a replica jersey of his or her favorite athlete, yet this applies to different athletes' jerseys throughout the year (with the changes unannounced). The fact that the school is willing to adopt a fluctuating, poorly communicated rule against displaying certain numbers clearly illustrates how important the fear of gangs is in governing the school.

In contrast, perceptions of threat in Fairway Estates High, most of whose students are middle-class and white, are not centered on any single issue. Instead, employees discuss the same potential safety threats that administrators and teachers discuss in every other school I studied, and presumably in schools across the country: fighting, drugs/alcohol, and the potential for what they often called a "Columbine-like incident." Administrators stress these issues as potential problems of youth and schools in general, and not as related to any characteristics of their particular students.

When considering the two mid-Atlantic schools, I find that perceptions of threat differ across the two schools, and in ways that seem to be influenced by student demographics. In Unionville High, which has a large proportion of black students, fears of school crime are focused on a small group of students who are reportedly anti-authority, defiant, and generally insubordinate. The most common complaint I heard from employees at this school is that there are several of these problem students, and that they wish these students could be expelled, but the school cannot get rid of these troublemakers because the district does not have a sufficient number of alternative placement spots. As Mr. Brook (a dean of discipline) stated:

> If you're here threatening teachers, if you're here threatening other students, you're constantly disrupting class, you're constantly walking the halls, you're constantly leaving. You know, get on the bus, come here in the morning, get off the bus and go to Burger King and come back at two o'clock to catch the bus [to go home]. Why am I wasting my time doing paperwork on that kid who has no desire to change his behavior? And I'm spending, I would say I spend ninety percent of my time dealing with ten percent of the students. (I)

These insubordinate students are repeatedly referred to as "frequent flyers," due to their frequent visits to school disciplinarians. One day a white male teacher at this school suggested to me that, since these students have no interest in learning, the school should:

> round up all the students who are failing, and just sit them in a big room and "make them color Ronald McDonald's nose all day," [because] this would keep them occupied and out of trouble. (FN)

When I observed the youth who are seen as continually insubordinate being punished, they were almost always black. The language I repeatedly heard used to describe these students—insubordinate, disrespectful of authority, threatening—closely resembles stereotypes of African Americans as aggressive and disorderly.[7] Moreover, this image of disorder among black students is reminiscent of the 1960s segregationists' warnings of disorderly, violent schools if desegregation were to occur. Consider, for example, George Wallace's 1963 inaugural address as governor of Alabama, known as the "segregation now, segregation forever" speech, in which Wallace links desegregation to general violence in Washington DC, blurring the line between school violence and violence in surrounding communities:

In the name of the greatest people that have ever trod this earth, I draw the line in the dust and toss the gauntlet before the feet of tyranny . . . and I say . . . segregation today . . . segregation tomorrow . . . segregation forever.

The Washington DC school riot report is disgusting and revealing. We will not sacrifice our children to any such type school system—and you can write that down. The federal troops in Mississippi could be better used guarding the safety of the citizens of Washington DC, where it is even unsafe to walk or go to a ballgame—and that is the nation's capitol. I was safer in a B-29 bomber over Japan during the war in an air raid, than the people of Washington are walking to the White House neighborhood.[8]

To be fair, these perceptions of danger at Frontera High and Unionville High are at least somewhat related to actual problems these schools face. Though I observed no gang violence at Frontera High, several individuals told me that the surrounding neighborhood does have a gang violence problem, and it is impossible to miss the graffiti painted around the neighborhood (which is gang-related, according to the police officer and others at the school). At Unionville High it is common to see students being disruptive and aggressive, either with one another or with teachers (e.g., cursing loudly in the hallways or at teachers, pushing other students, etc.). Despite this, the fact that the concerns about violence and disorder in these two schools resemble stereotypes associated with the racial/ethnic groups that compose their student bodies is important, and coincides with prior research that illustrates how social class and race/ethnicity shape teachers' and administrators' views of potential problems within schools.[9] These stereotypes can shape administrators' perceptions of the threat of violence beyond the actual problems they face, resulting in overly severe punishments for students who display stereotypical behaviors.

A second difference across schools is that students in the schools with more middle-class white students have greater power to appeal their punishments. In each of the two mostly middle-class white schools, it is common for teachers, administrators, or other school personnel to complain about students and their parents contesting the school's authority to punish. In Fairway Estates High several respondents complained to us that when students are sent to an administrator for punishment, students often call their parents on the way down to the office, and a parent might appear at the office to contest any punishment even before the student arrives. Here and at Centerville High I often heard complaints about wealthy parents whose children "could do no wrong" and who blamed the school for their children's misbehaviors. For example, one Latina teacher stated:

> What I have found is that [parents here] are not as supportive [as at other schools] because they don't think their kid ever does anything wrong. In special ed[ucation] I have learned that most of our students are risky, at-risk, or they don't have a lot, they're not as affluent [of a] family and so you don't get a lot of garbage. . . . If I was gonna be an administrator . . . I would wanna work at some place like [another high school in the district] . . . because [at the other school] you have just middle-class people, the parents know their kids aren't perfect and no kid is perfect. . . . But it does give you a lot of good practice in dealing with discipline and parents if you don't have these affluent parents coming in and saying my kid does no wrong and bla bla bla bla, so . . . And the thing is, is like with the whole cell phones, every kid in here, this kid has a lot of wealth, so every kid has a cell phone and when they get down to [in-school suspension] because they're tired, they just call mommy and daddy and they excuse their tardy and they can come back to class. And you don't get that at, like, [the other school]. (I)

Most parents of students in the two middle-class schools have more social capital than parents in the lower-income schools. Many of them hold white-collar jobs or are well educated, and I often heard about friendships between these parents and school employees. This social capital empowers them to challenge the school and equips them with the knowledge of how to do so effectively.[10] In contrast, when I observed parents interact with school officials or when I heard school officials talk about parents in the two lower-income schools, I rarely observed or heard about parents appealing the school's punishments. Parents may either accept the school's authority or become hostile toward it, but this hostility is usually a general response to perceived unfairness rather than an organized appeal of a specific punishment.

As a result of this disparity in social capital, one can notice a difference in the level of care given to following rules and documenting discipline procedures. Teachers and disciplinarians at the more advantaged schools are more careful to apply the school rules appropriately (i.e., "by the book") so that they can defend their actions if challenged. For example, at Unionville High one of the deans of discipline rarely calls parents to inform them their child has been suspended, despite the fact that the school rules say he must do so, because he claims to be too busy. I never observed violations of punishment procedures like this at either advantaged school (Fairway Estates High and Centerville High).

At times school administrators at Unionville High seemed to count on the fact that the mostly lower-income parents would be unwilling or unable to challenge the school's authority. During a meeting about school discipline between the principal, assistant principals, police officer, and deans of discipline, the principal, a white male, spelled out the strategy he wanted to pursue for the students who present the most difficult behavior problems:

> Principal Howley stressed the importance of the school district's rule that before returning from a suspension, each student must have a parent come to the school for a conference. Principal Howley insisted that the school not allow students to return if a parent doesn't come. Mr. Brook asked about a student [who had previously been discussed as a repeated behavior problem], and said that her mother won't come in anymore, because she's done it too often. Principal Howley said that if a parent doesn't come in, then that student can't be with the general school population. He added that "one of two things will happen. Either the parent gets upset and the student finally gets it, or the parent will get sick of coming in and will send the child somewhere else." (FN)

Making conditions difficult enough for students and their parents that they want to withdraw from Unionville High is consistent with teaching to the rules, since it seeks to exclude students by using harsh rule enforcement rather than addressing the causes of their behavior, and thus it is somewhat consistent with how rules are enforced in each school. Yet nowhere else did I notice such a deliberate effort to discourage problem students from coming to school.[11] The middle-class parents at Centerville High or Fairway Estates High would be more able to seek behavioral help for their students outside school, and to negotiate with the school to resolve the problem rather than having the child withdrawn from the school or being forcibly reassigned to an alternative school.[12]

A third difference among schools is the frequency of punishment. There is substantial regional variation in punishment, as the suspension rates are far greater in the mid-Atlantic state than the southwestern state. More important, though, within each state, the school with more lower-income and minority students has a higher suspension rate. The results presented in figure 2.2 leave no doubt that suspensions are handed out far more frequently in the schools with more disadvantaged youth.

This disparity among schools is consistent with results of the prior research on racial disproportionality of school punishment, which is an important and unavoidable conclusion about contemporary school punishment policies.[13] Yet a comparison of punishment rates—to which the prior literature has largely been limited—does not tell the entire story, since it fails to capture the way similar policies have been adopted across disparate schools, and how these policies influence students' educational experiences.[14]

Though there certainly are distinctions across schools that correspond to the racial/ethnic and socioeconomic statuses of their student bodies, there are also important similarities. The types of policies and practices once limited to urban schools or schools serving low-income youth of color are now used in middle-class white schools as well, even though the results of these practices are unequally distributed. The problems with school discipline that I discuss in the previous two chapters are present in all schools, not just in schools attended by mostly nonwhite youth. When considering how these policies take shape, it seems that school discipline policies reproduce the culture of control for *all* students.

At the national level, surveillance and policing in schools are pervasive. Though practices such as implementing police and using metal detectors at school entrances might have gained initial popularity only in urban schools, similar policies are now used throughout the United States. Consider, for example, comments from Ocean View, Delaware's police chief Kenneth McLaughlin, who was quoted in a Delaware *News Journal* article about how federal money is being used for security; Chief McLaughlin, whose town has a population of 1,100, stated: "Our little elementary school is more of a target than the White House. . . . We saw it in the Soviet Union. The Chechens took one. We can't let our guard down."[15]

Certainly there are differences across schools, with some variation in what kinds of strategies are used, and Chief McLaughlin's comment suggests an effort to protect youth rather than to punish them. It is true that schools with more low-income students are more likely to have metal detectors, while more affluent schools are more likely to have surveillance cameras. Some researchers describe this trend as suggesting that schools with white middle-class students use fluid, self-disciplining strategies (like surveillance cameras), in contrast to the rigid, hands-on, police-oriented practice of requiring youth to walk through metal detectors.[16] Yet a contrast between self-disciplining of middle-class youth and metal detector scans for lower-income youth does not explain why the very invasive practice of using drug-sniffing dogs occurs across each school stratum. Though their rate of use and the way they are used may vary across schools, schools across all demographic and regional groups have adopted new policing and surveillance practices.[17]

My research supports this observation of how universal new school discipline policies really are. Though none of the four schools uses either drug-sniffing dogs or metal detectors, all have police on campus and all use some form of a zero-tolerance policy. Each school responds fairly similarly to student misbehavior, in that it is quick to suspend students caught breaking rules. For example, each school in the mid-Atlantic state publishes a code of conduct that prescribes punishments for a range of infractions, and these stated punishments are relatively similar across the two schools—the distinctions that are evident show harsher punishments at Centerville High, not Unionville High (as one might expect). For a relatively common and mundane offense, such as leaving school without permission, the prescribed punishment (in the code of conduct) in Centerville High is a detention or suspension for the first offense, and a three-to-five-day suspension for subsequent offenses; in Unionville High the code of conduct calls for one to three days of in-school suspension, in sequential order.

As noted, all four schools teach to the rules. Students in each school are treated as powerless objects of punishment rather than partners in the discipline process. Surprisingly, students at all four schools are treated fairly similarly despite their very different social statuses and levels of cultural capital, and despite the different perceptions of threat across schools. What became clear is that because they are youth, *all* students are powerless relative to the adults who create and enforce the school rules. In other words, even wealthy white students with powerful parents still have less immediate power than the adults who make, monitor, and enforce the rules of their school.[18]

The data thus illustrate how contemporary school discipline and security practices have effects that are more complex than one might assume based on social reproduction theory. There are indeed clear differences between schools, consistent with this theory: schools with more lower-income youth of color have substantially higher suspension rates than their more advantaged counterparts; the reduced social capital of lower-income parents can influence the punishment process; and the racial/ethnic and social class composition of schools' student bodies can shape perceptions of threat. Yet there are surprising similarities across schools, despite the racial/ethnic and class disparities of the schools' student bodies.

Comparisons of Students Within Schools

The above comparisons are helpful, since they demonstrate not only how similar policies can be enacted differently across schools, but also how a punitive regime has spread. Yet it is still important to think about whether different groups of students within the same schools are treated differently, especially along lines of sex and race/ethnicity.

I gave juniors at all four schools a survey that asked about their experiences with school rules and punishments.[19] When answering whether they had been "in trouble" at school in the past twelve months, males at each school were more likely than females to say yes. Yet school punishment is not limited only to boys, since 24.1% of females at Fairway Estates High and 36.4% at Frontera High reported being in trouble at school in the past year, as shown in figure 5.1.

In Fairway Estates High and Unionville High, white students reported being in trouble less often than either Latino/a or black students. White students reported the highest frequency of trouble in Frontera High, but given that there were only 12 white respondents in this school (out of 440), one should not make much of this anomalous result. We also see that Latino/a students reported the lowest frequency of getting in trouble at Centerville High, but this result, too, is based on only 13 respondents (out of 295). Thus, as figure 5.2 illustrates, overall white students are less likely than others to receive school punishments.

Certainly, there are several explanations that might fit the relationships we see in figures 5.1 and 5.2, and these competing explanations should be taken into consideration (statistically controlled for) to isolate the influence of race/ethnicity and sex in shaping school punishments. To do this, I analyze a subset of the above data, using only the surveys from the two mid-Atlantic schools (see the appendix). These data allow me to consider whether getting in trouble is a function of students' overall behaviors, or whether racial/ethnic minority youth and males are targeted for punishment.

Using these data, I predict the likelihood of students getting into trouble at their schools, based on a number of variables, including each student's sex, race and ethnicity, grades, a general delinquency measure, criminal history, and how often he or she skips classes. In table 5.1 I summarize the important findings from these statistical models. This table shows how each of these variables shapes the odds that a student had gotten in trouble at school. Importantly, these results are produced after statistically controlling for (removing the influence of) all other predictor variables. Thus, the models tell us how race, sex, and other factors shape the likelihood of getting in trouble, while accounting for a student's criminal history, general delinquency, and history of skipping classes.

The results under the column for model 1 tell us about the relationship between sex and getting into trouble, as well as between race and getting into trouble.[20] Females are less likely to be in trouble than males, and African Americans are more likely to get in trouble than white students.[21] Yet these results change when I also take into consideration students' delinquency and school misbehavior (in model 2). Here I find nearly the same result of African Americans being far more likely to get into trouble than whites, but now there is no visible difference between males and females. This is because males are more likely than females to skip classes, have been arrested, or be delinquent generally. In other words, males are apparently more likely than females to be punished not because of selective targeting, but because they misbehave more. But the results also suggest that disproportionate punishments for African Americans are *not* due to their general delinquency, their criminal histories, or whether they skip classes. To the extent that these delinquency variables capture a student's propensity for acting out in school, one can conclude that African Americans are targeted by school actors because of some reason other than their actual misbehaviors.

FIGURE 5.1

Percent of Male and Female Students Who Report Being in Trouble, by School

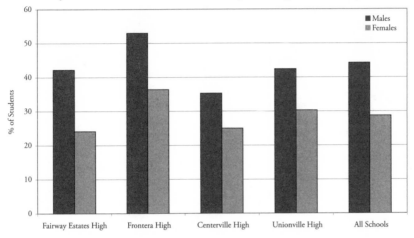

FIGURE 5.2

Percent of Students Who Report Being in Trouble, by Race/Ethnicity and School

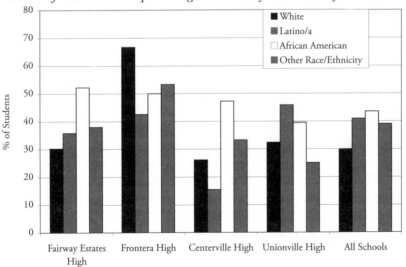

TABLE 5.1

Change in Odds of Getting into Trouble Associated with Each Predictor Variable

Predictor Variable	Model 1	Model 2: Adding Delinquency Variables	Model 3: Adding Grades
Female	-34%	-	-
African American	63%	68%	-
Ever arrested		-	-
Delinquency scale		73%	71%
Skipped classes		19%	-
Grades			-25%

Note: Only statistically significant values reported.

Adding the variable for students' grades (model 3) changes this result yet again, eliminating much of the observed difference between African American and white students. This suggests that African Americans may be more likely to be punished than whites, but it is largely because they are already marginalized within the official school status system due to poor academic performance.[22] This result helps explain why racial/ethnic minority youth are more likely than others to be punished. School staff may not target black students per se, but they target students who struggle academically, and such students are more likely to be African Americans. This is consistent with social reproduction theory, which argues that structural inequalities are hidden and made legitimate by an apparent meritocracy. I find the same for school punishment: African Americans are more likely to be punished because they get worse grades than whites, but their chances of school success are not equal to begin with. The fact that grades mediate the effect of race on getting into trouble illustrates how racial disproportionality in school punishment is veiled and made to seem fair.

This result raises questions about how intentional this process is, and whether it is partly a response to the pressures of standardized testing and school accountability. Since schools whose students perform poorly on standardized tests are punished as part of the No Child Left Behind law, it is in schools' interests to get rid of academically failing students. One way to do this is to suspend these students and eventually expel them, or to encourage them to drop out by using punishments to make the school a less hospitable environment for them. The strong link between academic performance and likelihood of school discipline suggests that this might indeed be occurring, as has been argued by prior scholars such as Lizbet Simmons.[23] But for this to be an intentional strategy, teachers, disciplinarians, and administrators would all have to share information about students' grades; though this is certainly plausible, I did not observe it in any of the four schools I visited. Rather, I find that although the discipline process may have the function of pushing out students who are unlikely to test well, academically underperforming students seem more likely to be disciplined because they disrupt class more often than others, and because they develop a reputation for being troublemakers, which shapes how school staff treat them.

School Staff and Subjective Authority

Academic Performance

These quantitative results match the themes I found based on the interviews and observations at the four schools. For one, it is easy to see how academic performance can mediate the effect of race on the likelihood of being punished. School employees commonly voice the opinion that students' behavior problems often stem from frustration in the classroom, as stated by Principal Ruiz at Frontera High:

I think sometimes you have students who misbehave out of frustration because they're not getting what they need. Educationally sometimes, students who have been given a shotgun education, a little here, a little there, a little everywhere, but no continuity built into it, because they either moved around a lot or been misdiagnosed, or maybe ADHD or some issues like that, they tend to act out more because of their frustration. Sometimes it's not their fault because they've been misdiagnosed or their parents have moved around a lot and there's just not continuity of education, and they're frustrated because they don't understand what's happening in their classes. (I)

This student echoed Principal Ruiz's comments:

I have a different opinion on school safety and security and that stuff, and I think a lot of it has to deal with the actual education students are getting that they actually care about what they're learning. If they care more then they're less likely to wanna commit any crimes if they're actually interested in school. So I don't think the problem with safety . . . uh, I think it has to do more with the actual learning they do, rather than the actions they take. . . . If I wanted to increase the safety of a school I'd improve on the curriculum of it instead of trying to put more police officers and other stuff like that. (I)

Students who are frustrated or afraid of being exposed for not understanding the material are more likely to skip classes or to act out during class; this way they avoid embarrassment and obtain attention on their own terms.

In addition to academic failure causing misbehavior, it is also true that teachers and other school staff respond differently to students based on their academic reputations. Students who do well in class are referred to as "good kids" and teachers are less likely to report their misbehaviors to administrators. For example, in the following interview transcript a Latino teacher at Frontera High talks about how an administrator punished "good" students, though the teachers who observed the misbehavior (leaving school grounds) were willing to look the other way:

Some very high excelling and, you know, highly active children in school politics . . . had a rule enforced on them. They weren't supposed to leave a certain area and they did, and [the teachers present] were expecting them to come back, and the main administrator refused to let [the students] reenter. . . . The instructors, however, were waiting for the administrator to leave so that they could let the kids back, because they know the kids are good and so they made exceptions [for] the[se] individual[s]. And I'm sure if it would have been any other student that they've had a problem with they would have been OK with the principal's decision. But because it was some, because it was children that they knew on a more personal level, they were willing to make exceptions. (I)

Perceptions of students with learning disabilities also illustrate how academic achievement can affect discipline, as some school employees assume that students enrolled in "special education" classes are repeat behavior problems, or "frequent flyers." For example, Mr. Brook at Unionville High discussed how he feels constrained in his ability to punish special education students, who he said committed the majority of the misbehaviors at the school (according to the school's profile, 11% of the student population is enrolled in special education curriculum):

> I would say out of all the students that I have files on that have done something discipline-wise, 50% of them are special ed. kids, but their folders are probably twice as thick. So their occurrences usually you know, a special ed. kid might do two things, two infractions while that regular ed. kid is doing one, so I guess that makes sense. (I)

Yet according to a white female special education teacher who had been teaching at Unionville High for twenty years, special education students benefit from extra attention and parent-school cooperation, which prevent them from misbehaving as often as other students:

> TEACHER: Special ed. kids are much better behaved than the regular population.
>
> INTERVIEWER: Really?
>
> TEACHER: My special ed. kids don't cause problems.
>
> INTERVIEWER: OK, is that just in your class or everywhere?
>
> TEACHER: Pretty much everywhere. These kids come up through [the district's] special ed. [system, where] you're contacting the parents no less than twelve times a year. You have direct contact with those parents, they know what's happening with their special ed. kid, they're not gonna cause problems. The kids know I have a direct line to their mother. So they're not gonna give me any crap or anybody else because we're gonna call home. (I)

Though I cannot tell which of these two very different views is correct, they do illustrate how special education teachers and other school staff have different views of special education students' propensities for misbehavior. Many school employees believe that students with educational disabilities misbehave more often; this in turn predisposes them to look for such misbehaviors more often and respond more punitively. Importantly, prior research documents that racial/ethnic minority students are more likely to be diagnosed as having special education needs than white students, thus again we see how apparently race/ethnicity–neutral mechanisms disproportionately affect youth of color.[24]

It is not surprising that better performing students are protected from punishment while lower performing students are targeted, since this seems to reflect a widespread norm. A recent front-page article in Delaware's *News Journal* describes a case where a student had been expelled from a local middle school for bringing a utility knife to school. The article begins:

> Marie Perkin's seventh-grade daughter had no history of school disciplinary problems.
>
> Generally an A and B student, she made the sixth-grade honor roll twice. She served as treasurer of the school's chapter of Family, Career and Community Leaders of America.[25]

The article then goes on to describe the mother's outrage at her daughter's expulsion, and the mother's quest to eliminate the district's zero-tolerance policies. What I take to be important from this quote is that the student's academic and extracurricular achievements are presented as crucial background information, presented in the second sentence of this front-page article. Clearly, the journalist and editor assume that readers will evaluate the fairness of the student's punishment based largely on her academic and extracurricular activities.

Though this may seem reasonable to many, it is important to remember that overall, black students do substantially worse than white students in terms of academics. For example, in the most recent state standardized test, 44% of black Unionville High students passed the reading/language arts portion and 22% passed the math portion; for white students, 71% and 56% passed. As a result of disparities like these, black students are more likely to be targeted for punishment based in part on their academic deficits.

Once these students become known as troublemakers, or "frequent flyers," this becomes a very difficult label to shed. The "troublemaker" characterization can follow students throughout their academic careers. Further, it can affect their behaviors, since they may begin to identify with the negative perceptions others hold of them, and thus opportunities for improving their reputations become limited.[26] My research confirms this effect, since I also observed how the label of troublemaker becomes attached to particular students, and how it shapes the ways that school staff respond to these students.

Ironically, perpetuating a student's reputation as a troublemaker is often discussed in positive terms by school staff, since it involves working as a team and sharing information. For example, in both Centerville High and Unionville High all freshmen attend classrooms clustered in a wing of each building, in order to group teachers together and facilitate sharing information about students. At Unionville High freshmen are assigned to one of two groups, and everyone in each group shares the same teachers; this allows the teachers to communicate easily with one another and find the best strategies for working with particular students. This is probably true, and many students can be helped in some ways by such an approach, but this practice also means that teachers warn one another about troublemaking youth, thereby predisposing teachers to suspect these students of misbehaving. As another example, consider how Centerville High manages its list of students on behavioral contracts (students who have repeatedly violated rules and may be close to being sent to an alternative school). Whenever anyone in that school accesses the computerized record of one of these students (which is necessary for tasks such as recording his or her grades, recording attendance, or looking up what class he or she is in), the fact that the student is on a behavioral contract appears on a pop-up screen. Further, all the student's teachers are e-mailed regularly, especially prior to the discipline committee's meeting about each of these students, at which point they are asked about the student's recent behavior. Again, these are helpful strategies for communicating and working effectively as a group, but they also mean that a student's label as a troublemaker spreads rapidly among teachers and administrators and is difficult to shed.

I also found evidence of these labels' effects; school staff are quicker to suspect known troublemakers of misbehaving, more likely respond to a troublemaker's misbehavior, and more likely to punish such a student. One day I was standing in the hallway of Unionville High with one of the deans of discipline, Mr. Brook, when he pointed out a student walking by:

MR. BROOK: I can almost guarantee you that he will spend a large part of his life in prison.

AARON: Why, is he always getting into trouble?

MR. BROOK: Yeah, always.

AARON: Is it for big things, or lots of little things?

MR. BROOK: Mostly little things. But teachers know him, and they just kick him out of class now before it has a chance to become a big thing. (FN)

Another time, Mr. Brook told me that when he receives a report of misbehavior about a student, he first checks the student's behavioral record. If the student has a record of misbehavior, then he assumes the report is legitimate and that the student is lying when he or she denies doing anything wrong. Of course, it's likely true that the best predictor of future behavior is one's past behavior; but this process also hinders students' abilities to improve their behavior (by expecting the worst from them) and means that responses to behavior vary based on a student's reputation.

Race/Ethnicity: "Because They're Brown"

Race and ethnicity also have an important direct effect on discipline. Above I note how perceptions of school crime and disorder correspond to racial and ethnic stereotypes of the student bodies at each school, and how school policies often reflect this (for example, the rule at Frontera High prohibiting clothing with certain numbers). I also observed ways in which stereotypes of African Americans and Latino/as shape how students are treated. Such disparate treatment is hard to observe, since it requires that the staff member's response is based on the student's race/ethnicity rather than his or her behavior; nonetheless there were moments when such biases became evident.

One behavior that elicits disparate treatment is horseplay or bodily touching. Though not very common, I observed occasions when African American and Latino/a students touched others and were reprimanded or given referrals by teachers, who perceived their actions as threatening. Yet this is less often the case for white students, whose actions are usually viewed as harmlessly playful and therefore ignored. In one case, a white middle-aged teacher at

Centerville High, Ms. Hemlock, wrote a referral for a black male student who, she claims, harassed females in the class:

> Ms. Hemlock described yesterday's incident to the administrator whom I was shadowing, and discussed why she thought he should be punished. According to her, Harold took a beaker with water and tossed the water at a girl near him. The girl saw the water coming and moved, so she didn't get wet, but Ms. Hemlock saw it clearly. She told him that this is completely inappropriate, that he broke the lab rules against horseplay, and she wrote a referral. Harold objected, saying he didn't hurt anyone, that it was just water, and he didn't see why it was a big deal. She said that even today he didn't see why it was a big deal. She then discussed how he doesn't respect personal distance [in general] and is too "hands-on" with the girls. He is always touching them in ways Ms. Hemlock finds offensive. She noted that the girls never complain, that they even defend Harold by saying it's no big deal, and that Ms. Hemlock doesn't know why they defend him. She said he usually does this with the black girls, but the girl he threw water at was Asian. To illustrate her point, she described his actions a few days ago. A girl was sitting on a stool at a lab desk; Harold came up behind her and leaned all the way over her (his chest on her back and his head over her head). Ms. Hemlock said she was "very offended" by this. Ms. Hemlock added that one day Harold even hugged her, and she was upset by that—she told Harold she found that "offensive." While describing it to us, she said since she was offended, it was really an offensive touching (suggesting he should be charged with a criminal offense). (FN)

Ms. Hemlock perceived Harold's behavior (including a hug) as threatening. It is true that Harold may have acted inappropriately, but my interpretation of his actions (as described by Ms. Hemlock and based on several observations of Harold outside this class) is that he is a normal adolescent experimenting with ways to relate to people. Though his actions may be inappropriate at times and he may need to learn to respect other people's personal boundaries, the actions Ms. Hemlock describes hardly seem worth the formal school punishment and criminal charges she seeks. My interpretation may be naive, but it also seems true that Ms. Hemlock is predisposed to dislike Harold, since I observed a lot of similar behaviors among white students that did not garner such a response. It is also noteworthy that although Ms. Hemlock describes a pattern of similar behavior, she chose to write a referral for it when the horseplay was directed at an Asian female student instead of a black female (his usual target).

A black female school employee helped make sense of how this happens and why black youth are punished more than often than white youth:

> In the African American culture, we, as you see [she is moving her hands while talking], we use our hands. We raise our tone, a lot of teachers are offended when you move your hands when you're talking, and they look at that as being more defiant, more threatening. So a lot of the problems, they're cultural differences. You know, black males, a lot of them, that's not saying that all black males are that way or white males don't, but I can tell you one thing, we definitely use our hands a lot. You know, that's one of the problems when I'm doing presentations, I'm concentrating: "keep your hands down." (I)

This view also resonates with the comments of Mr. Majors that I referred to in chapter 2, describing his understanding that, due to repeated mistreatment, black males may react more angrily than whites to confrontation:

> African American males, in my experience here, are more likely to react angrily if confronted with anger. You know, if I were to come at somebody in a harsh way, for whatever reason, because I stayed up too late last night or because I'm having a rotten day or whatever, some students will get very quiet and understand that, "Wow, Mr. Majors is really serious and you know I better [back down]." And other students have a more oppositional approach to that. And only through working with my colleagues [have I come to] understand that you know, when you've been mistreated by white males in authority . . . be they, you know, managers at stores or law enforcement, or fill-in-the-blank, then you have a different reaction to that, and it comes from your experience. (I)

Because of staff members' perceptions and students' responses to their treatment, African Americans, especially males, are more likely than whites to be perceived as threatening by school staff members, even if the student has done nothing wrong.[27]

Others expressed an opinion that begins similarly, yet reaches a very different conclusion: that due to racial differences minorities are indeed more disruptive than whites. The key difference between these views is that this explanation focuses on the students' worse behaviors, not on staff members' perceptions. In the following transcript, a white female teacher at Unionville High describes why African Americans are more likely to receive school punishments than whites:

TEACHER: It's the way they act. I mean it's disproportionate, if you walk through the halls in the morning, just take a look at, let's say, loudness. It's disproportionate, the black females and black males will tell you this, are so much louder than any group in the building. Is that racially identifiable? Of course it is, because that's who's the loudest. I mean you, people need to get over the fact that we're saying black, white, red, green, yellow. If that's what they're doing, then that's what they're doing, and that's how they're getting punished. Are we picking on the black kids? No, not that I see at all. I mean, I can tell you every teacher that I've been with, they pick on the kid that's the asshole, white, black, red, or green, so, you know.

INTERVIEWER: How else—what other ways are they acting differently? They're louder, are they . . . ?

TEACHER: They are quicker, they have a quicker trigger. This thing about "you don't respect me." You know, "you're dissing me" comes very quickly in a black child as opposed to a white child. For what reason, I cannot tell you. I know for a fact my kids at home have never said that teacher didn't respect me, so, it's never come, they were born with the fact that if they're older, they get respect, irregardless. I believe in the black community, they think you need to respect them immediately and if you don't, you're dissing them, and it's a difference in society, not necessarily in this school. But they have a quick trigger, and they're fast to pull it out. So, I mean, say something to a black child and see what they say to you, even look at them, and the trigger, bang, you set it off. Now I can look at many white kids and never get that. If you walk down the hall and see a group of black kids and you look a certain way, do the same thing with a group of white kids, you're gonna see a totally different reaction, and I don't believe that's from us, I think that's from society. But people here don't recognize that. So do we have to approach certain kids differently? Absolutely. (I)

I heard similar statements made about Latino/a students as well.[28] Some school employees, such as the white male security guard quoted below, described how Latino/as are more likely than white students to misbehave:

You know we'll have a large Hispanic group sometimes that cling together and when they're new to the school and new to the country, their manner-isms sometimes aren't tolerated by our young ladies. You know sometimes, we had a real bad [problem] last year where the boys were catcalling and whistling and, you know, saying stuff, of course not in English so then the girl's really intimidated, so we had to put a stop to that. (I)

Others describe how Latino/a students are more likely than others to be tar-geted for punishment. An instance of this occurred while I was observing Fron-tera High, at the same time in 2006 that there were organized marches in many major cities against proposed anti-immigration legislation. Principal Ruiz explained to me how the local police—whom he had called to help protect the students who marched—ticketed and towed the students' parents' cars:

PRINCIPAL RUIZ: Yesterday I told you we had a march, and I told the kids that if they stayed in school all this time, I would have marched with them. Well, I was having a meeting like this until four o'clock. I went outside and there's the police officers that I contacted, asking them to escort us so that nothing happened, and what were they doing? They were giving tickets to the parents who were leaving off the kids for the march. And one of the parents didn't have her insurance with her, so they towed her car away. And I'm talking to the police officer, and I said, "You know what? It looks like this is a retaliation to the march. I don't understand why you're giving tickets." And they said, "Well, go talk to my sergeant, he's over there." I went to the sergeant and talked to him and he got upset that I was even questioning him. And he said, "See that sign right there? We enforce the law." And I said, "Man, I've been here five years, and none of you have ever been here to enforce the law before. Why today? Of all days, why today? And not only are you not giving them a warning, you're giving them a ticket and you're towing the car away? You don't think that's overkill?" So [sigh] I just want things to be fair and equitable all the way through. If they had been enforcing that law from day one [slaps hands together] it's easier to swallow, it's easier to explain to parents. But when it only gets enforced the day that they're going to march, because I asked them to make sure the roads were clear, can they do that? It puts a bad taste in my mouth, and then it correlates to what the kids said. Because the kids told me that, you know, how they get mistreated by the police, and I see that happen, and I say, "You know, they got a point."

INTERVIEWER: Because of their ethnicity, the kids say?

PRINCIPAL RUIZ: Because they're brown. (I)

Importantly, when school employees talk about either perceptions of racial/ethnic minority youth or their behaviors, they talk about youth getting in trouble for petty offenses: talking back, being insubordinate or confrontational, or cursing. None of them claim that youth of color are more likely to bring a weapon to school, fight other youth, or use drugs on campus. This helps clarify how these negative perceptions of youth of color shape the discipline process. African American and Latino/a youth are more likely than white youth to be written up for minor rule violations, since these offenses involve more subjectivity in deciding whether a rule has been broken. Biases and negative perceptions influence how school staff perceive the behaviors of racial/ethnic minority youth, such as Harold's hugging that I describe above, and lead staff to subjectively perceive these actions as violating school rules. When we recall from chapter 2 how the most frequent offenses at these schools are minor ones such as insubordination, it becomes apparent how important negative perceptions of minorities can be in shaping school discipline.[29] Moreover, the largest discrepancies between rates of punishment of white students and either black or Latino/a students are for violence and disrespect/defiance of authority, as is clear in figure 5.3. These offenses—especially defiance/disrespect—involve great subjectivity in detection; one must possess some chemical or alcoholic substance to be punished for a drug/alcohol violation, but disrespect is in the eye of the beholder, and violence can be as minor as one student playfully pushing another while waiting in line for lunch.

FIGURE 5.3

Percentage of Students Who Report Getting in Trouble for
Various Behaviors, by Race/Ethnicity

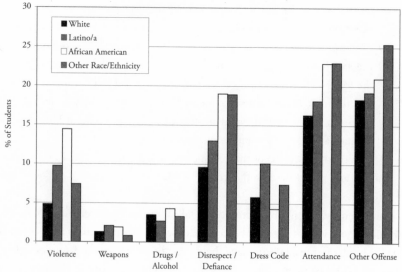

Indeed, at all four schools I observed much less consistency of enforcement for minor rule violations than for more serious ones. At Fairway Estates High, for example, the administration had implemented a strict policy for tardiness, which was followed by some staff but not others. Teachers are supposed to lock their doors at the start of class, and all tardy students must go to ISS for the period (this is called "going to sweep") and be marked absent for that class. Yet one day I came across a classroom door with a sign taped to it, titled, "If you are tardy." It instructed students to not let the door slam, to not interrupt class, and to take a seat quietly at the back of the class. In other words, the teacher in this classroom had a sign on the door that gave instructions that directly contradicted the school rules. This is not surprising, given how inconsistently this rule and other rules against low-level offenses (e.g., dress code violations) are enforced at each school.

Not only are youth of color more vulnerable than whites to subjective appraisals of misconduct, but they also are less likely to respond in ways that avoid punishment. Prior studies consider this to be a problem of cultural capital. Since schools are predicated on middle-class, white behavioral norms, poor students and youth of color are less likely to abide by these norms.[30] This means that they are more likely to talk to teachers or administrators in ways perceived as confrontational. As a result, not only are youth of color more likely than whites to be suspected of wrongdoing, but their responses to these suspicions are likely to make the matter worse, whereas a student who is well versed in middle-class norms of communication and negotiation may be able to negotiate his or her way out of the situation. This explanation stems from the work of sociologist Annette Lareau, who demonstrates how middle-class families impart a type of cultural capital in children that teaches them how to force institutions, such as school, to adapt to them.[31] In contrast, working-class and lower-class children are not taught these mechanisms, and thus have little skill in negotiating and manipulating institutions to conform to their individual needs.

The importance of these problems has likely grown in recent years with the arrival of the new school discipline regime. Serious offenses—such as violence leading to injury, possession of weapons, or drug use on campus—were against school rules prior to the harsh rules and practices now in place; the new discipline regime, however, widens the net of school misbehavior to define and detect a greater number of behaviors as violating the rules. Put differently, zero-tolerance policies against weapons primarily affect students who bring nail clippers or other petty "weapons" to school; students who brought guns or knives would have been in trouble prior to these policies as well. For example, in her analysis of zero-tolerance policies in Texas, Augustina H. Reyes finds that the vast majority of students suspended (96%) or expelled (86%) under zero-tolerance laws are punished for a discretionary offense—ones for which suspension or expulsion are not required under the policy—rather than for a mandatory offense.[32] Thus, negative perceptions of African Americans and Latino/as increase their risk of getting in trouble for minor misbehaviors, while the contemporary discipline regime encourages schools to define more minor misbehaviors as violations. The problem is circular: students who are punished eventually develop reputations as troublemakers, and their behaviors are monitored more closely and interpreted in a negative light. Though on its face the new school discipline regime is race/ethnicity–neutral, in fact it exacerbates the disadvantages faced by racial and ethnic minorities.

Social Class

Though some respondents' comments help to clarify the particular effects of race and ethnicity on school punishment, others offer similar comments but couch them in terms of social class instead. That is, several describe how poor students act differently than middle-class students, either because of deviant norms or unstable home lives. This is unsurprising, given the sensitivity of stating that black or Latino/a students behave worse than white students, or that teachers and administrators treat nonwhite students worse than whites. The following quote from Officer Malvern at Centerville High captures this theme well; prior to the following statement, he had explicitly stated that social class, not race, shapes whether students get in trouble at school:

> You know because of where they're from, they have more of a survival instinct and . . . the defiance and the insubordination isn't so much them being defiant and insubordinate, it's more of a survival instinct. That's how they treat everybody they deal with. And because they haven't learned the other way to treat somebody. What you know, the funny thing is, it's like profanity, the use of the word "fuck." We are alarmed and offended by that because of how we were raised and our upbringing. To us, it's abnormal, it's profane. To a student, depending on where they coming from, that's common language, there's nothing obscene, profane, or wrong about it. It's a normal part of their language. So you have two different viewpoints on just that one issue alone and that causes a conflict. Because if you have a teacher and she hears you use this word "fuck," but you use it commonly in your household, "pass the fucking butter," or your parents say, "you get the fucking butter yourself," it's normal, common language. So when you come to a school and you're using what's normal to you, but the person you're using it around views it as abnormal, [then] there's gonna be a conflict and before you know it, there's defiance and insubordination. [These are] the two [most common offenses] in the building, and that's how it happens, you know. (I)

Though it is possible that he is using class as a "code word" for race, it is important to note that attributed effects of race/ethnicity and class often intermingle when school staff discuss misbehaving youth. Most school staff assume that poverty causes misbehavior, and that within their schools poverty disproportionately affects minority students. These two issues are distinct and each is important on its own, though the limitations of my data do not allow me to treat them separately in a way that they deserve. That is, I have no way of discerning whether Officer Malvern really had in mind a poor family, a black or Latino/a family, or a poor black or Latino/a family, just as I have no way of knowing whether the attributions of misbehavior for low-income black and Latino/a students are due to the poverty or race/ethnicity of the students. Moreover, prior research clearly establishes how both social class and race contribute to how students are treated in school.[33] Given the research design of my study, in which I compare schools with middle-class white students to schools with lower-income Latino/a and black students, I observed interactions in schools where these two factors are perceived in conjunction with one another. The following field note illustrates this by describing a conversation in which a white dean of discipline at Unionville High talks about how he would expect students at a mostly white, middle-class school to be better behaved than the students at Unionville High, but without articulating whether race/ethnicity or class is the source of the family problems he notes:

Mr. Sussex asked me about other schools where I was doing research. When I told him that I was studying a [nearby] school with more middle-class, white students, he asked about differences. I told him that there were fewer differences with behavior problems than one might think. He said this surprised him, since "I would guess that there are more two-parent families there. Right?" [I said yes.] "They're probably better able to give kids the things they need at home to avoid problems. I mean, a lot of our kids here, they don't know their dads, their mom works hard to support them, but may have to work two jobs and isn't able to spend much time with them, and they have other family problems. Kids from families like that are just going to have more problems than kids from two-parent families." (FN)

It's hard to know whom, specifically, Mr. Sussex has in mind when thinking about "families like that" as compared to "kids from two-parent families"; I assume that race and social class merged together in his mind and are symbolized by the absence of two-parent families.

Gender

Recall that more males get in trouble at school than females. Yet when controlling for delinquency record and whether students skip classes, there is no significant difference between males and females in the multivariate results (see table 5.1). This suggests that males are more likely to get in trouble because they misbehave more often. But there is a problem with such an interpretation: it ignores the gendered ways that boys' and girls' behaviors are viewed. As criminologists who study female delinquency have repeatedly shown, gendered views of male and female behavior make official data on their rates of misbehavior questionable. For example, according to official arrest statistics female delinquency has been increasing relative to male delinquency over the past ten years.[34] One interpretation might be that girls are becoming bolder and less afraid to commit crimes that have traditionally been male-only behaviors, like violence and theft. But scholars such as feminist criminologist Meda Chesney-Lind very convincingly debunk this myth. Chesney-Lind and colleagues argue that it is policing that has changed, not girls' behaviors. In years past, police would have ignored girls' misbehaviors as harmless, but now they are more likely respond to this misbehavior with arrests, meaning that changing gender norms (how police should treat girls) influence both criminal punishment and delinquency statistics.[35]

Similarly, it is easy to spot the influence of gender norms on school rules and punishment when looking at the dress codes of each school. Though the dress codes prohibit styles most often worn by black and Latino/a students—baggy pants, do-rags, bandanas, and gang-affiliated numbers—these are usually applied to boys, not girls, in an effort to prevent gang violence. In contrast, each school's dress code also includes a number of prohibitions against female clothing items, but with the clear intent of preventing displays of female sexuality (rather than preventing violence).[36] Items such as spaghetti straps, visible thongs, short skirts, and low-cut shirts are prohibited in an effort to keep girls' bodies concealed. These rules enforce existing gender norms, since they seek to teach girls how females ought to dress and punish them for violating these norms.

Of the four schools, Fairway Estates High is particularly concerned with how female students dress. In this mostly middle-class white suburban school, girls' violations of the school dress code is one of the school problems most frequently mentioned by staff. School employees often complained to me about how girls dress, and it is evident that many of the female students wear items on the banned clothing list. But according to several school employees, the dress code is inconsistently and rarely applied. As one white security guard stated:

HENRY: Come lunchtime and fifth and sixth hour I'll be darned if I'm gonna' [give a] dress code [violation to] these girls that are wearing, like, puny clothes. It's like, where have you been for four hours?

INTERVIEWER: But you'll do it earlier in the day?

HENRY: I'll do it earlier, I'll probably, I'll do lunchtime dress codes. But there's kids, I've seen at three o'clock in the afternoon I'm watching them walk by, I'm going, I can't believe this girl hasn't been dress-coded with nearly no top on. You know, or everything exposed, or shorts so short that I don't know how they fit, things like that. (I)

Reasonable people may disagree on whether teenagers should be allowed to dress at school the way Henry describes. The bigger problem is that this policing of sexuality only occurs for girls. There are no dress code rules for boys obviously aimed at policing their sexuality (e.g., no prohibitions against tank tops, mesh shirts, or shirts being unbuttoned or too tight). Moreover, I found that male students can walk through Fairway Estates High's campus shirtless—passing assistant principals along the way—and receive no reprimand. I observed this more than once standing in the school courtyard prior to the break between classes; the weight room is in a separate building on the other side of the student parking lot, so students who lift weights during physical education class must walk through the lot and the school's courtyard to return to the locker room before the class session ends. When I saw them do so, many male students wore only their shoes and gym shorts. Granted, these observations occurred late in the school year in the Southwest, and it was very hot out—but even on a warm day, the fact that nobody ever reprimanded these shirtless boys amazed me, given the ubiquitous concerns about girls wearing revealing clothing.

With such an emphasis placed on policing girls' sexuality through the school's dress code, I expected to find that female students far outnumbered male students when it comes to who gets punished for dress code violations.

FIGURE 5.4

Percentage of Male and Female Students Who Report
Getting in Trouble for Various Behaviors

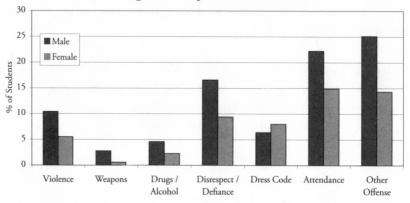

Yet females are only slightly more likely than males to get in trouble for how they dress; in contrast, they are far less likely than males to be in trouble for every other offense, as shown in figure 5.4. In fact, for most of the other categories, the percentage of males in trouble is almost twice that of females. Thus, though girls only slightly outweigh boys regarding dress code violations, this is a large jump relative to their representation in every other offense category. In sum, though it is very difficult to compare how frequently boys and girls actually misbehave, it is clear that gendered views of appropriate behavior and dress shape school punishment.

Unequal Discipline

The analyses of race/ethnicity, class, and gender throughout this chapter lead me to two somewhat contrasting conclusions. The first conclusion has to do with comparing different schools to one another. When I compare what happens in mostly white, middle-class schools to mostly nonwhite, lower-income schools, I see greater similarity than one might expect. Despite some important differences, the practices that were once reserved for schools serving nonwhite youth are now implemented in middle-class white schools as well. These punitive and surveillance-oriented strategies now affect all students, though in varying degrees.

This conclusion offers empirical support for Jonathan Simon's argument about governing through crime in schools. He maintains that though only a small number of schools experience serious problems with violence, the logic of governing through crime assumes that all students have a high likelihood of victimization, and that this viewpoint has reshaped school discipline and security in schools across the United States.[37] Harsh contemporary school policies that initially came about in response to perceptions of violence in inner-city schools, attended mostly by lower-income youth of color, have since spread to suburban schools as the practice of governing through crime makes these policies seem worthwhile for all student populations. Though racial and ethnic minorities are far more likely to be punished, all youth are now subjected to a qualitatively similar style of discipline.

The second conclusion considers differences among students within schools to better isolate how their experiences vary. Though on their face, school policies appear color-blind and gender-neutral, the ways they are enacted allow for stereotypes and biased perceptions of minority groups, poor youth, and females to shape the discipline process. At times this effect is indirect, in that African Americans tend to get worse grades than white students, and students' grades influence discipline. But at times these effects are direct, such as when the horseplay of youth of color is perceived as more threatening or aggressive than the behavior of white youth. The effects of such biases become clear when analyzing more closely how school rules are enforced.

This is hardly news. The argument about disproportionate punishments has been made many times before in previous studies.[38] Nevertheless, the analyses I present in this chapter contribute to our understanding of the effects of race, ethnicity, class, and gender on school discipline in a number of ways. For one, though several studies illustrate racial/ethnic disproportionality in punishment, few are able to explain this disproportionality by understanding how biased perceptions shape the punishment process.[39] Additionally, given the focus of this book, my analyses contextualize this disproportionality within the contemporary school discipline regime. The school discipline and security practices that have come about lately—ratchetting up punishments for misbehaviors, increasing surveillance over students, and the like—may be ubiquitous, but they do not affect all students equally. Rather, they compound the difficulties already faced by disadvantaged youth, especially low-income youth of color. These students may have always faced biased perceptions and disproportionate punishments in school, but the consequences of these problems only grow as we watch over students more closely, punish students more harshly, and incorporate police officers into the schools as standard practice. Thus, the negative consequences of the contemporary school discipline regime that I have described throughout this book exacerbate the educational and social marginalization faced by poor youth of color.[40]

Additionally, at first glance gender does not appear to have a significant role in shaping school discipline. Yet when looking at what rules are in place and how they are enforced, it becomes clear that gender norms are enforced through school punishment. This is particularly evident in the dress codes and their enforcement at Fairway Estates High. Though in one way this is good for girls, since they are less likely than boys to be subjected to harsh punishments, there are much deeper problems with gendered rule enforcement. The fact that school rule enforcement is shaped by gender stereotypes reinforces social inequality by socializing girls into gendered behavioral expectations. Moreover, the lack of attention to female offending also means that girls' victimization is likely to go unnoticed.[41]

CONCLUSION

Undoing the Harm

The following appeared in the *Arizona Republic*:

A student at Mountain Ridge High School was arrested
Friday by Glendale police and accused of plotting to stage
a food fight.

The boy, a 17-year-old junior, was taken into custody at
the Glendale school and then placed in a juvenile-deten-
tion center on a charge of disrupting an educational facility,
police said.

Jeff Payne, the student's father, said the food fight
never happened, so he can't understand why his son was
arrested. . . .

School officials have taken further action by slapping
the student with a suspension. . . . The food fight, planned
on a Web site, was supposed to occur Thursday, but school
officials got wind of the plot . . .

Extra teachers and security were posted in the school
cafeteria and nothing happened. . . . Officials were back on
guard Friday and again foiled a possible outbreak of tossed
food, [a school district spokesperson] said.

School administrators were specifically singled out as food-
fight targets, police Officer Mike Peña said. The boy was taken
into custody after he became very uncooperative, he said.[1]

This example of arresting a student for planning (but not actually engaging in) a food fight may seem over the top, but it is consistent with
what I have described throughout this book: that schools have overreacted to
potential threats so that students are at risk of arrest and harsh school punishment, strategies that do not address the actual problems students face. The

teachers, administrators, and other school staff I met during this research clearly care about the youth in their charge, but they work within a flawed system—one that prioritizes rules over children's needs, that focuses on punishment over problem solving, that alienates youth rather than integrating them into the school, and that unnecessarily punishes and hurts the future chances of many. Though harsh school discipline and tight security practices are found in schools with white middle-class students as well as schools with lower-income youth of color, the differences in how—and how often—they are enforced exacerbate educational and professional disadvantages of racial/ ethnic minorities and poor youth.

This does not mean that our schools are failing, or that we should further weaken traditional public schools through disinvestment via school vouchers or charter schools. It does, however, suggest that many of the policies that have spread across the country over the past two decades, which have cost taxpayers a great deal of money, are bad ideas that were implemented and are spreading in the absence of critical thought.

Below I offer several recommendations for how schools can reshape their policies and practices to be more fair, effective, and helpful to students, teachers, and administrators. I make these recommendations understanding my limited perspective: I am a sociologist who teaches at the university level, not a high school teacher, so I have never had to respond to a disruptive adolescent while trying to teach to thirty others. Yet sometimes an outsider's perspective can clarify problems that might not be apparent to an insider. Moreover, the literature in the fields of sociology, education, and criminology is fairly clear about practices likely to reduce school misbehavior, and it is evident from studying these four high schools how far they have strayed from several of these evidence-based strategies.

The problem with school punishment and security is not a simple matter of bad policies. The problem is also with the overall climate of school discipline, which prioritizes rules and rule enforcement over students' needs. Improving how schools maintain safe learning environments thus requires much more than implementing better rules—it also means that schools recognize how this disciplinary climate hurts students and prevents effective strategies from taking flight. This requires a critical conversation within the school community, whereby school officials begin to question their practices and the very way they think about school security, rather than blindly accept that more security and more punishment will benefit the school. The result can be high schools that more effectively maintain safe learning environments, and that do so in a way that better encourages students' social and emotional development.

Creating Rules

Each school has a code of conduct that specifies prohibited behaviors and their resulting punishments. A good first step to improving school discipline would be to revisit not just the code of conduct but also the process by which it is created. Typically the code of conduct is a product of state mandates, district rules, and school-level decisions made by a discipline committee and the principal. Often parents are involved as well, either through parent-teacher associations, town meetings, or a school committee. But students usually are precariously absent from the rule-making process.

There are good reasons to include students in the rule-making process, especially when it comes to student misbehavior.[2] Students know best what goes on in the school. As several school staff said to me, the students want their school to be safe and orderly; they have more at stake in a safe school than anyone else, since they are the ones most likely to be victimized or skip school out of fear. Students are a great resource for identifying the school's biggest behavior problems, and they might also be able to distinguish between concerns over actual problems the school faces as opposed to unrealistic fears. Another important reason for requesting student input is that it would be a big step toward creating a democratic and inclusive school climate, one of the most important factors associated with safe schools. Allowing students a voice in how they are treated would empower them, make them feel a part of the school community, and increase their bonds with the school. It would also make them more likely to view the school's rules as fair and legitimate, which is another crucial factor in preventing misbehavior.[3]

Allowing students a voice in creating school rules might seem idealistic, and some might criticize it out of the belief that students would do their best to create a lax environment with passive discipline. Obviously there must be limits to students' power in shaping the rules so that the school administration's goals are preserved throughout the process, even if there is student push back.[4] But through such a dialogue students would gain experience honing their negotiation skills, and open-minded administrators might become aware of previously unforeseen problems with certain rules. At the very least, vetting rules in this way would force administrators to enact only policies for which they have solid justification, rather than ones that are arbitrary or unfair, such as allowing baseball caps but not allowing headwear such as "do-rags" that are usually worn only by black students. The goal of encouraging student participation should be to create a more inclusive and democratic environment and to draw from students' expertise, not to allow students to pursue an agenda that is contrary to that of the school.[5]

There is no evidence of which I am aware that suggests students would intentionally water down rules and punishments. In fact, in my interviews with students I was repeatedly surprised when students expressed desire for *harsher* punishments and *more* rules. As one Asian American male student stated:

> I don't think people, if they don't want to learn, they shouldn't—they should just not come to school. I think that's maybe a bit radical, but you see a lot of students, like for example, my study hall, just packed with students who just, I got my study hall because I had, I fulfilled all my half-year courses, like health and gym, so I had no more space for another class, so I had to be like stuck with a study hall, but, when you see the trend going on with study halls and these people don't wanna learn and they just goof around. So what's the point of letting them come to school if they don't wanna learn? It's a waste of taxpayers' money. (I)

Another student—a white male at Unionville High who is known as a "frequent flyer" and who is currently on a behavioral contract for offenses including skipping classes and possession of alcohol—endorsed the ideas of metal detectors in school, security cameras outside the school building to help catch students skipping classes (which he admitted to doing regularly), and stricter punishments for those caught breaking school rules. Students want to learn in safe environments, and they are willing to have firm discipline so long as it is exercised fairly.[6]

In *Judging School Discipline*, Richard Arum voices a variation of this criticism of student participation, arguing that contemporary schools are in a crisis of moral authority because students have successfully used legal action to challenge school rules and punishments.[7] Though I agree with his overall point—that student challenges cannot be so deep as to undermine the school's authority—I disagree with the way Arum interprets what has happened in schools over the past few decades. The fault is not with the students who complained about unfair treatment or with the courts that sided with students, but rather with the schools that acted unfairly, thereby necessitating legal intervention. For example, consider education scholar Gerald Grant's compelling story of a high school that lost its moral authority in the 1970s, *The World We Created at Hamilton High*.[8] Chaos ensued at Hamilton High when students began to invoke the language of legal rights to challenge the school's authority, threatening to sue teaches or the school at every turn and refusing to abide by school rules. This situation of student over-empowerment only began during desegregation and with a series of race riots, when racism and educational inequality came to light, thus eroding students' and parents' trust in the schools.[9] The chaos was then fueled by the school itself, which relinquished control to the students rather than instituting fair, consistent, and reasonably strict discipline—but the crisis only occurred because the school was seen as unfair and thus not a legitimate authority.[10]

In *Moral Education*, Emile Durkheim clearly and repeatedly emphasizes that although firm rules are crucial for teaching morality, these rules cannot be excessive and the discipline must be fair. When defending the idea that students ought to participate in the process of enforcing school rules (against the assumption that student participation contradicts the necessity of the teachers' dominance), Durkheim states: "A class in which justice is dispensed by the teacher alone, without securing the support of the group, would be like a society in which the judges render sentence against actions that the public does not condemn. Such judgments would lack both influence and authority. The teacher must gain the support of the class when he punishes or rewards."[11] Moral authority comes when students see the school's discipline as legitimate and when they are emotionally invested in the school rules. These are conditions that would improve, not deteriorate, if students were allowed greater input in creating rules.

Legal action against the school is certainly a problem because it can cause uncertainty among teachers, who may not know what current rules are or who may not have confidence that their actions will be supported.[12] It is certainly unfortunate that courts were forced to side with a number of students who brought legal challenges, but this is necessary for restoring moral authority when schools take actions such as suspending seventy-five students for demonstrations in support of observing Black History Week (without any hearing, notification of charges, or opportunity to present evidence on the students' behalf, as in *Goss v. Lopez*, 1975), or suspending students for wearing black armbands in a political protest (as in *Tinker v. Des Moines Independent Community School District*, 1969). School rules that are unfair or unhelpful should be challenged, and schools should be open to that challenge. A free, democratic dialogue—within limits that preserve the school administration's right to make final decisions—would help, not hurt, the school climate, prevent discipline problems, and improve the school's moral authority by improving its legitimacy.

Collaboration with students at some level already occurs in the schools I studied; each has a student council, though it is clear that students' voices are marginalized in most. But at Centerville High, Principal Miller talked to me about her efforts to involve students in school government through focus groups with randomly selected students:

INTERVIEWER: The focus groups that you have with the students, do you do that regularly?

PRINCIPAL MILLER: Yeah, I meet monthly with them and they're randomly selected out of the student homerooms and they tell me everything. . . . The biggest [complaint] last month was, "Could you replace the locks on the bathroom doors because the doors don't lock?" So that was my goal, [to] get the locks back on the bathroom doors, and I did. They got replaced last week, soap in the bathroom dispensers. . . . But you know we start to talk about, you know, IDs were the big hit topic in October and November, [with students asking:] "Why do we have to wear them, why are we doing this?" You know, so, it's the little things.

INTERVIEWER: So each month it's a different group of kids?

PRINCIPAL MILLER: Uh huh, yep. . . . I feed them breakfast and listen to them for an hour. (I)

Though the students were unable to force change on something the administration wants to do—require students to wear ID badges—they were able to alert the principal to a problem with the bathrooms and obtain a solution.

Efforts to include students in the governing process should be encouraged and made more central to the rule-creation process, which happens before the school year starts; this is especially important in schools with large populations of minority and lower-income youth, who are less likely to feel empowered to begin with.[13]

Of course, in addition to improving the process by which rules are created, it is also important to keep an eye on the content of school rules. The most apparent need for improvement is to eliminate zero-tolerance policies, as has been suggested by several organizations, including the American Psychological Association, the American Bar Association, the American Civil Liberties Union, and the National Council on Crime and Delinquency. Zero tolerance policies have been repeatedly shown to fail at their primary missions of reducing school misbehavior and increasing consistency of school discipline.[14] These policies also make schools less democratic, lead to unnecessary escalation of punishment in unwarranted circumstances, and exacerbate racial disparities in punishment.[15] Zero tolerance is not only a bad strategy, but a bad message to send to our children—tolerance and forgiveness are values that we ought to teach our children, as even youth who need to be removed from a school because of their behavior deserve a chance at redemption. This does not mean that the school cannot suspend or expel a student, but that these decisions must be made on a case-by-case basis, involve a dialogue and student participation, and be reviewable.

Though many school staff members with whom I spoke voiced support for zero-tolerance policies, others complained that these policies go too far in limiting administrators' discretion. A few others suggested that their school does not "really" have a zero-tolerance policy, since everything is somewhat negotiable, such as Ms. Doherty, a black administrator at Centerville High School:

INTERVIEWER: How do you feel about zero-tolerance policies, are you in favor of them?

MS. DOHERTY: As long as they're not discriminatory. I find that with zero-tolerance policies, zero ain't on certain students, they're basically geared toward helping the disadvantaged students—I mean, hurting those students.

INTERVIEWER: In general or do you think that's how it works here?

MS. DOHERTY: In general, in general. A lot of, again, some of them aren't zero. If you have money, and you can get an attorney, zero becomes more than zero. So that's why I have the problem. If you have good advocates, there are exceptions to the rule. Whether the advocate has money or position, there are exceptions. (I)

If this characterizes how zero-tolerance policies work elsewhere too, it suggests that these policies are even more harmful, for they conceal inconsistencies in a way that makes the rules appear to be equally enforced for all. Additionally, zero tolerance rules provide cover for school administrators to make unfair decisions. When a punishment seems unfair, an administrator can hide behind the cloak of zero tolerance, as if he or she has no choice but to suspend or expel a student, when really the administrator chose to prescribe such harsh punishments.

Relatedly, schools should rely less on exclusive punishments, primarily suspension. Though sending home a student can help by quelling a flare-up or preventing further conflict among students (or between a student and staff member), schools should not rely heavily on the practice. Removing a student from the school means that he or she falls behind, academically, and also that he or she usually spends time unsupervised. If a student is acting up out of boredom or because he or she does not understand course material, then a suspension might be more of a reward than a punishment. Keeping students in school makes far more sense; instead of removing troublesome students, the school can deny them privileges given to others, require detention, or create a new version of in-school suspension in which students actually do work or receive instruction.

By devising penalties short of excluding students from the school, schools would also avoid an excessive penalty scheme. As Durkheim notes, punishments become less effective when they are applied as opposed to threatened, and therefore punishments become ineffective when a school prescribes severe penalties too quickly: "Nothing, then, is so dangerous as having too brief a scale of punishment. Since one runs the risk of going through it too quickly, the threat-value of the penalty which retains its full force only so long as one has not been subjected to it may be rapidly exhausted. This is the weakness of Draconian laws. Since they move immediately to extremes of harshness, they are soon driven to repeat themselves; and the influence of punishment declines with frequency of repetition."[16] Though it is important that schools punish students for violating school rules, these punishments should start out as minor and eventually escalate, rather than beginning with suspensions (as is dictated for many offenses in the code of conduct at each school I studied).

It is also important that the school staff be more sensitive to rules that target racial/ethnic minorities or only one sex. This was evident at Fairway Estates High, for example, where a strict dress code is based almost entirely on preventing the display of female body parts, while males who exercise in the weight room are allowed to walk back to class shirtless. Or, consider the following rule about head wear at Frontera High, listed among the student rules: "[Students] shall not wear hairnets or other hair coverings, including bandanas, and dew rags [sic] except in cases of recognized religious beliefs or for medical reasons." While bandanas and do-rags, which tend to be worn by Latino/a and African American youth, are explicitly prohibited, the more commonly worn baseball hat is not. Rules like these are one reason why youth of color are more likely to be punished than white youth; while it may be very difficult to rid schools of stereotypes that create the problem of disproportionate punishment, it would be relatively easy to amend schools' codes of conduct with this problem in mind.

Communicating Rules

Communicating the school's rules to students and parents is something that schools tend to do well. Each of the four schools I studied sends home a code of conduct and requires a parent's signature of receipt at the beginning of the school year. I also saw behavioral expectations listed on posters hung in hallways and very often in classrooms. This is entirely consistent with one of the "best practices" of school behavior management, in that the school rules must be clearly communicated to students.

I suggest that schools continue with these efforts but go a step further by reaching out to parents and beginning a conversation about behavioral expectations, not just gathering a signature. This suggestion came from a Latino assistant principal at Frontera High School, Mr. Cordero, who told me he used to do this when teaching:

I used to call their parents and say, you know, "This is Mr. Cordero, I'm calling from so-and-so high school and the purpose of this call is to say that I have your son in my classroom and I just wanted to say that if there is anything you ever need let me know, and from time to time I'll be calling." Well, it only takes—you make one or two calls a [day], and it only takes you know, three to four weeks and you've called through your whole list of students. And . . . now you've established some common ground so if there's any time you have to make that tough call saying, "You know your son is not, or your daughter is not acting in accordance to what I believe to be right and appropriate," now you've broken that ice. But if the first call is a cold call and you call on a discipline point, there, at times can be a little bit more . . . defensive[ness] or resistan[ce]. . . . Another key thing is the kid's gonna go, "You called my dad?" I said, "Yes." . . . He goes, "Why did you call?" I said, "Just to say who I am and that I'm glad that you're in my class." He goes, "Wow, I've never had a teacher call my house." (I)

By reaching out to parents early in the school year, Mr. Cordero was able to approach parents with good news, something that many of them probably weren't accustomed to. He enlisted their support in reinforcing positive behaviors (e.g., complying with school rules, performing schoolwork), and in the process showed students that he cared. As a result he claims great success, in that students very rarely misbehaved in his classes. Reaching out to parents in this way enlists them as partners, communicates classroom and school expectations to them, and reinforces these expectations in a real way for students.

But one note of caution about this suggestion is in order. Schools' tendency to teach to the rules might be reinforced by posting the rules throughout the school, since everyone is constantly reminded of the priority these rules take. My suggestion is that posted rules should be present, but not dominant in the school's landscape; they should be accompanied by messages to students that help them in other (non-discipline) realms of life, such as posters listing healthy study habits, healthy eating and exercise habits, social and behavioral resources available to students within the school and the community, and so forth.

Another suggestion for the communication of rules is that when schools distribute their codes of conduct, they also distribute a set of expectations for (not just of) students. Schools should communicate to students what they will do to ensure that students are treated fairly, and students should know what their rights are in disciplinary situations (e.g., what type of personnel have the authority to issue a suspension, or whether they must consent to a police search in school). Doing so would help students view the school's authority as legitimate rather than arbitrary or coercive.

Enforcing Rules in the Classroom

Teachers are the most crucial gatekeeper to the school punishment process, since most punishments begin with a teacher who writes a referral for a misbehaving student. Therefore, one of the most efficient and effective steps a school could take to reduce student misbehavior would be to help teachers improve their classroom management skills. Better classroom management would mean that many cases of misbehavior could be stopped or prevented before they escalate to where the teacher writes a referral; in turn, fewer referrals would mean that the school disciplinarians (deans, interventionists, assistant principals) would feel less overwhelmed and have more time to help students. With fewer behavior problems reaching their desks, principals and assistant principals would have more time to focus on improving instruction, promoting athletic programs, and other positive features of the school.

Surprisingly, the four schools I studied do little by way of classroom management training. Teachers are all evaluated, usually by assistant principals, and the evaluations include the subject of classroom management—thus, it is not ignored. Yet given its importance in the discipline process, it is shocking that more is not done in this area, such as classroom management workshops or guest speakers. One possibility would be to regularly recognize teachers who are skilled at managing their classrooms, and have these teachers discuss with other teachers what they do to prevent student misbehavior.

Throughout my observations of classrooms and interviews with teachers, I noticed very wide disparities in classroom management skills. Some teachers speak confidently about how they rarely have student behavior problems because they prevent small problems from becoming big ones. For example one white male teacher at Frontera High stated:

TEACHER: I learned this in elementary school, by the second year I was teaching, [that] the kids are gonna test you. They're gonna figure out what they can get away with, what they won't get away with. But deep down inside they really wanna succeed. They want your approval. They want to be cool. They wanna be good at something, and unfortunately, for some kids, the only thing they can be really good at is being a pain in the ass or being bad or being the toughest. Maybe they're flunking the class, but they can flunk it better than anyone else and they'll be proud of that. So, when you get a few kids like that, sometimes, what you have to do is you have to find what to flip them, you know? . . . If they do something better than anyone else, then you make a big point of it, and after a relatively short time, the other behavior gets extinguished.

INTERVIEWER: So just highlighting their strengths and what they do well?

TEACHER: Yeah, it's a little more than that, but yeah, exactly, exactly. (I)

Teachers such as this one should be recognized for their effectiveness, and other teachers should have an opportunity to learn from them. Certainly, many teachers would feel that this is condescending, since they might be offended by the presumption that a colleague is being recognized as superior to them, and they might also object to additional meetings. Perhaps such workshops should be voluntary; yet if they are effective at helping other teachers, many teachers would soon recognize the benefit to their daily working environment (in the form of fewer behavior problems) and participation would grow. Moreover, even if these workshops are sparsely attended, the recognition of outstanding behavior management would send a message that this skill is prized within the school.

Though attention to classroom management training in the four schools I studied was sparse, there is one positive example of this. Again, I find it in Centerville High, where a pilot program, "Instructional Support Teams" (IST), was being formed while I was conducting my research. The idea of the program is to have trained case managers available to help students, parents, or teachers who initiate the IST process. The manager then meets with the student, teacher, and parents, with the goal of changing the behavior of both teacher and student to reach a positive pattern of interaction. The program begins with an academic assessment, out of the understanding that most misbehavior is rooted in learning problems, and then proceeds to look at other behavioral issues. The IST program is nonevaluative and confidential, meaning that teachers are not hurt in their annual evaluation for requesting help. Though my research ended before the program began, it inspires hope that the school would implement an evidence-based program that seeks to support teachers in dealing effectively with students.

Efforts to teach effective classroom management need to focus on instructional skills and behavior management as inherently linked. Almost every teacher with whom I spoke discussed how students who are engaged with class material and are "on task" (performing the appropriate schoolwork) behave better than others, and this is acknowledged by the training given to IST program case managers. Students who are uninterested or confused often misbehave in order to escape the boredom, bring positive attention to themselves, or reaffirm their identity as cool.[17] Obviously, then, teachers who can make lessons interesting, often by making the material seem relevant to the students' lives, and who can prevent large numbers of students from struggling with the material, will have fewer disruptions than others.[18]

When prevention fails and students disrupt class, it is crucial that teachers engage with the students rather than confronting them or immediately punishing them. The effective teachers I observed vary in how they do this. Several state that they ask to speak to the student outside the classroom for a moment, thus avoiding a public display. These teachers usually talk calmly to the student about what's wrong, and rely on the rapport with the student that they have already developed to calm the student down. Other effective teachers take a different approach by not reacting, thereby refusing to give attention to the misbehavior. One, for example, describes how in doing so she is usually able to extinguish behavior problems (despite having to give out a rare referral and remove a student on the day of this interview):

TEACHER: The one young man that I removed [from class] today, he's removed from every class, every day, but mine. Because he's looking for attention and I won't give it to him, the type where he's removed and he's one-on-one, you know that's just not gonna happen. There comes a point though when he disrupts the entire class, for the entire period that you have to say, "OK wait. You know, let's back up." Which is what happened today. I just don't give in, you know, I don't know how to say it . . .

INTERVIEWER: So you ignore him, or—?

TEACHER: I act appropriately. If he's trying to draw for attention, I'll say nicely, "You know, [student], could you please stop?" And he'll focus his attention on me instead of the other areas that he was. And then he'll try to get my attention which I can easily avoid, so most of the class periods, he's worried about focusing on me to get my attention and I can ignore him and he's no problem to the rest of the class. Today he just wanted everybody's attention, all period, so. He wanted out, is what he wanted. So, he got it. (I)

These approaches have important features in common. They show respect to students; they avoid escalating a problem by yelling, scolding, or getting angry at the student; and they rely on a rapport between teacher and student rather than authority alone to settle the problem.[19] It is important to talk to students about why they are misbehaving; even if the student's response is a typical adolescent "I dunno," engaging with the student in a calm, caring manner can go a long way toward building a rapport. And if the student does give a real response, the teacher has a window into solving an actual problem rather than simply exercising authority or teaching to the rules.

Certainly there will always be times when teachers—even those with the best classroom management techniques—will have to remove students from class, if the students don't respond to the teacher's attempts to settle things down. It is understandable for a teacher to remove a student who misbehaves and impedes a difficult lesson plan, especially given the current pressure on teachers to impart the knowledge that will be on standardized exams. But although teachers' time is so limited and they are under such pressure, it is important to engage with rather than dismiss even the most demanding and intractable students as an investment both in the functioning of future lesson plans and in the school climate overall. Students are removed from class far more often than necessary for minor offenses such as talking during instruction. Consider, for example, the following field note, in which a student is first kicked out of class and then sent to in-school suspension because he fell asleep in class (something that students in my classes do painfully often):

While Mr. Sussex and I were talking, an African American male student entered his office. The student said he'd been kicked out of a class. Mr. Sussex asked him what he'd done, and the student said he fell asleep. Mr. Sussex said, "Well you can go to ISS, you can probably sleep there." (FN)

Perhaps engaging with this student and requiring him to participate in class would have been more constructive than kicking him out of class.

When attempts to stem a problem fall short and students do miss class because of school punishment, it is crucial that the teacher or the school compensate for the missed time with tutoring. Students who miss class time for punishment receive no compensatory lesson, meaning that students who may be acting up because they do not understand the class material will only fall farther behind and be more of a problem when they return. Perhaps it is too much to ask already overburdened teachers to hold one-on-one tutoring sessions after school; in that case, the school could couple removals from class with mandatory group after-school sessions, whereby large numbers of students could be grouped by the subjects they miss and given at least some help with their work. Though this still would require time and effort, it is another investment that would eventually free up resources by reducing future behavior problems.

Not only would improved classroom management reduce misbehavior, but it would also reduce the flow of referrals to disciplinarians and allow them time to relate more constructively with youth. It would also mean that fewer cases result in suspension, each of which require an assistant principal's signature, thereby demanding less of the administrators' time and allowing them to work on other elements of the school. Further, if the constant stream of referrals in a school like Unionville High were reduced, it is possible that its self-image of a school in crisis would go away, which might in turn reduce the school's reliance on punishment as a way to restore order out of perceived chaos.[20]

Rule enforcement within the classroom can also be improved through greater sensitivity to social class, race/ethnicity, and gender dynamics. Some teachers I spoke to described their efforts to do just this. According to one such teacher:

You know, one-parent families, no-parent families, they're homeless, I mean I could never imagine that kids would be homeless and then going to school. You know they're living out of a car maybe or something like that. So those are the things that I don't think we, I don't think the schools, our school, and maybe a lot of schools address. You know the kids with money go to the private schools, because those parents are like, "I don't want them to deal with kids that don't have it and have all those issues," so consequently the public schools have a lot of the kids with those issues. And I don't think we do enough to handle that. Which I think causes some of the educational difficulties. . . . Yeah, the kid comes in and he's hungry or he's cold, the last thing on his mind is going to class and learning, probably. Maybe we just need to feed him. (I)

Some administrators, as well, discussed how they try to be sensitive especially to race/ethnicity, and self-aware of any unintended biases they may have. More of these efforts are needed, since both the prior research and my analyses illustrate disproportionate punishments by race/ethnicity.

My point is not that school staff should expect one group of students to misbehave more than others, or that different groups should be held to different standards. Rather, school staff need to be aware of how their disciplinary decisions may be shaped by stereotypes, such as being more likely to view minority youth as threatening or disrespectful. Greater attention to the fact that biases have been repeatedly shown to influence school punishments in schools across the United States could lead to increased self-awareness among teachers, which would, hopefully, help reduce the scope of this problem.

Assigning Punishments

Throughout my research I probably spent more time observing students receiving punishments, or "consequences" for misbehavior, than any other type of action. As I discuss throughout this book, this process revolves around teaching to the rules rather than fully listening to students or helping them with their underlying problems. This is an enormous failing of schools that needs to be fixed.

The first and most basic change to how school staff respond to student misbehavior is to listen more carefully to students. This is hard to do, and takes a great deal of effort. Students who receive referrals should be asked about what happened during the incident, how they are doing in their classes, and whether they are having any problems generally—and then the adult must listen carefully to the students' responses. Many students will of course offer excuses, justifications, and arguments of innocence; some of these are likely true, while most will be attempts to avoid punishment. The point is not to allow students a trial at which they can argue their way out of punishment, but to use punishment as an opportunity for school staff to respond to students' problems and prevent future misbehavior. These problems often hinge on personal conflict with a particular teacher, for example, and in response a dean can schedule a follow-up meeting with the teacher and the student to work out the problem. If it becomes clear that students are acting up because they do not understand class material, then they can be referred to a tutor. In response to student-student conflict, disciplinarians can schedule mediation or intervention sessions.[21] In response to chronic tardiness or absence, punishment meetings can be an opportunity to revisit the student's schedule in case it conflicts with work or family obligations; I observed this problem a number of times, especially among the large number of immigrant students at Frontera High School who worked part-time jobs. Other students might be responding to more complicated issues such as emotional problems, addiction, or physical abuse, which may be beyond the capacity of the school's disciplinarian; these students should be referred immediately to the school psychologist or other trained clinician.[22] If schools use punishment meetings as an opportunity to learn more about rather than simply punish a student, they would be able to prevent future misbehavior and better serve their students.

This issue was the focus of a July 2008 program on Philadelphia's NPR station, in reference to school security in Philadelphia public schools. One participant on the program, Karla Mota, a student at the Kensington Creative and Performance Arts School in Philadelphia, argued very eloquently for counseling and communication:

I think if a counselor comes in and talks to a student and gets down to the bottom of what really happened, maybe that will calm the student down. . . . Maybe the student just reacted to something the teacher said, and the teacher just reported it. But they didn't get down to what really happened in the classroom. . . . Sometimes teachers aggravate students, and they say stuff, like, it's happened before in the classroom, and the teachers tell the students something, and we're like, "You're a teacher, you're not supposed to address us like that." And a lot of students, like, don't have the patience, they don't think about what they're going to say, so they just react and just start talking. I think if there's a problem that deep, a counselor should come in. They should talk to the parents about what's going on at home.[23]

Her argument makes sense and is consistent with what I find in my research.

Importantly, punishment must still follow student misbehavior. As prior research has repeatedly shown, discipline is most effective when it is strict and fairly applied. Thus, listening to students and helping them should occur along with, but certainly not instead of, punishment. Moreover, by better listening to students, disciplinarians will be better able to understand what actually happened in any incident, and can punish students in a way that students will be more likely to see as fair.

When punishments are handed out to students, they need to be accompanied with an explanation for why their actions were wrong. In order to view school rules as legitimate, students need to understand why the prohibited actions are harmful to individual students, staff, or the school as a collective unit. Responding in a way that prioritizes the rules, and the rules alone, as a reason for misbehaving erodes student perceptions of legitimacy in the rules and fails to teach students important lessons about proper behavior. This suggestion echoes the parenting advice I read repeatedly in my effort to better discipline my own children, yet school disciplinarians usually fail to follow this well-rehearsed counsel.

Punishment meetings are also opportunities to deal more effectively with chronic behavior problems (the "frequent flyers," as staff at Unionville High call them). The fact that a student repeatedly receives referrals ought to be a clue that the school's standard punishment routine is not working. In response, students might receive a behavioral contract, which usually just means the standard approach to discipline is followed more rigorously and with escalated punishments—in other words, more of the same. These students require a different approach, something other than the portfolio that includes detention, in-school suspension, or out-of-school suspension, and something that keeps them in school rather than sending them to alternative learning environments. One option is to require that students who receive a certain number of referrals must see the school psychologist about their behavior. Though not every chronically misbehaving student will have problems that require a psychologist, many will. Moreover, this strategy would at least provide an opportunity for someone outside the school discipline team to learn about the student and respond to his or her reasons for misbehaving. I saw almost no link between the discipline and counseling staffs at the four high schools I observed, which needs to be changed in order to improve school discipline.

By improving their listening skills and better engaging with students' problems, school disciplinarians can reduce misbehavior both directly, by solving some problems, and indirectly, by improving students' perceptions of fairness and legitimacy of school authority. Yet this level of engagement carries risk as well, since disciplinarians must be careful to not alienate the teachers or others who write the referrals and send youth into these meetings. Though (as I state above) the point of listening to students is not to allow them a platform for presenting their innocence, there certainly are cases where students are wrongfully punished; by spending more time talking to students, disciplinarians would uncover more such cases. Since it would be unfair to punish students when it is clear that teachers have overreacted or made a mistake, disciplinarians should undo these mistakes. Doing this without upsetting teachers or making them feel unsupported is very difficult yet important, since teachers who do not feel supported in their efforts to discipline students will be less consistent and thorough with their discipline in the future.[24] Thus, schools face a serious challenge—to meet this challenge school administrators must hold teachers accountable when they make mistakes, encourage and reward fair and effective punishment practices, and provide resources to teachers to learn the difference between the two. The classroom management workshops I suggest above are one example of how administrators can negotiate this difficulty.

Security Personnel

Given that one of the most visible and striking features of contemporary school security is the presence of school resource officers, it is worth discussing what security personnel would be best able to maintain school safety and help students. The benefits of having officers in school are unclear. Prior research does not clearly show that their presence decreases crime in school, and there are a number of problems that can result from their presence: erosion of students' rights, escalation of punishments, growing surveillance over students and communities, redefinition of behavior problems as criminal problems, and the socialization of students to expect a law enforcement presence in their lives. But, as I discuss in chapter 3, one cannot ignore the fact that officers make students and school staff feel safer, and that it is always helpful to have additional role models available to youth.

I believe that few schools—only those with documented and serious crime problems—should have full-time officers. All other schools should have tight links to police departments through police liaisons. These liaisons would visit the school regularly and be familiar with its layout, students, and administration. This would allow school administrators the ability to consult easily with an officer and benefit from a quick response to a crisis. Schools should also continue with the practice of including a nonschool employee in the school community to whom students can confide. Yet police officers are poorly suited for this role, despite the good intentions among all the officers I observed. Instead, adolescent counselors who spend their days interacting with youth (not scheduling classes) would be better trained as counselors and could ensure confidentiality to students who open up to them. Having non-police as counselors, along with police liaisons who visit the school regularly but are not there full-time, would accomplish much of the benefits of the school resource officer program but without its harmful consequences.

For those rare unfortunate schools that do have problems with crime that necessitate police presence, changes to the school resource officer model are necessary. There must be greater training given to officers about how to interact with youth in ways that de-escalate problems rather than provoke further conflict. Officers should be encouraged to use arrest only as a last resort, when the law or school safety necessitates it, out of recognition that students should learn from their mistakes in ways that preserve their future life chances. Though officers work for the police, not the school, the school principal must be in contact with the officer's supervisor and must have some formal influence over how the officer does his or her job. Further, greater incentives should be offered to police who want to be SROs, such as additional vacation time when school is not in session, to ensure a competitive process in selecting officers for the position, with those who make this decision weighing both police skills and the ability to interact with children.

I also see little benefit to having security guards unless a school has a proven security problem. Recall that neither mid-Atlantic school has security guards, suggesting that they are not necessary even in schools that generate large numbers of referrals for misbehavior (such as Unionville High). That said, the open courtyard setting of both southwestern schools would make life difficult without guards, since there are too many areas on campus that require supervision. But aside from dealing with the difficulties imposed by such a campus layout, deans, interventionists, or assistant principals are perfectly capable of retrieving students for punishment meetings—especially if the number of referrals is reduced through improved classroom management.

As far as who should be assigning the consequences in response to referrals, each of the methods I observed appears to work, including a single dean at Frontera High, multiple deans at Unionville High, assistant principals at Fairway Estates High, and interventionists at Centerville High. My discussion above about necessary improvements in how these disciplinarians assign punishments is about what they do, not who is doing it. My one suggestion regarding disciplinarian personnel is that whoever has this job should have at least some training in adolescent development. Hiring individuals for their coaching expertise and giving them disciplinary responsibilities is unacceptable unless they receive extensive training both on why adolescents misbehave and on evidence-based ways to respond.

Surveillance Technologies

Surveillance technologies such as cameras, metal detectors, and drug-sniffing dogs are another important part of contemporary school security. Of these, the only one I observed was security cameras, which are used in each school except for Fairway Estates High, though the camera system at Frontera High is antiquated and barely functional. Although the systems at both Centerville High and Unionville High are technologically advanced, allowing users to access video images from their computers, the cameras are not commonly used in rule enforcement. I did observe some instances where disciplinarians used the camera systems to investigate an incident after the fact, and in these cases the cameras were clearly helpful. But since nobody regularly monitors the cameras they offer no opportunity to stop an incident in progress, and their inevitably limited coverage means that many incidents occurred in the cameras' blind spots—especially the classrooms, where most misbehavior occurs. Thus, they offer only limited help in the discipline process.[25]

Further, surveillance technologies come with social costs that offset this limited help. Video cameras and other surveillance devices facilitate schools' growing connections to criminal justice agencies, which can lead to students' unnecessary arrest and exclusion from school for minor offenses. Moreover, these technologies can create a climate of distrust and fear, since they send the message that students are not trusted or that there is something to fear within the school's halls.[26] Consider, for example, drug-sniffing dogs pulling police officers through hallways as they search students' lockers and students' bodies—practices like this are disturbing because they treat children like criminals and expose them to police-state tactics. In some ways metal detectors are even worse, since they can create long lines at front doors, causing students to miss instructional time, and can result in degrading and offensive treatment.[27] Again I argue that unless a school is responding to documented high crime rates within its walls, practices like these are unnecessary, of little benefit, and potentially harmful. Given how expensive surveillance technologies are, the funds used to purchase them could be more effectively used by financially strapped public schools.

Contrary to what one might expect, Columbine High School, the site of the most deadly and best-known high school shooting, is an example of a school that has sought to engage with students rather than implement security technology like metal detectors.[28] Dennis Barnebey, an education specialist at PCCY (Public Citizens for Children and Youth), and a Philadelphia public school teacher for thirty-two years, talked about what he learned of Columbine High:

The story that I often tell is meeting some students who actually went to Columbine High School. And they were in Philadelphia for the summer and they visited schools, and they saw these metal detectors, and they were shocked. And they said, "Why do you have to go through metal detectors?" And everybody said, "Well, don't you have to? You go to Columbine High School, where the shootings, the worst shootings in the country took place." They said, "No, we don't have metal detectors." And I was stunned, and I actually called a counselor at Columbine, just to talk with them about, "Well, what did you do?" And they said, "Well, we talked about it, and we decided we didn't want to create a jail-like atmosphere at the school." "Well, what did you do?" "We created, we hired lots of counselors to talk to kids. We hired and we created programs . . . where kids can talk to kids, and really create a basis for creating a small community." And the difference between how Columbine chose to deal with these kids and how [Philadelphia schools] chose to deal with these kids is stark. . . . I mean, it's, whether metal detectors are essential is always going to be a conversation, I'm sure. But it's the impact of how we respond when there's a problem. And I think that's what's important—let's get at what's affecting kids' behaviors.

It is very encouraging to hear this account of affairs at Columbine High, the site where such a horrible tragedy took place; despite the fears that must remain there, school officials chose to invest in student relations rather than surveillance.

One Step Forward, Two Steps Back?

The suggestions I list above would, hopefully, have several benefits, including: helping students learn how to solve their problems, strengthening their bonds to the school community, increasing their perceptions of legitimacy of the school's authority, and directing them to people who can help them with academic and emotional problems. Each of these, in turn, would likely lead to decreases in misbehavior and delinquency at school—at least this is what the prior research leads us to assume. But there are problems with these strategies as well. One is that they run the risk of implementing a hidden but coercive form of self-discipline that maintains students' powerlessness while appearing to do otherwise.

This issue is addressed in the work of postmodern scholars such as Nikolas Rose, who point to how state power is exercised not just *on* individuals, but *through* them, as individuals police themselves.[29] In contemporary society individual citizens assume growing responsibility for their own security, income, and other needs, while the government sheds the duties to its citizens that were assumed under a New Deal style of governance. As individuals are expected to provide for themselves needs that they often have no way of attaining by themselves (e.g., job security), corporations, other large institutions, and the government gain power and freedom, since they no longer face the burden of providing for individuals, nor do they receive blame when they fail to do so. I raise this here because my suggestions above somewhat resemble this pattern; by entreating schools to enlist students as partners in the discipline process, not just passive subjects, responsibility for discipline is partially transferred to students who participate in disciplining themselves.[30] For example school staff who enforce rigid rules that were approved by a student body have "cover" to act unfairly, since they can claim the students had a hand in creating the rules. In this way, schools may shed some of their responsibility to ensure that students are treated fairly, since more responsibility will be assumed by students themselves, all while meeting the school's disciplinary goals.

Though the likelihood of self-discipline is very real, there is room for both student involvement and real empowerment; student participation in governance does not necessarily mean that they become parties to their own subordination. Many of the school's goals are shared by the students, since both want an orderly, safe, and high-performing school. They may differ on how to achieve these goals, who should have power, and who bears responsibility for failing to meet these goals, but there is no reason that at least some of these topics cannot be open for discussion. If students become involved in school governance in ways that respect their autonomy, their opinions, and their preferences, rather than as mouthpieces of school administrators, then these changes can be empowering. For example, if students are able to voice their concerns and complaints without fear of reprisal and in a way that they find inviting—perhaps using technologies such as cell phones or an anonymous complaint field on a website—then they may participate in school governance in an open manner. These interactions must occur within boundaries that respect the school's authority, but they can be pitched in a way that allows students to offer their unique perspective to the discussion about school rules, thereby improving how the school's authority is exercised. Additionally, discussions about school discipline must not be constrained to talking about individuals' behaviors, since such a micro-view usually means that authoritarian systems remain unquestioned. Instead, students must be able to discuss the school's power structure, policies, and institutional practices, and they should be encouraged to think critically about such issues rather than accepting them unquestioningly. Such participation would help build collaborative school climates that are perceived to be fair, even if it occurs within boundaries that maintain the school's authority.

Another potential problem is that by encouraging schools to investigate students' emotional and behavioral problems and to engage more (and earlier) with parents, my suggestions risk increasing the school's reach into students' private lives. Students have a right to privacy and may not wish to share their problems with a school disciplinarian. More important, an investigation of a student's personal life may shed light on negative information that puts the student at a disadvantage. One can imagine, for example, a disciplinarian treating a student more harshly after learning about an older sibling's criminal history, since the disciplinarian may come to expect similar behavior from the current student. This would be unfair, but it is a reasonable expectation if schools begin to engage more with students by talking to them about their personal problems. There is a clear precedent for this type of control; several historians of early American education accuse early schools of a similar invasiveness, as educational reformers sought to use schools as a platform for teaching middle-class "American" norms to entire families of immigrant and lower-class children.[31]

There is no doubt that my suggestions entail such a risk of invasiveness. Yet investigating real reasons for student misbehavior also represents the best chance of helping youth. When sensitive information arises, school staff must remember their mission to help the student rather than only to punish. To help prevent against overly invasive scrutiny into students' private lives, students need to be aware of their rights to privacy and encouraged to invoke these rights when appropriate. Counselors, not just disciplinarians, must be used when sensitive problems arise, and the counselors must respect confidentiality of student information. Hiring nonschool employee counselors instead of police officers would help a great deal because it would mean students can talk to an adult in the school who is not under the control of the administration and who can respect students' confidentiality. By being aware of these potential problems, schools can improve the effectiveness and fairness of discipline while also limiting the risk of invoking new forms of discipline that are more invasive and self-driven.

Finally, my suggestions also risk masking structural problems by making them appear to be individualized ones. In *Bad Boys*, Ann Ferguson offers this criticism of counseling as a response to violation of school rules, since it assumes the student has a pathological personality rather than considering the impact of the student's environment.[32] For example, a student who comes to school and mirrors patterns of dress and language learned in his or her neighborhood might be in violation of the school's code of conduct; punishing the student as if he or she freely chose to violate rules (rather than choosing an equally accessible conformist option) ignores how the student's behavior and dress are shaped by his or her environment. This individualization of the problem fails to address the conflict between expectations in one's community and at school that many students face and that causes great stress.[33] This potential pitfall is absolutely true, and by advocating for greater involvement of counselors in the discipline process my suggestions might exacerbate the problem. Yet I have also suggested that students have an opportunity to participate in the rule-making process, during which neighborhood-school conflicts and unfair expectations might surface and be resolved. And, if schools can be more sensitive to race/ethnicity-, class-, and gender-based stereotypes, environmental problems like the ones Ferguson observes are less likely to arise.

Conclusion

I began studying school discipline and security because I found it to be an interesting extension of my prior research on punishing youth in juvenile and adult courts. But the further involved I became in this research, the more I realized that this isn't just an issue that interests me as someone who is fascinated by efforts to prevent and respond to youths' misbehaviors—it is also an issue in which I have a personal interest as a parent, citizen, and former adolescent. I care deeply about the schools where I will someday send my children and about the future citizens that schools produce.

Almost everyone I met during the course of my research convinced me that they care as well. Though there are substantial problems with contemporary school punishment and security, these are not because of a lack of caring among school staff. In some ways, part of the problem is that school staff care too much, that they are too invested in a faulty strategy of prioritizing rules and consequences over youth, their behaviors, and evidence-based practices.

Though Gerald Grant's aforementioned study was based on a school with a very different problem—there was too little discipline, too little rule enforcement, and too much student empowerment—in many ways my suggestions mirror those made by Grant. He argues that we need to create a *positive ethos* in schools: a climate in which students are taught to care for one another and for their community, where they are taught both moral and intellectual virtue.[34] My research a generation later finds that schools with too many rules that are too rigid and prescribe too harsh punishments suffer a similar problem—the difficulties I describe through this book impede the ability to create a positive ethos. Rules and punishments ought to be more fair, more democratic, and more attuned to solving students' problems.

Granted, my evidence in making this argument is based on only four public high schools, and thus I cannot claim that the argument applies to all schools in the United States. Yet the fact that these schools, located in far-separated regions and with very different student bodies, act so similarly suggests that there are substantial commonalities across schools. The similarities between what I find in my research and what others have written about adds to my confidence that these patterns describe public high schools generally.[35] In addition, I find that schools that try to work around the pitfalls of contemporary punishment and security have a hard time doing so because of the overall climate in which they operate, which also suggests that these patterns are widespread and based on systemic issues in how schools are organized.[36]

Not only have our public high schools eschewed evidence-based strategies for reducing school misbehavior, but they have spent a great deal of time and money pursuing punishment and security practices that have shown little success. These practices include police in schools, zero-tolerance policies, increased punishment for minor school infractions, greater reliance on school exclusion, and surveillance technologies. Because they focus on these practices and on making rules and rule enforcement so central to the school's mode of operation, schools fail to address—and often compound—students' underlying problems; they exacerbate existing social inequalities, especially racial/ethnic and class inequalities; and they teach students to uncritically accept power and authority.

EPILOGUE

I collected the data described throughout this book from 2005–2007. Since then (as of December 2009), I have become somewhat optimistic that the conditions of school discipline may be improving.

Though I have not had much contact with staff at the southwestern schools, I have been in touch with some of my contacts at the midatlantic schools, Unionville High and Centerville High. In particular, I have spoken several times with the police officer at Centerville High. Recently he described to me how arrests there have decreased substantially since the year I observed him (2006-2007). He noted that during his first year there – the year I observed him—he wanted to "send a message" by arresting all youth involved in a fight, regardless of who instigated it; but now he no longer does. He also talked about how he directs youth toward counseling services rather than treating students' problems only as criminal justice issues, a subject I rarely heard him discuss during my research.

I also received a positive update from Principal Howley at Unionville High. As I describe in the preceding chapters, I observed discipline at Unionville High soon after Principal Howley there, and it was clear that he was trying to "right the ship" by instilling firm discipline in a chaotic environment. When last I heard from him, in spring of 2009, he indicated that referrals had dropped significantly, largely due to a more stable environment. He wrote: "The consistency of the team, both administration and deans, has gone a long way in cleaning things up here."

I see encouraging signs beyond these schools as well. I recently had the opportunity to participate in a task force group organized by a Delaware state legislator to make suggested revisions to state laws regarding school punishments. The task force consists of a wide variety of stakeholders who one would expect to hold very different views: state legislators, school district superintendents, state police officers, members of the attorney general's office, defense attorneys, juvenile and family rights activists, academics, representatives from the state civil liberties union, and juvenile justice system reform advocates. Yet the participants all seem to be on the same page in wanting to improve school discipline. At the most recent meeting, participants discussed ideas such as: reducing zero-tolerance laws, increasing school-based mentoring programs, improving teachers' classroom management skills, mandatory counseling sessions for youth who receive disciplinary referrals, and adding counselors to schools. One participant talked about the need to implement positive behavioral support programs in such a way that staff receive substantial training—this participant talked about the need to change the school culture so that the program is properly administered. Others discussed the need for more "evidence-based" programs that use documented "best practices."

These proposals are entirely consistent with the deficiencies I found throughout my research, and with my policy suggestions in the conclusion. I was delighted to hear and participate in the discussion. Moreover, I am surprised to hear such consistent views from such different stakeholders—the fact that the head of the state's civil liberties union and representatives of the state's attorney general's office are in accord speaks volumes about the widespread currency of these ideas, since prosecutors and civil rights advocates rarely seem to agree.

I am also hopeful that some of these ideas may come to fruition, since the hazards of zero tolerance policies were recently exposed in Delaware. Soon after this task force was formed a six-year-old in Delaware named Zachary Christie made national news for his suspension from school. Zachary had brought to school his cub scout fork/spoon/knife tool, and was removed from the school under the district's zero tolerance weapons policy. By rule, he had to attend an alternative school for 45 days before he could be readmitted to his first grade class. His mother alerted the media, and within days his case was national news – he even appeared on the Today show.[1] In response to public outcry (over 29,000 people signed an online petition to reverse his punishment), the school board unanimously agreed to revise its rule; by the revision, kindergartners and first-graders who bring a knife shorter than three inches long face only a three to five day suspension rather than a longer stay at an alternative school.[2] The case was embarrassing for the district and the entire state, and vividly illustrated how absurd zero tolerance rules and overreactive school discipline can be. Now seems to be perfect timing for revised legislation in Delaware.

Yet there are reasons for my optimism to be tempered. It is hard to imagine that any new programs will be implemented or new counselors hired in the current economic climate, in which schools have been forced to make major budget cuts. And though the public was outraged at the longterm suspension of a white middle-class six year old, that does not necessarily mean that policies directed at reforming how we punish older youth (who are more likely to be racial/ethnic minorities) will be as popular. Thus it is uncertain how much of what the task force recommends will become law.

Furthermore, even if new laws are enacted which seek to reduce punishments and instead respond to youths' problems, I am cynical about how well schools will be able to enact these policies. Recall in chapter four how I discuss schools' and individuals' efforts to avoid teaching to the rules – these tend to fail because they run contrary to the overall disciplinary climate. New policies will only succeed if the entire school staff "buys in" – if they begin to view students and student misbehavior in a different light, and approach security and discipline from a completely different perspective. This would be very difficult, given that problems with school discipline stem from the difficulties of dealing with unruly youth in an insecure, under-funded institution, but it is certainly possible.

Thus there are encouraging developments, both in my research sites and on the legislative arena in my home state. But one can also find signs that things are getting even worse. For example, a middle-school in Chicago recently had twenty-five students, ages 11 to 15, arrested for a food fight.[3] Hopefully, as events like Zachary Christie's punishment or the food fight arrests continue, citizens will become increasingly frustrated and provoke real change.

APPENDIX

Research Methods and Analysis

The original research described in the preceding chapters took place in four schools—two in a southwestern state and two in a mid-Atlantic state—and includes interviews, observations of schools, and surveys. I then supplemented these data with data from the Federal Department of Education's National Center for Education Statistics and the University of Delaware's Center for Drug and Alcohol Studies.

My selection of school sites proceeded in several stages. First, I chose four appropriate districts and schools based on student demographics within each of the two states: two districts/schools housing mostly middle-class white youth and two with mostly lower-income youth of color. Second, I leveraged professional contacts in an attempt to gain access to one of each of the selected districts and schools. Since I needed to secure the approval first of each school district and then of each principal, it helped when I was able to have a colleague who could introduce me to a member of the district or school community. Despite these efforts, however, I was denied access to research in one selected district in each state. I then proceeded to the second (equally appropriate, demographically) choice for each state; in both cases access was then granted.

Once I obtained permission from each school district and school principal, I then visited each school, accompanied by a graduate student research assistant. During this initial visit we met the school principal and assistant principals, toured each school, and obtained a primary contact to help with our initial visits (a dean of discipline at Frontera High and Unionville High, a "team leader" at Fairway Estates High, and an interventionist at Centerville High). For our first several visits we would find the contact and trail him or her; the contact then introduced us to other school staff, whom we could then trail and observe on subsequent visits. After several visits, we were able to meet and eventually observe all personnel involved in punishing students at each school.

Each research assistant had prior training and experience in qualitative data collection. Before entering each site, the research assistants and I discussed the theoretical issues being considered (e.g., governing through crime, cultural reproduction) and the particular technologies in which I was most concerned (e.g., student-disciplinarian interactions, the manner in which rules are enforced, etc.). I accompanied each research assistant on the first few site visits; after each visit we would compare field notes and discuss what we observed and how these observations should be recorded. This process led to a consistent format and tone of field notes, and helped established reliability in our data. I also read each field note carefully and met regularly with each research assistant to discuss the process of data collection.

Olivia Salcido, a graduate student at Arizona State University, and I collected data in the southwestern schools throughout the 2005–2006 school year, beginning at Frontera High and soon proceeding to Fairway Estates High, so that we were studying both schools simultaneously for most of the time. Olivia continued this research in the fall of 2006. Nicole Bracy, a graduate student at the University of Delaware, and I mimicked this procedure in the mid-Atlantic schools during the 2006–2007 school year; we began at Centerville High and then continued with Unionville High. For the first three months at each school we trailed school staff and observed interactions with students. We would shadow an administrator, police officer, security guard, or dean of discipline, sit in on classrooms, or observe common areas (e.g., cafeterias, hallways). We noted interactions between adults and students, particularly in response to perceived misbehavior among students. The majority of the interactions we observed were casual conversations in the hallways or classrooms, since this is the most common type of student-staff interaction. We observed hundreds of meetings between students who were given a referral (i.e., removed from class and sent "to the office") and were sent to either their dean of discipline, interventionist, or assistant principal (whoever handles referrals at each school), and we also observed arrests on campus and expulsion hearings (though these are far less common). Though I refer to what "I" observed throughout this book, the data collection was truly a team effort.

We logged at least one hundred hours of observational time at each school, with visits lasting two to three hours on average. We wrote field notes immediately upon leaving each research site, rather than in the field, so as to limit an observation/reaction bias. We would then revise these notes after several hours or the next day, adding any details that we remembered at that point. Because we kept our visits relatively short rather than observing entire days, we were able to recall our observations in detail (after experimenting, we found that two to three hours was the maximum amount of time in the field we could recall with confidence).

After we had established a rapport with the school staff responsible for handing out school punishments and after we had a good sense of how school discipline and security works at each school (two to three months at each school), we began collecting data through interviews as well. We conducted a total of 105 semi-structured interviews across the four sites (at least 26 at each), with each interview taking between twenty minutes and almost two hours (most interviews lasted about forty-five minutes). We interviewed a variety of individuals, including school administrators and (nonpolice) security (n = 31), teachers (n = 16), police officers (n = 4; one in each school), students (n = 43), and parents (n = 11). Ten of these interviews, all with students or parents, were conducted in Spanish by Ms. Salcido. School security and administration respondents were selected based on a purposive sample, whereby we interviewed the individuals most involved with discipline; for teachers, students, and parents, we used snowball sampling to collect a sampling frame, and then selectively invited participants so as to maintain a sample that included whites and racial/ethnic minorities as well as males and females. Interviews were digitally recorded and sent to a professional transcriber (except for the Spanish interviews, which Ms. Salcido transcribed). The interview guide varied depending on the role of the respondent, though each sought to acquire an understanding of the respondent's views of the school rules and punishments, his or her experiences with school discipline, and his or her perceptions of school violence and appropriate responses to it. In each interview we began with this guide and probed to explore relevant themes as necessary.

All data from both interviews and observations were coded and analyzed in Atlas.ti 5.2 to search for patterns and themes that helped us understand how school discipline takes shape in and across schools. Analyses were guided by three goals: (1) developing a general understanding of common patterns in rule enforcement at each school (i.e., how each school punishes students), (2) carefully considering differences across schools in these patterns, and (3) a grounded theory approach whereby data were coded for any unexpected processes or themes that could further contextualize school discipline.

We also collected survey data in each school. All juniors present at school on a predetermined day at each school were given a brief, anonymous, closed-ended written survey to complete. At Frontera High surveys were distributed during a required history course on November 28, 2006; at Fairway Estates High they were distributed during homerooms from November 29 to December 1, 2006; at Centerville High they were distributed on February 13 and March 5, 2007; and at Unionville High they were distributed on February 15 and March 1, 2007.[1] Questions on the survey asked about demographic information, school involvement, perceptions of school rules and punishments, students' experiences being punished at school, and (if they had such experiences) their perceptions of the fairness of these incidents. Several questions were modeled after questions on the School Crime Supplement to the National Crime Victimization Survey, collected by the U.S. Department of Justice and distributed by the National Center for Education Statistics. An early draft of the survey was piloted by distributing it to two classrooms at a separate high school in the southwestern state. Students in these two classes took the survey and then participated in focus group sessions where they reflected on the clarity and quality of the questions.

I supplemented these survey data from the mid-Atlantic state by collaborating with researchers at the University of Delaware Center for Drug and Alcohol Studies (CDAS). The CDAS conducts an annual survey of risky behavior for all juniors in public high schools in the state. My questions were included with this survey, and the CDAS allowed me access to students' responses to other questions as well. This was most helpful because it allowed me to include data I had not collected through my questions, particularly questions about students' experiences with alcohol and drugs, as well as their self-reported delinquent activity.

I also used data collected by the National Center for Education Statistics, a branch of the federal Department of Education, through their School Survey on Crime and Safety (SSOCS). This is a survey distributed to approximately three thousand randomly sampled elementary and secondary schools across the United States.[2] Principals or appropriate substitutes respond to the survey by anonymously providing information about misbehavior and crimes at school, schools' security efforts, and responses to student misbehavior. Appendix table 1, which uses these data to show the prominence of school security measures in high schools in 2003–2004 and how they vary along

APPENDIX TABLE I

Percentage of Public High Schools That Used Selected Safety and Security Measures, by School Characteristics: 2003–2004

	Limited access during school hours		Visitor requirements		Required to wear badges or picture IDs		Metal detector checks on students		Sweeps and technology			Clear or no book bags
	To buildings	To grounds	Sign-in/check-in	Metal detector	Students	Faculty/staff	Random checks[a]	Daily use	Random drug-sniffing dogs[a]	Random contraband sweeps[a,b]	Security cameras[a]	
Total	83	36.2	98.3	0.9	6.4	48	5.6	1.1	21.3	12.8	36	6.2
Percent minority enrollment[c]												
< 5%	81.6	22.4	96.1	‡	1	35.7	1.5	‡	28.5	11.3	36	4.2
5–20 %	84.6	30.2	98.5	‡	4.1	50.4	1.9	‡	23.6	9.8	36.9	4.7
20–50 %	83.1	39.3	98.4	‡	6.8	53.8	4.8	0.2	22.2	13.8	35.3	7.2
> 50 %	82.2	48.9	99.6	2.7	11.8	48.8	11.9	2.7	13.5	14.7	33.8	6.9
Percent eligible for free or reduced-price lunch												
0–20 %	88.6	30.9	97.2	‡	4	54.1	1.8	‡	18.7	8	39.3	4.1
21–50 %	81.8	29.3	98.1	0.3	4.9	46.1	3.7	0.7	28.7	13.8	35.3	5.1
> 50 %	80.7	45.2	99.1	1.9	9	46.1	9.3	1.8	16.3	14.8	34.8	8.3

‡ Reporting standards not met.
a One or more.
b For example, drugs or weapons. Does not include dog sniffs.
c These estimates exclude data from Tennessee because schools in this state did not report estimates of students by race/ethnicity.

racial and social class lines, is a reproduction of table 19.1 in the *Indicators of School Crime and Safety, 2006.*[3]

Although the data in this series are collected with federal tax dollars and are intended for public consumption, only a redacted version of the data is available to the public. Important variables such as the percentage of the student body who are racial/ethnic minorities or who receive free or reduced lunch are withheld from this publicly accessible data. These findings are restricted so that nobody can identify individual schools, despite the fact that it seems incredibly unlikely that anybody would be able to identify a particular school (out of a population of approximately eighty thousand) based on the available indicators. Nevertheless, I applied for a restricted-use data license so as to analyze the complete data set. After reapplying twice, obtaining the signature from my university's associate provost who supervises university research, and securing a dedicated, stand-alone computer for the data analysis (requirements included no Internet connection, password protection after five minutes of inactivity, and a warning posted on the computer monitor), my application was approved and I was sent these data.

I used them to analyze how different security practices are distributed across schools. With the help of another graduate research assistant at the University of Delaware, Megan Denver, I performed logistic regression analyses using only public high schools included in the SSOCS. The analyses were performed in SPSS 15.0. I performed a series of logistic regression models that consider whether a variety of potentially important variables (crime and disorder, parental involvement, school size and location, and student body characteristics) are related to a school using any of a number of security practices: security cameras, locked gates around the school, metal detectors, drug-sniffing dogs, any law enforcement officer or security guard, any armed guard or officer, and any full-time law enforcement officer. Appendix table 2 reports the full results for these logistic regression models; the table includes Exp(B) coefficients, which indicate the change in odds of a school using each security practice, associated with an increase in one of each independent variable, while controlling for all other independent variables.

Overall, the results in this table suggest that the level of violence and disorder at schools is unrelated to whether schools use any of the above policies. I include seven variables to measure a variety of students' misbehaviors: violent crimes, thefts, weapons offenses, alcohol use, vandalism, threats, and a "disorder scale."[4] These variables show almost no statistically significant relation-ship with the security measures: of the forty-nine opportunities for any of these seven variables to predict any of the seven security measures, there are only three statistically significant relationships—this is about what one would expect by chance alone even if there were no real relationship between the variables.[5] Yet even if one does assume that the relationships between misbe-havior and security mechanisms are valid, this effect is most pronounced for the disorder scale (which includes student verbal abuse of teachers, student disorder in classrooms, student acts of disrespect, and student gang activities), not violence, property crime, or other offenses. Looking at this cynically, one could argue that there is no evidence of a relationship between student mis-behavior and school security; if one were more confident in the results, she could argue that minor acts such as disrespect, acting up in classrooms, and perceived gang affiliation (but not gang violence, which would be included in the violence variable) are related to security—but there is no evidence that schools with greater violence, theft, vandalism, alcohol, or other serious mis-behavior problems are more likely to use security mechanisms such as drug-sniffing dogs or law enforcement officers.

We do, however, see that larger schools are more likely to have locked gates, some form of law enforcement or security, or a full-time law enforce-ment officer, and that city schools are more likely to have some form law enforcement or security guard than other schools. The most consistent and robust results have to do with school region: schools in the South are much more likely than schools in the Northeast (the comparison in these models) to have random dog searches or any type of guard or law enforcement offi-cer. We also see some important results regarding race/ethnicity and poverty. Schools with larger proportions of racial/ethnic minority students are more likely to have locked gates and metal detectors, but less likely to use random dog searches or have any armed guard. Schools with more students receiving free or reduced lunch are more likely to have locked gates, metal detectors, or random dog searches. This is the case even while statistically controlling for students' rates of misbehavior and crime in school.

These results suggest a few things to keep in mind as we consider school discipline and security. One is that it is very common for schools to have a school resource officer, armed guard, or other law enforcement officer on campus. A second is that student crime and disorder are, at best, very tenu-

APPENDIX TABLE 2

Logistic Regression of School Security Practices on School and Student Characteristics (Exp[B])

	Surveillance cameras	Locked gates	Metal detectors	Random dog searches	Any law enforcement or security guard	Any armed guards	Full-time law enforcement officer
Region (compared to Northeast):							
Midwest	0.92	1.24	1.28	3.48 ***	1.17	1.90	1.03
South	1.39	1.80 *	1.93	8.55 ***	2.17 *	6.70 ***	3.49 ***
West	0.50 **	1.56	0.08 ***	1.73 *	1.46	1.96	1.12
Student population (in 100s)	1.02	1.05 ***	1.04	1.02	1.20 ***	1.03	1.10 ***
Crime near school	0.90	0.99	1.20	0.75	2.08	0.85	0.85
Area (compared to urban):							
Urban fringe	0.81	1.48	0.55	1.36	0.24 *	0.64	0.61
Town	0.93	0.81	0.76	1.67	0.18 **	0.72	0.39 *
Rural	0.64	1.21	0.77	1.22	0.13 **	0.82	0.42 *
Parental involvement	0.84	1.09	0.74	1.06	1.07	0.89	0.93
Crimes and misbehavior at school:							
Disorder	1.01	1.09	1.06	1.24	1.87 **	1.21	1.04
Violence	1.01 *	1.00	1.01	1.00	1.01	1.01	1.00
Thefts	0.99	0.99	0.99	1.00	1.01	1.00	1.00
Weapons	1.01	1.05	0.99	0.97	1.07	1.01	1.00

	Surveillance cameras	Locked gates	Metal detectors	Random dog searches	Any law enforcement or security guard	Any armed guards	Full-time law enforcement officer
Crimes and misbehavior at school (*continued*):							
Alcohol	1.00	1.00	1.00	1.00	0.99	0.99	1.01
Vandalism	1.00	1.01	0.98	1.01	0.95 **	0.99	1.00
Threats	1.00	1.00	1.00	1.00	1.00	1.01	1.01
Student characteristics:							
Attendance	0.98	1.01	0.92 **	1.05 *	0.94	1.04	0.98
% ESL	0.98 *	1.01	0.99	1.00	1.04	1.02	0.98
% Special education	0.99	0.99	0.99	0.98	1.00	0.98	0.97
% Low stand. test scores	0.99	0.99	0.99	1.00	1.01	0.99	1.00
% College-bound	0.99	1.00	1.00	0.99	1.00	1.01	1.00
% Academics important	1.00	1.01	0.99	0.99	1.00	0.99	1.00
% Racial/ethnic minority	0.99	1.01 **	1.02 **	0.97 ***	1.00	0.98 **	1.00
% Free/reduced lunch	1.00	1.01 *	1.02 *	1.02 **	1.00	1.02	1.01
Constant	32.86	0.03 *	188.62	0.01	35.98	0.10	13.96
-2 log-likelihood	1141.57 ***	1079.93 ***	482.95	1008.37 ***	623.26 ***	470.30	660.45 ***

* p < .05; ** p < .01; *** p < .001.

ously related to the likelihood that schools rely on specific security practices. A third is that region of the country, race/ethnicity of the student body, and social class of the student body are the best predictors of a school's security measures. Rather than the most violent or disorder-plagued schools using the most invasive security practices, it is southern schools and schools with more poor students that do so.

Importantly, since these data were all collected at the same time, we cannot infer any causality from them; for example, if the two are related we cannot determine whether the level of violence shapes school policies or vice versa. Rather, I use these analyses to explore how these different security measures are distributed across schools.

I also report abbreviated results of data analysis in chapter 5, where I predict the likelihood of individual students within the mid-Atlantic state getting into trouble at school. Appendix table 3 displays the full results for these analyses, a series of logistic regression models performed in Stata SE 9.0. The dependent variable in each model is whether the student reported having been in trouble in the past school year. Independent variables include demographics (sex, race/ethnicity), the student's report on what grades he or she usually receives (coded 1 = mostly Fs, 2 = mostly Ds, 3 = mostly Cs, 4 = mostly Bs, 5 = mostly As), whether the student states that he or she intends to go to college, the number of extracurricular activities he or she is involved in, parental involvement (how often the parents contact the school, and how often parents help with homework), and misbehavior (whether the student reports ever having been arrested, a general delinquency scale,[6] and how often the student reports to skip classes [from 1 = never to 6 = almost every day]). I also include a dummy variable for Centerville High to control for differences between schools. These models include a robust standard error to account for similarities among students within each school.

Like before, I am also limited in inferring causal direction with these analyses. For example, it is unclear whether students who get bad grades get punished because poor-performing students are targeted, or whether students who are punished in school subsequently receive worse grades. Both are likely to occur at the same time. Due to my focus on the outcome of school discipline rather than academic performance, I discuss the former in chapter 5. Future analysis should reconsider this issue using longitudinal data in order to better understand the temporal order behind the sequence of these events.

Logistic Regression of Self-Reported Trouble (Exp[B])

	Model 1	Model 2: Adding Delinquency Variables	Model 3: Adding Grades
Female	0.66 *	0.77	0.8
Race/ethnicity (contrast = white):			
African American	1.68 *	1.74 *	1.58
Latino	1.12	1.28	1.19
Other race/ethnicity	0.97	1.13	1.14
College ambition	0.6 *	0.66	0.77
# extracurricular activities	0.83 *	0.85 *	0.88
Parental contact	0.67 **	0.71 **	0.72 **
Parental help	1.3 **	1.28 *	1.24 *
Centerville High	0.79	0.74	0.69
Ever arrested		0.98	0.95
Delinquency scale		1.75 **	1.72 **
Skipped classes		1.19 *	1.15
Grades			0.75 *
Log pseudolikelihood	-312.16 ***	-290.24 ***	-286.34 ***

* p < .05; ** p < .01; *** p <.001

NOTES

INTRODUCTION

1. All names throughout this book are pseudonyms. I have also altered the characteristics of some individuals I describe in order to protect their anonymity. When possible I describe (without alteration) the race/ethnicity and sex of interview respondents and individuals I observed. Even though I explicitly focus on race/ethnicity and gender and their effect on school discipline only in chapter 5, race/ethnicity are crucial for understanding respondents' interactions and beliefs. See Amanda Lewis (2006) *Race in the Schoolyard: Negotiating the Color Line in Classrooms and Communities.* New Brunswick, NJ: Rutgers University Press.

2. See also Sara Rimer (2004) "Unruly Students Facing Arrest, Not Detention." *New York Times,* January 4, A1.

3. See Richard Lawrence (2006) *School Crime and Juvenile Justice* (2nd ed.). New York: Oxford University Press.

4. With the term "discipline," I refer to the group of policies and practices that are used to detect misbehavior and respond to it, including behavioral rules, surveillance practices, and punishments. Consistent with prior scholars who refer to discipline as a means of controlling, governing, and training populations, school discipline seeks to produce conformity and complacency among students. See Michel Foucault (translated by Alan Sheridan) (1995) *Discipline and Punish: The Birth of the Prison* (2nd ed.). New York: Vintage Books.

5. See Aaron Kupchik and Torin Monahan (2006) "The New American School: Preparation for Post-industrial Discipline." *British Journal of Sociology of Education* 27: 617–631.

6. Deciding whether such a search was constitutional was the issue in the recent Supreme Court case, *Safford United School District #1 v. Redding* (2009); the Court ruled in favor of the student.

7. See, for example, Dewey G. Cornell (2006) *School Violence: Fears Versus Facts.* Mahwah, NJ: Lawrence Erlbaum Associates.

8. David Garland (2001) *The Culture of Control: Crime and Social Order in Contemporary Society.* Chicago: University of Chicago Press; Jonathan Simon (2007) *Governing Through Crime: How the War on Crime Transformed American Democracy and Created a Culture of Fear.* New York: Oxford University Press.

9. See Richard Arum (2003) *Judging School Discipline: The Crisis of Moral Authority.* Cambridge, MA: Harvard University Press; Denise C. Gottfredson (2001) *Schools and Delinquency.* New York: Cambridge University Press; see also Lawrence (2006).

10. On the lack of federal funding for education, see Diane Orson (2005) "Connecticut Challenges 'No Child Left Behind.'" Broadcast on National Public Radio, August 22. Retrieved December 31, 2007, from http://www.npr.org/templates/story/story.php?storyId=4810586. On decreases for social services see Richard Wertheimer and Astrid Atienza (2006) *Vulnerable Youth: Recent Trends* (Report to the Annie E. Casey Foundation). Washington, DC: Child Trends.

11. About after-school programs, see An-Me Chung (2000) *After-School Programs: Keeping Children Safe and Smart.* Washington, DC: U.S. Department of Education. A small number of evaluations have shown that police in schools promote safety. See, for example, Ida M. Johnson (1999) "School Violence: The Effectiveness of a School Resource Officer Program in a Southern City." *Journal of Criminal Justice* 27: 173–192; John G. Schuiteman (2001) *Second Annual Evaluation of DCJS-Funded School Resource Officer Program.* Richmond: Virginia State Department of Criminal Justice Services. Yet these evaluations have been mostly impressionistic or methodologically weak, relying on opinions of stakeholders or trends in crime, without adequate comparisons such as a control group. For example, when evaluating the effect of police officers on offense rates in Birmingham, Alabama, schools, Johnson (1999) finds that offense rates were lower for some offense categories following placement of full-time SROs in school but higher in others, and concludes that SROs deter offenses. Importantly, though, these data were collected at a time of unprecedented decreases in juvenile crime nationally, and the research includes no comparison/control group, which cause me to question the validity of the results. For a discussion of police as ineffective and counterproductive, see Randall R. Beger (2002) "Expansion of Police Power in Public Schools and the Vanishing Rights of Students." *Social Justice* 29: 119–130.

12. This phenomenon closely parallels a part of Feeley and Simon's argument about the "new penology": that the state manages problem populations rather than try to treat the problems. See Malcolm Feeley and Jonathan Simon (1992) "The New Penology: Notes on the Emerging Strategy of Corrections and Its Implications." *Criminology* 30: 449–474.

13. Of course there is substantial variation in how teachers respond to misbehavior, as I describe in following chapters.

14. In describing the political and economic marginalization of youth, sociologist Murray Milner Jr. writes: "They cannot change the curriculum, hire or fire the teachers, decide who will be admitted to their school, or move to another school without the permission of adults. At the time of life when the biological sources of sexuality are probably strongest, in a social environment saturated with sexual imagery and language, they are exhorted to avoid sex. In many situations they are treated as inferior citizens who are looked upon as at best a nuisance. They are denied the right to buy alcohol or see "adult" movies and are subject to the control not only of parents, teachers, and police, but numerous petty clerks in stores, movies, and nightclubs who 'check their IDs.'" See Murray Milner Jr. (2004) *Freaks, Geeks, and Cool Kids: American Teenagers, Schools, and the Culture of Consumption.* New York: Routledge, 25.

15. See, for example, Arum (2003); Gottfredson (2001); Tom R. Tyler (1990) *Why People Obey the Law*. New Haven, CT: Yale University Press; Jason Sunshine and Tom R. Tyler (2003) "The Role of Procedural Justice and Legitimacy in Shaping Public Support for Police." *Law and Society Review* 37: 513–548.

16. Tamela McNulty Eitle and David James Eitle (2004) "Inequality, Segregation, and the Overrepresentation of African Americans in School Suspension." *Sociological Perspectives* 47: 269–287; John D. McCarthy and Dean R. Hoge (1987) "The Social Construction of School Punishment: Racial Disadvantage Out of Universalistic Process." *Social Forces* 65: 1101–1120; Russell J. Skiba, Robert S. Michael, Abra Carroll Nardo, and Reece Peterson (2000) "The Color of Discipline: Sources of Racial and Gender Disproportionality in School Punishment." Indiana Education Policy Center, Research Report SRS1; Shi-Chang Wu, William Pink, Robert Crain, and Oliver Moles (1982) "Student Suspension: A Critical Reappraisal." *Urban Review* 14: 245–303.

17. See, for example, McCarthy and Hoge (1987); Prudence L. Carter (2005) *Keepin' It Real: School Success Beyond Black and White*. New York: Oxford University Press; Skiba et al. (2000).

18. For discussions of how schools have long sought to teach proper behaviors, see Michael W. Apple (1979) *Ideology and Curriculum*. Boston: Routledge; David B. Tyack (1974) *The One Best System: A History of American Urban Education*. Cambridge, MA: Harvard University Press. John Devine ([1996] *Maximum Security: The Culture of Violence in Inner-City Schools*. Chicago: University of Chicago Press) discusses a separation whereby teachers work with students' minds and security staff work with their bodies.

19. Public Law 107-110, January 8, 2002. Retrieved November 2, 2009, from http://www.ed.gov/policy/elsec/leg/esea02/107-110.pdf.

20. See Jonathan Kozol (2005) *The Shame of the Nation: The Restoration of Apartheid Schooling in America*. New York: Crown Books.

21. Simon (2007).

22. Carter (2005).

CHAPTER 1

1. Daniel G. Meyer (2008) "Problem Students in Pipeline to Prison." *Boston Globe* May 28 (op-ed). Retrieved July 6, 2009, from http://www.boston.com/bostonglobe/editorial_opinion/oped/articles/2008/05/28/problem_students_in_pipeline_to_prison/.

2. Though I focus in this book on American schools, these trends are seen elsewhere as well. See, for example, Rebecca Raby (2005) "Polite, Well-Dressed, and On Time: Secondary School Conduct Codes and the Production of Docile Citizens." *Canadian Review of Sociology and Anthropology* 42: 71–92.

3. National Sheriffs' Association. "Keeping America's Schools Safe: Law Enforcement Promising Practices Series: School Resource Officers." Retrieved November 10, 2009, from http://www.sheriffs.org/userfiles/file/SchoolSafetyBrochure.pdf.

4. Rachel Dinkes, Emily Forrest Cataldi, and Wendy Lin-Kelly (2007) *Indicators of School Crime and Safety: 2007* (NCES 2009-022/NCJ 226343). U.S. Departments of Education and Justice. Washington, DC: U.S. Government Printing Office; J. F. DeVoe, K. Peter, P. Kaufman, S. A. Ruddy, A. K. Miller, M. Planty, T. D. Snyder, D. T. Duhart, and M. R. Rand (2002) *Indicators of School Crime and Safety: 2002* (NCES 2003-009/NCJ 196753). U.S. Departments of Education and Justice. Washington, DC: U.S. Government Printing Office.

5. Dinkes et al. (2007).

6. Vincent Schiraldi and Jason Ziedenberg (2001) *Schools and Suspensions: Self-Reported Crime and the Growing Use of Suspensions.* Washington, DC: Justice Policy Institute.

7. R. J. Skiba (2000) "Zero Tolerance, Zero Evidence: An Analysis of School Disciplinary Practice." Indiana Education Policy Center, Policy Research Report SRS2. This echoes findings by Russell J. Skiba and R. L. Peterson (1999) "The Dark Side of Zero Tolerance: Can Punishment Lead to Safe Schools?" *Phi Delta Kappan* 80: 372–376, 381–382; A. J. Imich (1994) "Exclusions from School: Current Trends and Issues." *Educational Research* 36: 3–11; C. Morgan-D'Atrio, J. Northrup, L. LaFleur, and S. Sepra (1996) "Toward Prescriptive Alternatives to Suspensions: A Preliminary Evaluation." *Behavioral Disorders* 21: 190–200; and others that show minor misbehaviors, such as defiance, disruption, and attendance problems, to be the most common triggers for school suspensions.

8. Cornell (2006); for an example of rhetoric about dangerous schools, see Estaban Parra and Ginger Gibson (2009) "School Violence Reflects Society, Educators Say." *News Journal,* January 10, A1.

9. Dinkes et al. (2007).

10. Ronald Burns and Charles Crawford (1999) "School Shootings, the Media, and Public Fear: Ingredients for a Moral Panic." *Crime, Law, and Social Change* 32: 147–168; J. F. DeVoe, K. Peter, M. Noonan, T. D. Snyder, and K. Baum (2005) *Indicators of School Crime and Safety: 2005* (NCES 2006-001/NCJ 210697). U.S. Departments of Education and Justice. Washington, DC: U.S. Government Printing Office.

11. E. Donohue, V. Schiraldi, and Jason Ziedenberg (1998) *School House Hype: School Shootings and the Real Risks Kids Face in America.* Washington, DC: Justice Policy Institute.

12. K. Brooks, V. Schiraldi, and J. Ziedenberg (2000) *School House Hype: Two Years Later.* Washington, DC: Justice Policy Institute; Dinkes et al. (2007).

13. Dinkes et al. (2007), vii. Though low, school crime and perceptions of safety among students do vary. Disparities among rates of school crime tend to mirror rates of community crime, since urban areas with high rates of violence also tend to have high rates of school problems. See Lawrence (2006). For example, in his ethnography of security in a New York City public high school, John Devine (1996) discusses the harsh reality of crime and violence that students there face. See also Arum (2003). Furthermore, Dinkes et al. (2007) report a slightly larger percentage of students in

urban schools (6%) who report avoiding an activity or place at school because of fear than students in rural or suburban schools (4%). See p. 52. Similarly, black and Hispanic students were more likely in 2005–2006 to report being afraid for their safety at school than were white students (see p. 50).

14. See, for example, Arum (2003); Gottfredson (2001); Gary D. Gottfredson, Denise C. Gottfredson, Allison Ann Payne, and Nisha C. Gottfredson (2005) "School Climate Predictors of School Disorder: Results from a National Study of Delinquency Prevention in Schools." *Journal of Research in Crime and Delinquency* 42: 412–444.

15. Note that the operationalization of "misbehavior" varies among studies; I focus on those that consider actual or perceived crime, violence, delinquency, or school rule violations, rather than the broader set of studies on student academic outcomes, and especially (but not exclusively) on those that consider high school students.

16. Wayne N. Welsh (2003) "Individual and Institutional Predictors of School Disorder." *Youth Violence and Juvenile Justice* 1: 346–368.

17. Gottfredson et al. (2005).

18. G. Roy Mayer (1999) "Constructive Discipline for School Personnel." *Education and Treatment of Children* 22: 36–54; U.S. Department of Education, Office of Special Education Programs. "Technical Assistance Center on Positive Behavioral Interventions and Supports: School-Wide PBS." Retrieved August 21, 2008, from http://www.pbis.org/schoolwide.htm; U.S. Department of Education, Office of Special Education and Rehabilitative Services (2000) *Safeguarding Our Children: An Action Guide*. Washington, DC: U.S. Department of Education. Retrieved August 21, 2008, from http://www.ed.gov/admins/lead/safety/actguide/action_guide.pdf.

19. Dennis Jay Kenney and T. Stuart Watson (1996) "Reducing Fear in the Schools: Managing Conflict Through Student Problem Solving." *Education and Urban Society* 28: 436–455; Vera Institute of Justice (1999) *Approaches to School Safety in America's Largest Cities* (Prepared for the Lieutenant Governor's Task Force on School Safety). New York: Vera Institute of Justice.

20. Gottfredson (2001); Clea A. McNeely, James M. Nonnemaker, and Robert W. Blum (2002) "Promoting School Connectedness: Evidence from the National Longitudinal Study of Adolescent Health." *Journal of School Health* 72: 138–146.

21. Gottfredson (2001), 85–86.

22. Travis Hirschi (1969) *Causes of Delinquency*. Berkeley and Los Angeles: University of California Press; for a recent application of the theory to school misbehavior, see Eric A. Stewart (2003) "School Social Bonds, Social Climate, and School Misbehavior: A Multilevel Analysis." *Justice Quarterly* 20: 575–604.

23. Tom Tyler and associates have produced a great deal of evidence and theoretical clarification of the concept; see Tyler (2003); Tyler (1990); Tom Tyler and Yuen Huo (2002) *Trust in the Law*. New York: Russell Sage.

24. Gottfredson (2001), 91.

25. For a discussion of how schools have chosen ineffective strategies, see Cornell (2006).

26. Ellen Jane Hollingsworth, Henry S. Lufler Jr., and William H. Clune III (1984) *School Discipline: Order and Autonomy*. New York: Praeger; M. J. Mayer and Peter E. Leone (1999) "A Structural Analysis of School Violence and Disruption: Implications for Creating Safer Schools." *Education and Treatment of Children* 22: 333–356; R. E. Shores, P. L. Gunter, and S. L. Jack (1993) "Classroom Management Strategies: Are They Setting Events for Coercion?" *Behavioral Disorders* 18: 92–102; Russell Skiba, Cecil R. Reynolds, Sandra Graham, Peter Sheras, Jane Close Conoley, and Enedina Garcia-Vazquez (2006) *Are Zero Tolerance Policies Effective in the Schools? An Evidentiary Review and Recommendations* (Report by the American Psychological Association Zero Tolerance Task Force). Washington, DC: American Psychological Association. Retrieved December 24, 2008, from http://www.apa.org/releases/ZTTFReportBODRevisions5-15.pdf; see also A. T. Adams (2000) "The Status of School Discipline and Violence." *Annals of the American Academy of Political and Social Science* 567: 140–156; Kevin P. Brady, Sharon Balmer, and Deinya Phenix (2007) "School-Police Partnership Effectiveness in Urban Schools." *Education and Urban Society* 39: 455–478; A. C. Insley (2001) "Suspending and Expelling Children from Educational Opportunity: Time to Reevaluate Zero Tolerance Policies." *American University Law Review* 50: 1039–1074.

27. Ramon Lewis, Shlomo Romi, Yaacov J. Katz, and Xing Qui (2008) "Students' Reaction to Classroom Discipline in Australia, Israel, and China." *Teaching and Teacher Education* 24: 715–724; Margaret Graham Tebow (2000) "Zero Tolerance, Zero Sense." *American Bar Association Journal* 86: 40–45.

28. Irwin A. Hyman and Donna C. Perone (1998) "The Other Side of School Violence: Educator Policies and Practices That May Contribute to Student Misbehavior." *Journal of School Psychology* 36: 7–27. The potential for such harm was recently cited by the Supreme Court in making its decision on *Safford Unified School District #1 v. Redding*, 557 U.S. 08-479 (2009).

29. See, for example, Advancement Project and the Civil Rights Project (2000, June) *Opportunities Suspended: The Devastating Consequences of Zero Tolerance and School Discipline Policies* (Report from a National Summit on Zero Tolerance, June 15–16, 2000, Washington, DC). Retrieved August 6, 2008, from http://www. civilrightsproject.ucla.edu/research/discipline/opport_suspended.php; Advancement Project (2005, March) *Education on Lockdown: The Schoolhouse to Jailhouse Track*. Washington, DC: Advancement Project; Anne Arnett Ferguson (2000) *Bad Boys: Public Schools in the Making of Black Masculinity*. Ann Arbor: University of Michigan Press; Linda M. Raffaele Mendez (2003) "Predictors of Suspension and Negative School Outcomes: A Longitudinal Investigation." In Johanna Wald and Daniel J. Losen (eds.) *Deconstructing the School-to-Prison Pipeline: New Directions for Youth Development*. San Francisco: Jossey-Bass; Pedro Noguera (2003) *City Schools and the American Dream: Reclaiming the Promise of Public Education*. New York:

Teachers College Press; Russell J. Skiba and M. K. Rausch (2006) "Zero Tolerance, Suspension, and Expulsion: Questions of Equity and Effectiveness." In C. Evertson and C. Weinstein (eds.) *Handbook of Classroom Management: Research, Practice, and Contemporary Issues.* Mahwah, NJ: Lawrence Erlbaum Associates; Skiba et al. (2000); R. R. Verdugo (2002) "Race-Ethnicity, Social Class, and Zero-Tolerance Policies: The Cultural and Structural Wars." *Education and Urban Society* 35: 50–75; Wu et al. (1982).

30. Wu et al. (1982).

31. Douglas B. Downey and Shana Pribesh (2004) "When Race Matters: Teachers' Evaluations of Students' Classroom Behavior." *Sociology of Education* 77: 267–282; McCarthy and Hoge (1987); Brenda L. Townsend (2000) "The Disproportionate Discipline of African American Learners: Reducing School Suspensions and Expulsions." *Exceptional Children* 66: 381–391.

32. See, for example, Edward Morris (2005) "'Tuck in That Shirt!' Race, Class, Gender, and Discipline in an Urban School." *Sociological Perspectives* 48: 25–48.

33. Skiba et al. (2000), 18–19.

34. Christine Bowditch (1993) "Getting Rid of Troublemakers: High School Disciplinary Procedures and the Production of Dropouts." *Social Problems* 40: 493–507; K. Brooks et al. (2000); Ronnie Casella (2001) *Being Down: Challenging Violence in Urban Schools.* New York: Teachers College Press; L. M. DeRidder (1990) "How Suspension and Expulsion Contribute to Dropping Out." *Educational Horizons* 68: 153–157; Insley (2001); Gary Sweeten (2006) "Who Will Graduate? Disruption of High School Education by Arrest and Court Involvement." *Justice Quarterly* 23: 462–480.

35. Brooks, Schiraldi, and Ziedenberg (2000); Paul Hirschfield (2008) "Preparing for Prison: The Criminalization of School Discipline in the USA." *Theoretical Criminology* 12: 79–101; Johanna Wald and Daniel J. Losen (2003) "Defining and Redirecting a School-to-Prison Pipeline." In Wald and Losen (2003).

36. Devine (1996); Elora Mukherjee (2007) *Criminalizing the Classroom: The Over-Policing of New York City Schools.* New York: New York Civil Liberties Union.

37. Advancement Project (2005).

38. *Tinker v. Des Moines* 393 U.S. 503 (1969).

39. See *New Jersey v. T.L.O.* 469 U.S. 325 (1985).

40. *Goss v. Lopez* 419 U.S. 565 (1975).

41. *Safford Unified School District v. Redding #1,* 557 U.S. 08-479 (2009); see p. 2 of Souter's opinion.

42. See p. 12 of Souter's opinion.

43. The remaining three justices, Ginsburg, Stevens and Thomas, each concurred in part and dissented in part with Souter's opinion.

44. Public Agenda (May 2004). *Teaching Interrupted: Do Discipline Policies in Today's Public Schools Foster the Common Good?* New York: Public Agenda. Retrieved August 15, 2008, from http://www.publicagenda.org/files/pdf/teaching_interrupted.pdf.

45. C. Henault (2001) "Zero Tolerance in Schools." *Journal of Law and Education* 30: 547–553.

46. E. Crouch and D. Williams (1995) "What Cities Are Doing to Protect Kids." *Educational Leadership* 52: 60–62; B. Kipper (1996) "Law Enforcement's Role in Addressing School Violence." *Police Chief* 63: 26–29.

47. Ronnie Casella (2006) *Selling Us the Fortress: The Promotion of Techno-Security Equipment for Schools.* New York: Routledge.

48. C. Maranzano (2001) "The Legal Implications of School Resource Officers in Public Schools." *NASSP Bulletin* 85: 76–80; A. Jackson (2002) "Police-School Resource Officers' and Students' Perception of the Police and Offending." *Policing: An International Journal of Police Strategies and Management* 25: 631–650.

49. SRO programs are based on a problem-oriented community policing model, under which schools and law enforcement agencies work together to identify and prevent crime in schools. Anne J. Atkinson (2002) *Fostering School–Law Enforcement Partnerships* (Guide 5 in *Safe and Secure: Guides to Creating Safer Schools*). Portland, OR: Northwest Regional Educational Laboratory..

50. N. Hopkins (1994) "School Pupils' Perceptions of the Police That Visit Schools: Not All Police Are 'Pigs.'" *Journal of Community and Applied Psychology* 4: 189–207; Jackson (2002).

51. Garland (2001), 170.

52. See Tyack (1974); James C. Carper (2001) "The Changing Landscape of U.S. Education." *Kappa Delta Pi Record* 37: 106–110; James G. Cibulka (2001) "The Changing Role of Interest Groups in Education: Nationalization and the New Politics of Education Productivity." *Educational Policy* 15: 12–40.

53. Cibulka (2001), 16.

54. Cibulka (2001); Peter Schrag (2007) "Schoolhouse Crock: Fifty Years of Blaming America's Education System for Our Stupidity." *Harper's Magazine* (September), 36–44.

55. The connection between these persists today; in the third and final debate between presidential candidates Barack Obama and John McCain (on October 15, 2008), both candidates explicitly discussed a failing educational system as a national security concern.

56. Lawrence Hardy (2004) "A New Minority 50 Years After 'Brown.'" *Educational Digest* 70: 23–28.

57. The Broad Prize for Urban Education (2007) *New York City Department of Education.* Los Angeles: Broad Foundation. Retrieved August 21, 2008, from http://www.broadprize.org/2007NewYorkBrief.pdf; U.S. Census (2009), http://factfinder.census.gov/servlet/STTable?_bm=y&-geo_id=16000US3651000&-qr_name=ACS_2008_3YR_G00_S0901&-ds_name=ACS_2008_3YR_G00_ (retrieved November 9, 2009).

58. Jonathan Kozol (1991) *Savage Inequalities: Children in America's Schools.* New York: Harper Perennial, 165–166. See also Jean Anyon (1997) *Ghetto Schooling: A*

Political Economy of Urban Educational Reform. New York: Teachers College Press; Kozol (2005); William Lyons and Julie Drew (2006) *Punishing Schools: Fear and Citizenship in American Public Education*. Ann Arbor: University of Michigan Press.

59. Simon (2007); Lyons and Drew (2006); see also Cornell (2006).

60. Karen Sternheimer (2006) *Kids These Days: Facts and Fictions About Today's Youth*. New York: Rowman and Littlefield, 3.

61. Lisa Nicita (2008) "Teenage Girls Are Open to Parent Input, Survey Says." *Arizona Republic*, August 13. Retrieved August 15, 2008, from http://www.azcentral.com/arizonarepublic/arizonaliving/articles/2008/08/13/20080813teensurvey0813.html.

62. Peter Schrag makes this point when comparing the burden placed on U.S. public schools to that of other nation's educational systems: "Because of the relative paucity of social services in this country—as opposed to the universal preschool, health care, and similar generous children's services provided in other developed nations—our schools are forced to serve as a fallback social-service system for millions of American children" (2007, 42).

63. For an excellent discussion of how economic and political isolation affect schools, see Anyon (1997).

64. To clarify the source of data throughout this book, I label field notes (FN) and interview transcripts (I). Readers should keep in mind that field notes may not be quoted exactly, though double quotation marks are used in cases to show confidence that a particular phrase or word is accurately reported.

65. The question, qn9e, is included in June Wave 1, with a sample of n = 822 adults.

66. Data retrieved from Gallup Brain, through the University of Delaware's library, on August 25, 2008.

67. Schrag (2007), 36.

68. For a discussion of how declines in public confidence in education and accountability measures are linked, see Robert L. Crowson (2003) "The Turbulent Policy Environment in Education: Implications for School Administration and Accountability." *Peabody Journal of Education* 78: 29–43.

69. For details, see http://www.ed.gov/nclb/landing.jhtml?src=pb (retrieved August 25, 2008).

70. John Gilliom (2009) "Lying, Cheating, and Teaching to the Test: The Politics of Surveillance Under No Child Left Behind." In Torin Monahan and Rodolfo Torres (eds.) *Schools Under Surveillance: Cultures of Control in Public Education*. New Brunswick, NJ: Rutgers University Press; Schrag (2007).

71. Lizbet Simmons (2007a) "The Public School, the Prison, and the Bottom Line: Expenditure and Expediency." Paper presented at the American Sociological Association annual conference, New York, NY; Simon (2007), as well, argues that because it is accountability- and consequence-driven, NCLB is an example of governing through crime.

72. Simon (2007), 209.

244 | *Notes to Chapter 1*

73. Simon (2007), 214. See Laurie E. Gronlund (1993) "Understanding the National Goals." *ERIC Digest.* Retrieved October 6, 2009, from http://www.ericdigests.org/1993/goals.htm.

74. See Casella (2006).

75. Adams (2000); *U.S. Code* 20 (1994), § 8921.

76. K. A. Chandler, C. D. Chapman, M. R. Rand, and B. M. Taylor (1998, March). *Student's Reports of School Crime: 1989 and 1995* (NCJ 169607). Washington, DC: U.S. Department of Justice, Office of Justice Programs, Bureau of Justice Statistics.

77. Insley (2001).

78. B. Brown (2006) "Understanding and Assessing School Police Officers: A Conceptual and Methodological Comment." *Journal of Criminal Justice* 34: 591–604; S. Burke (2001) "The Advantages of a School Resource Officer." *Law and Order Magazine* 49: 73–75.

79. Casella (2001).

80. Rachel Dinkes et al. (2007) *Indicators of School Crime and Safety: 2007.* U.S. Departments of Education and Justice. Washington, DC: U.S. Government Printing Office.

81. Emile Durkheim (translated by Everett K. Wilson and Herman Schnurer) (2002) *Moral Education.* Mineola, NY: Dover Publications, 79.

82. John Dewey (1916) *Democracy and Education: An Introduction to the Philosophy of Education.* New York: Macmillan.

83. Samuel Bowles and Herbert Gintis (1976) *Schooling in Capitalist America: Educational Reform and the Contradictions of Economic Life.* New York: Basic Books.

84. See also Jacques Donzelot (translated by Robert Hurley) (1979) *The Policing of Families.* New York: Knopf; Stanley William Rothstein (1984) *The Power to Punish: A Social Inquiry into Coercion and Control in Urban Schools.* New York: University Press of America; for a historical account of the marginalization of urban schools, see Anyon (1997).

85. Pierre Bourdieu and Jean-Claude Passeron (translated by Richard Nice) (1990) *Reproduction in Education, Society, and Culture* (2nd ed.). Newbury Park, CA: Sage Publications; for a fine distinction between types of capital, see Lewis (2006).

86. See Pierre Bourdieu (translated by Peter Nice) (2007) *Distinction: A Social Critique of the Judgment of Taste* (2nd ed.). Cambridge, MA: Harvard University Press.

87. Apple (1979), 12.

88. James Paul Gee (1996) *Social Linguistics and Literacies: Ideology in Discourse* (2nd ed.). Briston, PA: Taylor and Francis.

89. Political scientist Clarissa Rile Hayward refers to this as a mode of "de-faced power," in contrast to perspectives of "power with a face," which presume that power is held by individuals who control others. She argues that power in school works in very subtle ways through how the practices of teaching and learning are defined,

rather than as the result of hegemonic individuals' attempts to exercise power over students. See Clarissa Rile Hayward (2000) *De-facing Power*. New York: Cambridge University Press.

90. Paul Willis (1977) *Learning to Labor: How Working Class Kids Get Working Class Jobs*. New York: Columbia University Press; see also Peter W. Cookson and Caroline Hodges Persell (1985) *Preparing for Power: America's Elite Boarding Schools*. New York: Basic Books; Aaron V. Cicourel and John I. Kitsuse (1963) *The Educational Decision-Makers*. New York: Bobbs-Merrill; Jay MacLeod (1995) *Ain't No Makin' It: Aspirations and Attainment in a Low-Income Neighborhood* (2nd ed.). Boulder, CO: Westview Press; Jeannie Oakes (1985) *Keeping Track: How Schools Structure Inequality*. New Haven, CT: Yale University Press; Ray C. Rist (1973) *The Urban School: A Factory for Failure*. Cambridge, MA: MIT Press.

91. Carter (2005); see also Anyon (1997); Lisa Delpit (2006) *Other People's Children: Cultural Conflict in the Classroom*. New York: The New Press; Townsend (2000).

92. Kupchik and Monahan (2006).

93. See also Hirschfield (2008); William G. Staples (2000) *Everyday Surveillance: Vigilance and Visibility in Postmodern Life*. New York: Rowman and Littlefield.

94. Loïc Wacquant (2001) "Deadly Symbiosis: When Ghetto and Prison Meet and Mesh." In David Garland (ed.) *Mass Imprisonment: Social Causes and Consequences*. Thousand Oaks, CA: Sage Publications, 94–95 (emphasis in original).

95. See Enora R. Brown (2003) "Freedom for Some, Discipline for 'Others': The Structure of Inequality in Education." In Kenneth J. Saltman and David A. Gabbard (eds.) *Education as Enforcement: The Militarization and Corporatization of Schools*. New York: Routledge.

96. Lyons and Drew (2006).

97. See Adamma Ince (2001) "Preppin' for Prison: Cops in Schools Teach a Generation to Live in Jail." *Village Voice*, June 12. Retrieved August 13, 2009, from http://www.villagevoice.com/2001-06-12/news/preppin-for-prison/; Kenneth J. Saltman (2003) "Introduction" In Saltman and Gabbard (2003); Julie A. Webber (2003) *Failure to Hold: The Politics of School Violence*. New York: Rowman and Littlefield.

98. Foucault (1995).

99. See David Garland (1990) *Punishment and Modern Society: A Study in Social Theory*. Chicago: University of Chicago Press.

100. In his later work, Foucault further developed ideas about "governmentality," or how individuals are governed through self-discipline. See Michel Foucault (1991) "Governmentality" (translated by Rosi Braidotti and revised by Colin Gordon). In Graham Burchell, Colin Gordon, and Peter Miller (eds.) *The Foucault Effect: Studies in Governmentality*. Chicago: University of Chicago Press.

101. David E. Campbell (2006) *Why We Vote: How Schools and Communities Shape Our Civic Life*. Princeton, NJ: Princeton University Press.

102. See Jonathan Simon (2002) "Commentary: Guns, Crime, and Governance." *Houston Law Review* 39: 133–148.

103. Wacquant (2001); see also Ince (2001).
104. Foucault (1995).
105. This is what social reproduction theory suggests, as described above.
106. Durkheim (2002); see also Arum (2003).

CHAPTER 2

1. Kozol (1991), 36–37.
2. In a recent book, political scientists Gaston Alonso and colleagues add to work such as Kozol's by presenting the views of students of color who attend under-resourced inner-city schools. See Alonso et al. (2009).
3. James Q. Wilson and George L. Kelling (1982) "Broken Windows." *Atlantic Monthly* 249: 29–38.
4. Since this figure measures number of suspensions rather than individuals suspended, it includes multiple suspensions given to the same individuals. This is why Unionville High has a rate of ninety-six suspensions per hundred students. During that year, 43% of enrolled students received at least one suspension, with many students receiving multiple suspensions.
5. Each of the four schools uses paper referral forms as a response to misbehavior. Receiving a referral means that a paper form is filled out about an incident, describing a student's misbehavior, and submitted to the school's disciplinary personnel (a dean, interventionist, or assistant principal).
6. Jean M. Twenge (2006) *Generation Me: Why Today's Young Americans Are More Confident, Assertive, Entitled—and More Miserable Than Ever Before.* New York: Free Press. This principal also mentioned Annette Lareau (2000) *Home Advantage: Social Class and Parental Interaction in Elementary Education* (2nd ed.). Lanham, MD: Rowman and Littlefield.
7. The graduation rate is based on a five-year cohort.
8. See Casella (2001); Ferguson (2000); Skiba et al. (2000); Wu et al. (1982).
9. There were very few students who "choiced" into Centerville High during the 2006–2007 school year, because at the time it was the only traditional (nonvocational or specialized) high school in the district, but over three hundred choiced into Fairway Estates High during the 2005–2006 school year.

CHAPTER 3

1. Mukherjee (2007), 14. Portions of this chapter originally appeared in Aaron Kupchik and Nicole L. Bracy (2009) "To Protect, Serve, and Mentor? Police Officers in Public Schools." In Monahan and Torres (2009).
2. Mukherjee (2007), 25.
3. Ibid., 25–26.

4. Katherine S. Newman, Cybelle Fox, David J. Harding, Jal Mehta, and Wendy Roth (2004) *Rampage: The Social Roots of School Shootings.* New York: Basic Books, 281.

5. Ibid., 282.

6. See Vera Institute of Justice (1999).

7. See Dinkes et al. (2007).

8. See also Advancement Project (2005) *Education on Lockdown: The Schoolhouse to Jailhouse Track.* Washington, DC: Advancement Project; Elissa Gootman (2004) "Crime Falls as Citations Surge in Schools with Extra Officers." *New York Times,* March 25; Ince (2001); Rimer (2004).

9. Connie Mulqueen (1999) "School Resource Officers: More Than Security Guards." *American School and University* 71: 11; see also Joanne McDaniel (2001) *School Resource Officers: What We Know, What We Think We Know, What We Need to Know.* Report for School Safety Strategic Planning Meeting, U.S. Department of Justice. Raleigh, NC: Center for the Prevention of School Violence.

10. That officers of the same race or ethnicity as the citizens they police will appear more legitimate and trustworthy to these citizens is assumed by the Kerner Commission in its reports on urban riots of the 1960s. See also W. Marvin Dulaney (1996) *Black Police in America.* Bloomington: Indiana University Press. Prior research on relationships between racial/ethnic minority police officers and mostly nonwhite communities is mixed and, overall, inconclusive. Though some studies suggest that nonwhite officers will identify with community members better than white officers, others find no difference. For a review and discussion of research limitations, see Geoff K. Ward (2006) "Race and the Justice Workforce: Toward a System Perspective." In R. Peterson, L. Krivo, and J. Hagan (eds.) *The Many Colors of Crime.* New York: NYU Press. Some recent research suggests that integrated groups (though not feasible in schools with a single SRO) may be considered more legitimate than police of only a single racial/ethnic group. See Ronald Weitzer (2000) "White, Black, or Blue Cops? Race and Citizen Assessments of Police Officers." *Journal of Criminal Justice* 28: 313–324. It is also possible that the black youth at Unionville High and Latino/a youth at Frontera High will feel betrayed and become angry when confronted with a police officer of their same race/ethnicity, though it is beyond my data to test this.

11. A recent study using surveys of school principals shows strong support for school resource officers; see David C. May, Stephen D. Fessel, and Shannon Means (2004) "Predictors of Principals' Perceptions of School Resource Officer Effectiveness in Kentucky." *American Journal of Criminal Justice* 29: 75–93.

12. See Devine (1996); Mukherjee (2007).

13. Mukherjee (2007), 15.

14. Jeanne B. Stinchcomb, Gordon Bazemore, and Nancy Riestenberg (2006) "Beyond Zero Tolerance: Restoring Justice in Secondary Schools." *Youth Violence and Juvenile Justice* 4: 123–147; Beger (2002).

15. Devine (1996).

16. Jackson (2002).

17. Hopkins (1994).

18. See Hopkins (1994); Jackson (2002).

19. This took place just before Officer Bartol left Frontera High.

20. Johnson (1999); Schuiteman (2001). These studies have relied on opinions of stakeholders or trends in crime, but without adequate comparisons such as a control group. See the introduction for details.

21. See also Peter Finn and Jack McDevitt (2005) *National Assessment of School Resource Officer Programs Final Project Report* (Final Grant Report). Washington, DC: National Institute of Justice.

22. Dinkes et al. (2007).

23. Finn and McDevitt (2005), 46 (emphasis in original).

24. Beger (2002).

25. Despite their recommendation that all schools have SROs, Newman et al. (2004) acknowledge this point.

26. Newman et al. (2004).

27. Casella (2001), 112; see also David C. Brotherton (1996) "The Contradictions of Suppression: Notes from a Study of Approaches to Gangs in Three Public High Schools." *Urban Review* 28: 95–117.

28. See Garland (2001); Simon (2007).

29. Torin Monahan (2006) "Electronic Fortification in Phoenix: Surveillance Technologies and Social Regulation in Residential Communities." *Urban Affairs Review* 42: 169–192.

CHAPTER 4

1. Jonathan Simon makes a similar point, in reference to the small proportion of schools with serious crime problems, when he states that at these schools "Punishment and policing have come to at least compete with, if not replace, teaching as the dominant modes of socialization" (2007, 210).

2. See, for example, Gilliom (2009).

3. These two phenomena are linked in other ways as well. According to Stanley William Rothstein, for example, standardized testing is a method of surveillance and a form of discipline, since it facilitates the disciplinary functions of classifying and grouping students. See Rothstein (1984).

4. See Lyons and Drew (2006).

5. This is supported by prior research as well; see, for example, Anthony Palumbo and Joseph Sanacore (2007) "Classroom Management: Help for the Beginning Secondary School Teacher." *Clearing House* 81: 67–70; see also Lewis (2006).

6. Hollingsworth et al. (1984).

7. Rist (1973).

8. Lewis (2006), 70–71.

9. Stinchcomb and colleagues make a similar point when arguing for restorative justice responses to school misbehavior rather than zero-tolerance policies. See Stinchcomb et al. (2006).

10. Hayward (2000).

11. Ivan Illich (1971) *Deschooling Society*. New York: Harper and Row.

12. William Lyons and Julie Drew offer a similar observation about surveillance strategies, which they call a "logic of surveillance-itself-as-effective," in *Punishing Schools* (2006). They discuss a principal who says that drug lockdowns are successful regardless of outcome: the school either catches someone or confirms that there are no drugs in the school. See also Apple (1979).

13. Gee (1996).

14. In *Goss v. Lopez*, the Supreme Court ruled that students must receive hearings and have an opportunity to contest charges prior to any suspension or expulsion.

15. Casella (2001), 58–73.

16. Lawrence (2007); Milner (2004).

17. See Gerald Grant (1988) *The World We Created at Hamilton High*. Cambridge, MA: Harvard University Press

18. For a recent illustration of how American teenagers creatively respond to social and economic marginalization, see Milner (2004).

19. Frances Vavrus and KimMarie Cole offer a similar conclusion, that school suspension is often the result of a challenge to the teacher's ability or authority through a series of events. See Vavrus and Cole (2002) "'I Didn't Do Nothin'": The Discursive Construction of School Suspension." *Urban Review* 34: 87–111.

20. See Kupchik and Monahan (2006).

21. See Erving Goffman (1961) *Asylums: Essays on the Condition of the Social Situation of Mental Patients and Other Inmates*. Chicago: Aldine Publising.

22. Lyons and Drew (2006); see also Brotherton (1996); Augustina H. Reyes (2006) *Discipline, Achievement, and Race: Is Zero Tolerance the Answer?* Lanham, MD: Rowman and Littlefield; Stinchcomb et al. (2006); Webber (2003).

23. Casella (2001) likewise argues that zero-tolerance policies lead to a "slate-clearing approach" to fighting, where students are immediately removed from the school with no assessment of why incidents occurred.

24. Lyons and Drew (2006) do discuss zero-tolerance approach as part of a larger political culture, one that divests from democratic public spheres, and as a function of a zero-tolerance culture. Thus, though they are not offering a simple causal chain whereby zero-tolerance policies produce the problem of a zero-tolerance culture, they do still put greater emphasis on the causal role of zero-tolerance policies than do I.

25. As an example, see the 1955 movie *Blackboard Jungle*.

26. Devine (1996).

27. Lyons and Drew (2006).

28. Michelle Fine (1991) *Framing Dropouts: Notes on the Politics of an Urban Public High School.* Albany, NY: SUNY Press.

29. See Arum (2003); Grant (1988).

30. Retrieved October 10, 2009, from http://www.ade.state.az.us/disciplineinitiative/downloads/brochure1.pdf.

31. Arum (2003).

32. See, for example, Gottfredson (2001).

33. See, for example, Tyler (1990).

34. Shoko Yoneyama and Asao Naito (2003) "Problems with the Paradigm: The School as a Factor in Understanding Bullying (with special reference to Japan)." *British Journal of Sociology of Education* 24: 315–330.

35. A few of the security guards have completed the training, and they are usually the ones who conduct the session. The school also has similar policies in place whereby students who react angrily to teachers attend an anger management class, and students suspected of drug use are sent to a drug treatment class.

36. For more information on how these programs work, or how common they are, see: U.S. Department of Education, Office of Special Education Programs. "Technical Assistance Center on Positive Behavioral Interventions and Supports: School-Wide PBS." Retrieved August 21, 2008, from http://www.pbis.org/schoolwide.htm; U.S. Department of Education, Office of Special Education and Rehabilitative Services (2000).

37. Mary Douglas (1986) *How Institutions Think.* Syracuse, NY: Syracuse University Press.

38. Heinz-Dieter Meyer and Brian Rowan (2006) "Institutional Analysis and the Study of Education." In Heinz-Dieter Meyer and Brian Rowan (eds.) *The New Institutionalism in Education.* Albany, NY: SUNY Press, 5; see also John W. Meyer and Brian Rowan (1977) "Institutionalized Organizations: Formal Structure as Myth and Ceremony." *American Journal of Sociology* 83: 340–363.

39. Paul J. DiMaggio and Walter W. Powell (1983) "The Iron Cage Revisited: Institutional Isomorphism and Collective Rationality in Organizational Fields." *American Sociological Review* 48: 147–160.

40. The idea of the "iron cage" comes from Max Weber's warnings that increasing rationalization and bureaucratization of society would lead to an increasingly rule- and control-based world with limited freedoms. See Max Weber (translated by Talcott Parsons) (1996) *The Protestant Ethic and the Spirit of Capitalism.* Los Angeles: Roxbury Press; Max Weber (edited by Guenther Roth and Claus Wittich) (1978) *Economy and Society: An Outline of Interpretive Sociology.* Berkeley and Los Angeles: University of California Press. A more recent translation of Weber suggests that a more accurate interpretation is "steel hard casing" rather than "iron cage," which may better connote how bureaucratic life imprisons us from within (not from the outside) by a certain form of consciousness. See Max Weber (translated by Stephen Kalberg) (2008) *The Protestant Ethic and the Spirit of Capitalism, with Other Writings on the Rise of the West* (4th ed.). New York: Oxford University Press.

CHAPTER 5

A portion of this chapter was initially published as Aaron Kupchik (2009) "Things Are Tough All Over: Race, Ethnicity, Class, and School Discipline." *Punishment and Society* 11: 291–317.

1. Emily Bittner (2004) "Sideways Ball Cap Lands Scottsdale Teenager in Jail." *Arizona Republic,* March 13, A1.

2. Ferguson (2000); Edward W. Morris (2007) "'Ladies' or 'Loudies': Perceptions and Experiences of Black Girls in Classrooms." *Youth and Society* 38: 490–515.

3. For a more detailed discussion, see chapter 1.

4. Lyons and Drew (2006), 5; see also Hirschfield (2008).

5. For a description of security in urban schools with mostly youth of color, see Devine (1996); Ferguson (2000).

6. Simon (2007), 210; see also Staples (2000). Staples argues that though surveillance and discipline may vary across social strata in quantity and quality, they are becoming more democratic, spreading to populations that might previously have been exempt from their reach.

7. Ferguson (2000); see also Lincoln Quillian (2006) "New Approaches to Understanding Racial Prejudice and Discrimination." *Annual Review of Sociology* 32: 299–328.

8. Alabama Department of Archives and History. Retrieved September 17, 2007, from http://www.archives.state.al.us/govs_list/inauguralspeech.html.

9. Regarding social class, see Hollingsworth et al. (1984); regarding race, see Ferguson (2000); McCarthy and Hoge (1987); Morris (2005).

10. Lareau (2000); see also Noguera (2003).

11. See Bowditch (1993); Casella (2001); Fine (1991).

12. See Lareau (2000); Annette Lareau (2003) *Unequal Childhoods: Class, Race, and Family Life.* Berkeley and Los Angeles: University of California Press.

13. See, for example, McCarthy and Hoge (1987); Skiba et al. (2000); Wu et al. (1982).

14. Certainly a number of studies go beyond comparing rates of punishment and explain how these rates are produced. See, for example, Ferguson (2000); McCarthy and Hoge (1987). Yet few studies consider how school punishments are enacted and how this process compares across demographically diverse schools. For an exception, see Lyons and Drew (2006).

15. Mike Chalmers and Lee Williams (2007) "Federal Money Burning Holes in Delaware Pockets." *News Journal,* May 6.

16. Hirschfield (2008).

17. Appendix table 1 illustrates this point using data from the National Center for Education Statistics on school security measures and school characteristics.

18. See Milner (2004).

19. See the appendix for a description of methods.

20. I include only African Americans in this table because values for Latino/as and those of other race/ethnicities are not statistically significant, probably because of the small numbers of these students.

21. In contrast to prior research (e.g., Ferguson 2000), there was no significant effect of an interaction between race/ethnicity and sex in these models.

22. See also Gale M. Morrison and Barbara D'Incau (1997) "The Web of Zero-Tolerance: Characteristics of Students Who Are Recommended for Expulsion from School." *Education and Treatment of Children* 20: 316–335; Wu et al. (1982). Note that adding an interaction term between African American and grades to the analyses did not help explain getting into trouble, suggesting that the relationship is an intervening one rather than an interactive one.

23. Simmons (2007a); Lizbet Simmons (2007b) "Research Off Limits and Underground: Street Corner Methods for Finding Invisible Students." *Urban Review* 39: 319–347.

24. Jose Luis Gaviria Soto (2005) "Beyond Over-Representation: The Problem of Bias in the Inclusion of Minority Group Students in Special Education Programs." *Quality and Quantity* 39: 537–558; Russell J. Skiba (2000) *Minority Over-Representation in Indiana Special Education: A Status Report*. Bloomington: Indiana Education Policy Center, Indiana University.

25. Alison Kepner (2007) "Parents Want Christina to Rethink 'Zero Tolerance' Policy." *News Journal*, October 10, A1, A7.

26. See, for example, Edwin Schur (1971) *Labeling Deviant Behavior: Its Sociological Implications*. New York: Harper and Row.

27. See Carter (2005); Delpit (2006); Lewis (2006) for descriptions of how cultural conflict and miscommunication can cause class disruption and lead to school punishment.

28. This does not mean that African Americans and Latino/as face the same issues and biases. In contrast, as I describe above with my discussion of the dress codes at each school, the schools have rules that prohibit styles that correspond to stereotypes of each particular group. Additionally, at Frontera High, which is almost entirely composed of Latino/a students, several interview respondents told me that school staff members often show biases against the few black students and in favor of Latino/as. Though I did not observe evidence of this firsthand, it highlights how members each group face unique conflicts and constraints. Moreover, the fact that many of the Latino/a youth at Frontera High are immigrants further complicates a comparison to the experiences with African Americans, since tensions and discrimination might arise from a student's immigrant status in addition to his or her ethnicity. A discussion of these issues is beyond the scope of this chapter. My intent is to illustrate how, despite these complexities, both black and Latino/a students are more likely than whites to be disciplined, and one reason for this is the proliferation of an array of biases and perceptions about them.

29. This is consistent with prior research as well; see Carter (2005); Ferguson (2000); McCarthy and Hoge (1987); Russell J. Skiba, Reece L. Peterson, and Tara

Williams (1997) "Office Referrals and Suspension: Disciplinary Intervention in Middle Schools." *Education and Treatment of Children* 20: 295–315.

30. Carter (2005).
31. Lareau (2003).
32. Reyes (2006).
33. For examples of studies focusing on social class, see Lareau (2000, 2003); for race, see Carter (2005); Wu et al. (1982).
34. Charles Puzzanchera (2009) *Juvenile Arrests, 2007.* Washington, DC: Office of Justice Programs.
35. See Lyn Mikel Brown, Med Chesney-Lind, and Nan Stein (2007) "Patriarchy Matters: Toward a Gendered Theory of Teen Violence and Victimization." *Violence Against Women* 13: 1249–1273.
36. See also Raby (2005).
37. Simon (2007).
38. See, for example, Wu et al. (1982); Skiba et al. (2000).
39. For exceptions, see Carter (2005), Ferguson (2000); McCarthy and Hoge (1987).
40. See Alonso et al. (2009); Anyon (1997); Kozol (2005); Noguera (2003).
41. For a very powerful description of this, see Jody Miller (2008) *Getting Played: African American Girls, Urban Inequality, and Gendered Violence.* New York: NYU Press.

CONCLUSION

1. Brent Whiting (2006) "Student Jailed for Planning Food Fight at Glendale School." *Arizona Republic,* May 20, B1.
2. See Carter (2005); Noguera (2003).
3. Udi Ofer, Angela Jones, Johanna Miller, Deinya Phenix, Tara Bahl, Christina Mokhtar, and Chase Madar (2009) *Safety With Dignity: Alternatives to the Over-Policing of Schools.* New York: New York Civil Liberties Union.
4. For an example of students' rights and empowerment taken too far, so that teachers' authority is constantly questioned, see Grant (1988) (discussed below).
5. For a discussion of the balance between order (through school discipline) and autonomy for students and teachers, see Hollingsworth et al. (1984).
6. Durkheim (2002) made this point almost a century ago: "Children themselves are the first to appreciate good discipline" (152). Hollingsworth et al. (1984) found similar results in their research as well.
7. Arum (2003) argues that pro-student (or anti-school) court decisions are responsible for contemporary school discipline problems. Yet it is not clear how a court climate lasting only from 1969 to 1975 (and in which pro-student decisions were always outnumbered by pro-school decisions) is responsible for the erosion of moral authority in today's schools.

8. Grant (1988).

9. For a discussion of the importance of relational trust among students, teachers, and parents in improving schools, see Anthony S. Bryk and Barbara Schneider (2002) *Trust in Schools: A Core Resource for Improvement*. New York: Russell Sage.

10. In the epilogue, Grant (1988) reports a statement from Hamilton High's first black teacher, who defended the violence in Hamilton High while it was undergoing desegregation, saying it was the only available outlet for the students' frustrations at racial discrimination.

11. Durkheim (2002), 243.

12. Grant (1988).

13. Lareau (2003).

14. See Skiba et al. (2006).

15. Lyons and Drew (2006); Reyes (2006); Skiba et al. (2007).

16. Durkheim (2002), 199.

17. Prior research illustrates that the problem of student defiance is complex, with factors as varied as student social networks and students' popularity shaping the likelihood of a student misbehaving in class—yet even when accounting for individual-level items, teaching style and classroom organization are still important predictors of student misbehavior. See Daniel A. McFarland (2001) "Student Resistance: How the Formal and Informal Organization of Classrooms Facilitate Everyday Forms of Student Defiance." *American Journal of Sociology* 107: 612–678.

18. See, for example, Palumbo and Sanacore (2007).

19. See Donetta J. Cothran, Pamela Hodges Kulinna, and Deborah A. Garrahy (2003) "'This Is Kind of Giving a Secret Away . . . ': Students' Perspectives on Effective Class Management." *Teaching and Teacher Education* 19: 435–444.

20. In subsequent communication with Principal Howley over a year after my field work ended, he told me that suspensions had in fact decreased substantially at Unionville High.

21. As I show in chapter 4, this does occur at Frontera High, though in a very superficial way.

22. See Ofer et al. (2009).

23. *Radio Times with Marty Moss-Coane*, WHYY, July 7, 2008.

24. Arum (2003); Grant (1988); for a discussion of how teaching cultures grow (in part) in response to teachers' interactions with students, with one another, and with the school administration, see Mary Haywood Metz (1986) *Different By Design: The Context and Character of Three Magnet Schools*. New York: Routledge.

25. Prior research in other settings finds that surveillance cameras fail to prevent violent crime in general; see Jason Ditton, Emma Short, Samuel Phillips, Clive Norris, and Gary Armstrong (1999) *The Effect of Closed Circuit Television Cameras on Recorded Crime Rates and Public Concern about Crime in Glasgow*. Edinburgh: Scottish Office Central Research Unit; Mark Rice-Oxley (2004) "Big Brother in Britain: Does More Surveillance Work?" *Christian Science Monitor*, Feb-

ruary 6. Retrieved October 12, 2009, from http://www.csmonitor.com/2004/0206/p07s02-woeu.html.

26. This is discussed at length in Torin Monahan (2006) "The Surveillance Curriculum: Risk Management and Social Control in the Neoliberal School." In Torin Monahan (ed.) *Surveillance and Security: Technological Politics and Power in Everyday Life.* New York: Routledge.

27. Mukherjee (2007).

28. I learned of this when listening to the Philadelphia NPR program *Radio Times with Marty Moss-Coane,* mentioned above.

29. Nikolas Rose (1996) *Inventing Our Selves.* Cambridge: Cambridge University Press. Much of this work by Rose and others is based on Michel Foucault's later work on "governmentality"; see Foucault (1991).

30. See Raby (2005).

31. See, for example, Tyack (1974); see also Donzelot (1979) for a discussion of how the state penetrates families through the school, reaching parents through their students.

32. Ferguson (2000).

33. See Carter (2005).

34. Grant (1988).

35. See, for example, Casella (2001); Lyons and Drew (2006); and others cited throughout the text.

36. Private schools and charter schools, however, may be organized very differently—hopefully future research will consider this question.

EPILOGUE

1. He appeared on the show on October 13, 2009.

2. Jennifer Price, 2009, "Public Not Tolerating Latest 'Zero Tolerance' Verdict." *News Journal,* October 13. Retrieved December 4, 2009, from http://proxy.nss.udel.edu:2061/pqdweb?did=1878169231&sid=1&Fmt=3&clientId=8331&RQT=309&VName=PQD.

3. Susan Sauly, 2009. "25 Chicago Students Arrested for a Middle-School Food Fight." *New York Times,* November 10. Retrieved December 4, 2009 from http://www.nytimes.com/2009/11/11/us/11foodfight.html.

APPENDIX

1. There were two dates at Centerville High and Unionville High to accommodate teachers with a scheduling conflict on the initial day, though each student received the survey only once.

2. See http://nces.ed.gov/surveys/ssocs/index.asp (retrieved November 27, 2009).

3. Dinkes et al. (2007).

4. The disorder scale includes responses about the frequency of student verbal abuse of teachers, student disorder in classrooms, student acts of disrespect, and student gang activities (Chronbach's alpha = 0.790).

5. Statistical significance is based on the probability of obtaining results that are due to chance alone rather than to a relationship between variables, and assumes that one will occasionally obtain significant results even if no real relationship exists. For a full explanation of statistical significance, see Ronet Bachman and Raymond Paternoster (2004) *Statistics for Criminology and Criminal Justice* (2nd ed.). New York: McGraw-Hill.

6. The general delinquency scale is the averaged score of students' responses to how often (from 1= never to 6 = almost every day) they: steal from a store, break into a car or house, sneak money from an adult's wallet/purse, or damage/destroy property that is not theirs. These items were selected based on high loadings during an exploratory factor analysis using principal component analysis with Varimax rotation; the Cronbach's alpha for the scale is 0.704.

INDEX

ABOUT THE AUTHOR

AARON KUPCHIK is Associate Professor in the Department of Sociology and Criminal Justice at the University of Delaware, and author of *Judging Juveniles: Prosecuting Adolescents in Adult and Juvenile Courts*, winner of the 2007 American Society of Criminology Michael J. Hindelang Award for the Most Outstanding Contribution to Research in Criminology (NYU Press).